HARCOURT

Science

CALIFORNIA EDITION

Harcourt School Publishers

Orlando • Boston • Dallas • Chicago • San Diego

www.harcourtschool.com

Cover Image
This butterfly is a Red Cracker.
It is almost completely red on
its underside. It is called a
cracker because the males make
a crackling sound as they fly.
The Red Cracker is found in
Central and South America.

Authors

Marjorie Slavick Frank
Former Adjunct Faculty Member at
   Hunter, Brooklyn, and Manhattan
   Colleges
New York, New York

Robert M. Jones
Professor of Education
University of Houston-Clear Lake
Houston, Texas

Gerald H. Krockover
Professor of Earth and Atmospheric
   Science Education
School Mathematics and Science
   Center
Purdue University
West Lafayette, Indiana

Mozell P. Lang
Science Education Consultant
Michigan Department of Education
Lansing, Michigan

Joyce C. McLeod
Visiting Professor
Rollins College
Winter Park, Florida

Carol J. Valenta
Vice President—Education,
   Exhibits, and Programs
St. Louis Science Center
St. Louis, Missouri
Former teacher, principal, and
   Coordinator of Science Center
   Instructional Programs
Los Angeles Unified School District
Los Angeles, California

Barry A. Van Deman
Science Program Director
Arlington, Virginia

Senior Editorial Advisor

Napoleon Adebola Bryant, Jr.
Professor Emeritus of Education
Xavier University
Cincinnati, Ohio

Program Advisors

Michael J. Bell
Assistant Professor of Early
   Childhood Education
School of Education
University of Houston-Clear Lake
Houston, Texas

George W. Bright
Professor of Mathematics Education
The University of North Carolina at
   Greensboro
Greensboro, North Carolina

Pansy Cowder
Science Specialist
Tampa, Florida

Robert H. Fronk
Head, Science/Mathematics
   Education Department
Florida Institute of Technology
Melbourne, Florida

Gloria R. Guerrero
Education Consultant
Specialist in English as a Second
   Language
San Antonio, Texas

Bernard A. Harris, Jr.
Physician and Former Astronaut
(STS 55—*Space Shuttle Columbia*,
STS 63—*Space Shuttle Discovery*)
Vice President, SPACEHAB Inc.
Houston, Texas

Lois Harrison-Jones
Education and Management
   Consultant
Dallas, Texas

Linda Levine
Educational Consultant
Orlando, Florida

Kenneth R. Mechling
Professor of Biology and Science
   Education
Clarion University of Pennsylvania
Clarion, Pennsylvania

Barbara ten Brink
Science Director
Round Rock Independent School
   District
Round Rock, Texas

Reviewers and Contributors

Kathy Harkness
Retired Teacher
Brea, California

Roberta W. Hudgins
Teacher, W. T. Moore Elementary
Tallahassee, Florida

Libby Laughlin
Teacher, North Hill Elementary
Burlington, Iowa

Kari A. Miller
Teacher, Dover Elementary
Dover, Pennsylvania

Julie Robinson
Science Specialist, K-5
Ben Franklin Science Academy
Muskogee, Oklahoma

Michael F. Ryan
Educational Technology Specialist
Lake County Schools
Tavares, Florida

Judy Taylor
Teacher, Silvestri Junior High School
Las Vegas, Nevada

UNIT A

LIFE SCIENCE
Survival of Living Things

UNIT B

EARTH SCIENCE
The Solar System

v

UNIT C

P H Y S I C A L   S C I E N C E

Investigating Matter and Energy

UNIT C

PHYSICAL SCIENCE
(continued)

Extension Chapters

Introduction and References

Using Science Process Skills

When scientists try to find an answer to a question or do an experiment, they use thinking tools called process skills. You use many of the process skills whenever you think, listen, read, and write. Think about how these students used process skills to help them answer questions and do experiments.

Maria is interested in birds. She carefully observes the birds she finds. Then she uses her book to identify the birds and learn more about them.

Try This Find something outdoors that you want to learn more about. Use your senses to observe it carefully.

Talk About It What senses does Maria use to observe the birds?

Process Skills

Observe — use your senses to learn about objects and events

Charles finds rocks for a rock collection. He observes the rocks he finds. He compares their colors, shapes, sizes, and textures. He classifies them into groups according to their colors.

Try This Use the skills of comparing and classifying to organize a collection of objects.

Talk About It What other ways can Charles classify the rocks in his collection?

Process Skills

Compare— identify characteristics of things or events to find out how they are alike and different

Classify— group or organize objects or events in categories based on specific characteristics

Katie measures her plants to see how they grow from day to day. Each day after she **measures** she **records the data**. Recording the data will let her work with it later. She **displays the data** in a graph.

Try This Find a shadow in your room. Measure its length each hour. Record your data, and find a way to display it.

Talk About It How does displaying your data help you communicate with others?

Process Skills

Measure — compare mass, length, or capacity of an object to a unit, such as gram, centimeter, or liter

Record Data — write down observations

Display Data — make tables, charts, or graphs

An ad about low-fat potato chips claims that low-fat chips have half the fat of regular potato chips. Tani **plans and conducts an investigation** to test the claim.

Tani labels a paper bag Regular and Low-Fat. He finds two chips of each kind that are the same size, and places them above their labels. He crushes all the chips flat against the bag. He sets the stopwatch for one hour.

Tani **predicts** that regular chips will make larger grease spots on the bag than low-fat chips. When the stopwatch signals, he checks the spots. The spots above the Regular label are larger than the spots above the Low-Fat label. Tani **infers** that the claim is correct.

Try This Plan and conduct an investigation to test claims for a product. Make a prediction, and tell what you infer from the results.

Talk About It Why did Tani test potato chips of the same size?

Process Skills

Plan and conduct investigations— identify and perform the steps necessary to find the answer to a question

Predict—form an idea of an expected outcome based on observations or experience

Infer— use logical reasoning to explain events and make conclusions

You will have many opportunities to practice and apply these and other process skills in *Harcourt Science.* An exciting year of science discoveries lies ahead!

Safety in Science

Here are some safety rules to follow.

① Think ahead. Study the steps and safety symbols of the investigation so you know what to expect. If you have any questions, ask your teacher.

② Be neat. Keep your work area clean. If you have long hair, pull it back so it doesn't get in the way. Roll up long sleeves. If you should spill or break something, or get cut, tell your teacher right away.

③ Watch your eyes. Wear safety goggles when told to do so.

④ Yuck! Never eat or drink anything during a science activity unless you are told to do so by your teacher.

⑤ Don't get shocked. Be sure that electric cords are in a safe place where you can't trip over them. Don't ever pull a plug out of an outlet by pulling on the cord.

⑥ Keep it clean. Always clean up when you have finished. Put everything away and wash your hands.

In some activities you will see these symbols. They are signs for what you need to do to be safe.

Be especially careful.

Wear safety goggles.

Be careful with sharp objects.

Don't get burned.

Protect your clothes.

Protect your hands with mitts.

Be careful with electricity.

Survival of Living Things

UNIT A

Survival of Living Things

Unit Project   ## Naturalist's Handbook

Observe the plants and animals that live around you. Make notes and sketches about your observations. Use tools like a hand lens, ruler, and thermometer to help you make your observations. Use reference materials to identify and describe the living things. Organize the information you find in a handbook to share.

Chapter 1

How Plants Grow

Plants grow almost everywhere on Earth. Plants come in many sizes. Some are tall, like oak trees. Others are smaller, like rosebushes. But each plant has the same basic needs. These needs must be met in order for the plant to live and grow.

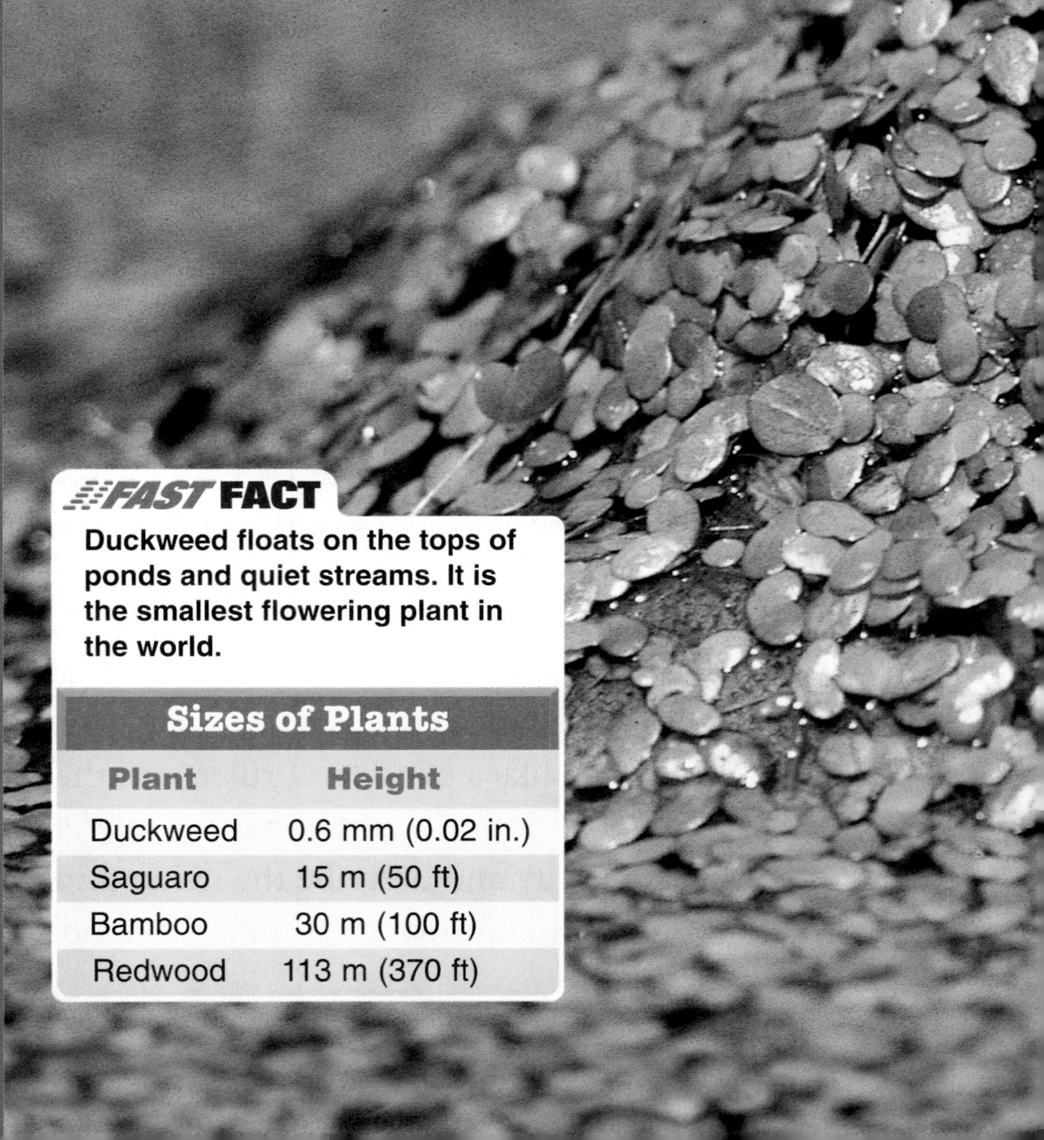

FAST FACT

Duckweed floats on the tops of ponds and quiet streams. It is the smallest flowering plant in the world.

Sizes of Plants

Plant	Height
Duckweed	0.6 mm (0.02 in.)
Saguaro	15 m (50 ft)
Bamboo	30 m (100 ft)
Redwood	113 m (370 ft)

Vocabulary Preview

- root
- stem
- leaf
- seed
- germinate
- seedling
- photosynthesis
- chlorophyll

Frog in duckweed

The largest cactus is the saguaro. It can be 50 feet tall and can weigh 14,000 pounds! In fact, it would take about 200 8-year-olds to match the weight of one giant saguaro.

What Do Plants Need?

In this lesson, you can . . .

 INVESTIGATE plant needs.

 LEARN ABOUT how plants meet their needs.

 LINK to math, writing, art, and technology.

INVESTIGATE

Needs of Plants

Activity Purpose Plants need certain things to live and grow. In this investigation you will **observe** changes in plants. Then you will **compare** your observations to find out some of the things plants need to grow.

Materials

- 6 young plants
- 6 paper cups
- potting soil
- marker
- brown paper bag
- water
- ruler

Activity Procedure

1. Put the plants in the paper cups and add soil. Make sure all six plants have the same amount of soil. Label two of the plants *No Water*. Put these plants in a sunny window. (Picture A)

◀ **The radishes you eat are roots.**

Plants	Day 1	Day 3	Day 5	Day 7	Day 9	Day 11
No Water						
No Light						
Water and Light						

2 Label two plants *No Light*. Place these plants on a table away from a window. Water the plants. Then cover them with a paper bag.

3 Label the last two plants *Water and Light*. Water these plants. Put them in a sunny window.

Picture A

4 Every other day for two weeks, **observe** the plants. Check to make sure the plants labeled *No Light* and *Water and Light* have moist soil. Add enough water to keep the soil moist.

5 Make a chart like the one shown. On the chart, **record** any changes you **observe** in the plants. Look for changes in the color and height of each plant. (Picture B)

Picture B

Draw Conclusions

1. Which plants looked the healthiest after two weeks? Why do you think so?

2. Which plants looked the least healthy after two weeks? What was different for these plants?

3. **Scientists at Work** Scientists often **compare** observations to reach their conclusions. Compare your observations of the plants to tell what things plants need to grow. Make a list.

Process Skill Tip

When you **compare**, you tell how things are the same and how they are different. You may compare objects, events, or observations.

What Plants Need

Plant Needs

FIND OUT

- four needs of plants
- how roots, stems, and leaves help plants live
- some different shapes and sizes of leaves

VOCABULARY

root

stem

leaf

These bluebonnets and Indian paintbrush flowers get what they need to live from nature. ▼

Plants are living things. They live in places all over the world. Plants grow in deserts, in rain forests, and in your back yard. But no matter where they grow, all plants need the same things to live. As you learned in the investigation, these things include water and light. Plants also need soil and air.

Most plants live and grow without human care. They get what they need from the sun, the air, the rain, and the soil. Different kinds of plants need different amounts of these things. For example, a cactus needs very little water. Other plants, such as water lilies, need a lot of water. This is why the kinds of plants in one place may be very different from those in another place.

✔ **What four things do all plants need?**

The sun provides plants with light. ▼

Rain gives plants the water they need. ▼

A6

Plant Parts

A tall oak tree looks very different from a daisy. A rosebush looks different from a dandelion. Yet all these plants have the same parts.

The **roots** of a plant are underground, where you often don't see them. A **stem** connects the roots with the leaves of a plant and supports the plant above ground. You may have seen a thin green stem on a flower. The thick, woody trunk of a tree is also a stem.

Leaves are plant parts that grow out of the stem. Most plants have many leaves.

✔ **How does water in the soil get to a plant's leaves?**

Roots, stems, and leaves are parts of a plant. They help the plant get what it needs to live.

The stem carries water from the roots to other parts of the plant.

Leaves take in the air and light a plant needs.

Roots hold a plant in the ground. They take in water and minerals from the soil.

Soil contains the minerals plants need. ▼

A7

Leaf Shapes

Leaves help plants get the light and air they need. You may know that most leaves are green. But did you know that leaves have many shapes and sizes?

Many leaves, such as those from maple and oak trees, are wide and flat. Others, such as those from the jade plant, are small and thick. Leaves can be many different shapes. A leaf may have smooth or rough edges. Some leaf shapes may remind you of other things you have seen in nature. The way a leaf looks can help you tell what plant the leaf came from.

✔ **When you observe a leaf, what can help you tell what plant the leaf is from?**

▲ **The black oak leaf is long and wide, with rough edges.**

◄ **The leaf of the beech tree is oval and has rough edges.**

The leaf of the sweet-gum tree is star-shaped. Its edges are rough. ▼

The jade plant has leaves that are small and thick. The edges are smooth. ▶

The ginkgo leaf is fan-shaped with smooth edges. ▶

Summary

Plants need water, light, soil, and air to live and grow. Roots, stems, and leaves help a plant get what it needs to live. Roots take in water from the soil. Stems carry this water to other parts of the plant. Leaves help the plant use light and air. Leaves have different shapes and sizes.

Review

1. Name four things a plant needs to live.
2. How does a plant take in water from the soil?
3. What plant part supports the leaves and branches of a tree?
4. **Critical Thinking** How might you care for an indoor plant?
5. **Test Prep** The plant parts that take in water and minerals from the soil are the —

   A flowers   **C** leaves
   B roots   **D** stems

LINKS

MATH LINK

Graphing Leaf Sizes Gather five to ten kinds of leaves. Use a ruler to measure the length of each leaf from the bottom of its stem to its tip. Make a bar graph to show the lengths of the leaves.

WRITING LINK

Informative Writing— Description Most states have a state tree and a state flower. What are these plants in your state? Write a description for your teacher of each.

ART LINK

Leaf Album Make drawings or crayon rubbings of your favorite kinds of leaves. Show the different shapes, sizes, and colors of the leaves. Label each drawing, and put it into a booklet.

TECHNOLOGY LINK

Learn more about plants and what they need by visiting the National Museum of Natural History Internet site.
www.si.edu/harcourt/science

LESSON 2

What Do Seeds Do?

In this lesson, you can . . .

INVESTIGATE what seeds need to sprout.

LEARN ABOUT why seeds are important.

LINK to math, writing, technology, and other areas.

Sprouting Seeds

Activity Purpose Cucumbers, carrots, and apples come from very different kinds of plants. But as different as these plants are, they all started as seeds. Seeds need certain things to sprout and grow. In this investigation, you will **observe** seeds to find out what they need to grow into new plants.

Materials

- 3 kinds of seeds
- paper towels
- 3 small zip-top bags
- scissors
- water
- tape
- hand lens

Activity Procedure

1 Start with a small amount of mixed seeds. Use size and shape to sort the seeds into three groups.

◀ **These corn seedlings have roots, stems, and leaves.**

Seeds	Days				
	1	2	3	4	5
Group 1					
Group 2					
Group 3					

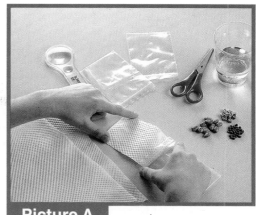
Picture A

2 Cut two paper towels in half. Fold the towels to fit into the plastic bags. Add water to make the towels damp. Do not use too much water or you will drown the seeds. (Picture A)

3 Put one group of seeds into each bag, and seal the bags. Label the bags *1*, *2*, and *3*. Tape the bags to the inside of a window.

4 Use a hand lens to **observe** the seeds every school day for 10 days. Use a chart like the one shown to **record** your observations. (Picture B)

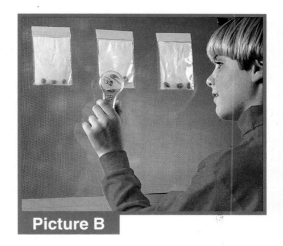
Picture B

Draw Conclusions

1. What changes did you **observe** in the seeds?

2. How quickly did the changes take place in the different kinds of seeds?

3. **Scientists at Work** Scientists **observe** their investigations closely to get new information. How did observing the seeds help you understand more about seeds?

Investigate Further Repeat the investigation steps, but place the bags in a dark closet instead of in a window. **Predict** what will happen. **Compare** your prediction with the actual results.

Process Skill Tip

When you **observe,** you use your senses to gather information. Observing sprouting seeds over time will help you understand more about how plants grow.

Growing Plants from Seeds

FIND OUT

- how plants reproduce
- what seeds need to sprout and grow
- four ways seeds are spread from one place to another

VOCABULARY

seed
germinate
seedling

What Seeds Are

Have you ever found seeds inside an orange or apple you were eating? Many plants reproduce, or make more plants like themselves, by forming seeds. The **seed** is the first stage in the growth of many plants.

Seeds may be large or small. They may be round, oval, flat, or pointed. Seeds may be many colors, too—they may even be striped. A seed looks very different from the plant that grows from it. But all seeds become plants that look like the plants they came from.

✔ **What does a seed do?**

After a sunflower seed germinates, a new sunflower plant will grow.

This cone from a pine tree produces many seeds.

What Seeds Need

In the investigation, you observed that seeds began to grow into new plants when you gave them water. When the small plant breaks out of the seed, we say the seed **germinates**.

As a seed begins to sprout, a root grows from it. Next, the seed breaks open and a young plant, or **seedling**, appears. The seedling begins to form the parts it will need as an adult plant. The roots grow longer, and the stem begins to grow. Soon the seedling breaks through the soil. As the plant grows larger, leaves begin to form.

✔ **What do both seeds and plants need to grow?**

This summer squash is ready to eat. It is filled with seeds that could grow into new plants. ▼

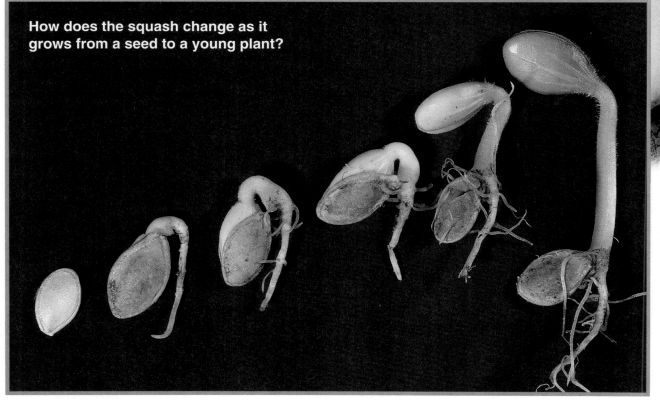

How does the squash change as it grows from a seed to a young plant?

A13

Some Plants Make Seeds

Plants that reproduce by seeds usually form more than one seed at a time. These seeds carry the information needed to grow into plants that look very much like the adult plant they came from.

Two groups of plants form seeds. In one group are the plants that have flowers. You may have seen flowers growing on bushes, on trees, or on small plants.

In the other group of seed-forming plants are plants that have cones. Some evergreen trees, such as pine trees, have cones. The cones have hard scales that protect the seeds under them.

Some plants can be grown from other plant parts. For example, if you place a leaf or a piece of a stem in water, it may form roots. Once roots form, you can put the plant part in soil, and it will grow into a new plant. The leaf or piece of stem used to grow the new plant is called a cutting. Underground plant parts such as tubers and bulbs can also be used to grow new plants.

✔ **Name five plants that form seeds.**

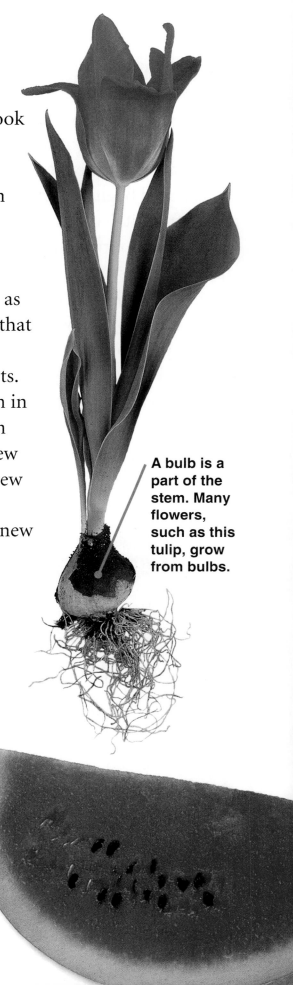

A bulb is a part of the stem. Many flowers, such as this tulip, grow from bulbs.

◀ Dandelions form many seeds that are easily blown by the wind.

The seeds in a watermelon are protected by its fruit. ▶

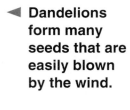

Seed Parts

Seeds may be many different shapes, sizes, and colors. But all seeds have the same parts. Seeds are like packages with tiny plants inside. The "package" is wrapped by the seed coat. Inside the seed coat is a seedling and food for the seedling.

✔ **What are the parts of a seed?**

The Parts of a Seed

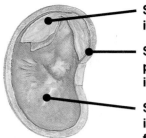

Seedling: A seedling lives inside every seed.

Seed coat: The seed coat protects the young plant inside the seed.

Stored food: Most of the inside of a seed is stored food. The young plant uses the food to grow when the seed sprouts.

THE INSIDE STORY

Sizes of Seeds

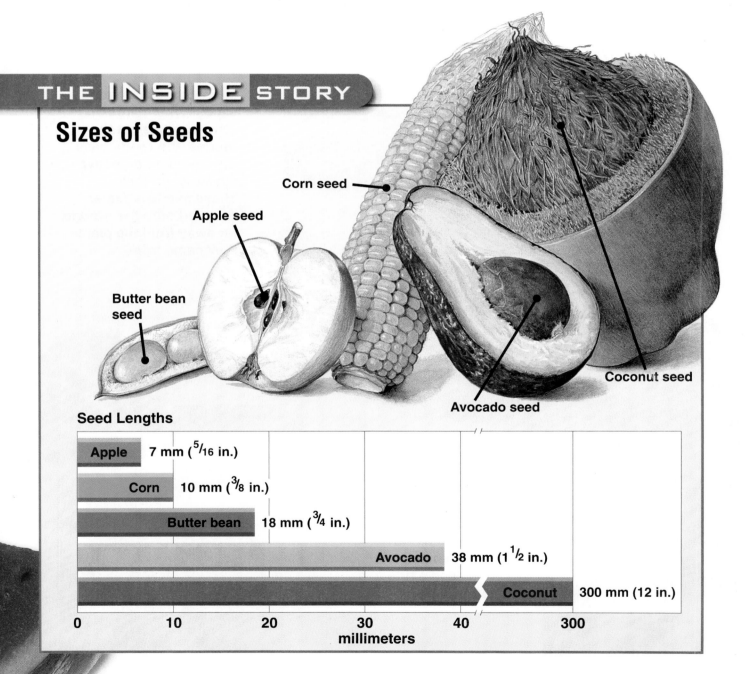

Corn seed

Apple seed

Butter bean seed

Coconut seed

Avocado seed

Seed Lengths

Apple	7 mm ($^5/_{16}$ in.)
Corn	10 mm ($^3/_8$ in.)
Butter bean	18 mm ($^3/_4$ in.)
Avocado	38 mm ($1^1/_2$ in.)
Coconut	300 mm (12 in.)

0   10   20   30   40   300
millimeters

How Seeds Are Spread

Many seeds do not simply fall off the adult plants and sprout in the soil. Instead, they are scattered and moved to new places. Seeds are spread to new places in many ways. Some seeds are shot out of the adult plant like cannonballs from a cannon! Other seeds are spread by air, water, and animals.

✔ **What are some ways seeds are spread from one place to another?**

The fluffy parts of these milkweed seeds help them float away on the wind. ▶

▲ Many berries contain seeds. When birds and other animals eat the berries, the seeds pass through their digestive systems unharmed. These seeds are later dropped onto the ground far away from the plant they came from.

◀ A cocklebur has hooks that grab onto fur or clothing. An animal or a person may give this seed a ride to a faraway place.

Water carries these mangrove seeds to new places. ▶

▲ Witch hazel plants shoot their seeds to spread them. This is called bolting.

Summary

Some plants form seeds to make new plants. Some plants also can be grown from plant parts. Seeds grow to look like the adult plants they came from. Although they may look different from one another, all seeds have the same parts and need water to sprout. Seeds are often spread to new places by air, water, and animals.

Review

1. What is a seedling?
2. What are some ways plants make new plants?
3. Describe some ways an animal can carry a seed from one place to another.
4. **Critical Thinking** If two seeds look alike, will they always grow into plants that look the same?
5. **Test Prep** What happens when a seed germinates?
   A The seed breaks open and a seedling appears.
   B The seedling breaks through the soil.
   C Leaves begin to form.
   D A root grows from the seed.

LINKS

MATH LINK

Counting Seeds Working with a partner, cut open an apple. Count the seeds inside. How many seeds in the whole class? Group the seeds by tens.

WRITING LINK

Narrative Writing—Story Write a creative story for a younger child about the life of a seed.

SOCIAL STUDIES LINK

Seeds Are Food Research the kinds of seeds people eat. Share with the class what you learn.

ART LINK

Fruity Posters Collect seeds from your favorite fruits. Use them to make a poster that tells about each fruit and its seeds.

TECHNOLOGY LINK

Visit the Harcourt Learning Site for related links, activities, and resources.

WELCOME TO THE LEARNING SITE

www.harcourtschool.com/ca

Food Factories

Activity Purpose
How do plants get food? They make it! To make food, plants must use the things around them. In this investigation, you will **observe** a plant making food. Then you will **infer** what plants need to make their food.

Materials
- scissors
- elodea
- dowel or pencil
- twist tie
- empty 0.5-L plastic bottle
- water
- brown paper bag
- watch or clock

Activity Procedure

CAUTION

1. **CAUTION** **Be careful when using scissors.** Use scissors to cut a piece of the elodea (el•oh•DEE•uh) as long as the bottle.

2. Wrap the elodea around the dowel. Use a twist tie to attach it to the dowel. (Picture A)

LESSON 3

How Do Plants Make Food?

In this lesson, you can . . .

 INVESTIGATE what plants need to make their own food.

 LEARN ABOUT photosynthesis.

 LINK to math, writing, language arts, and technology.

◀ Lemon trees make their own food.

A18

3 Put the elodea into the bottle, and fill the bottle with water. (Picture B)

4 Put the bottle in a place away from any windows. Cover the bottle with the brown paper bag. After 10 minutes, remove the bag. **Record** any changes you **observe.**

5 This time, place the bottle in bright sunlight and don't cover it with the brown paper bag. After 10 minutes, **observe** the bottle. **Record** any changes you observe.

Picture A

Draw Conclusions

1. Did the elodea and water in the bottle look different after Steps 4 and 5? If they did, tell how they were different.

2. What did you change between Steps 4 and 5? What remained the same in Steps 4 and 5?

3. **Scientists at Work** From what you **observed,** what can you **infer** about the bubbles you saw?

Picture B

Investigate Further Scientists often **measure** what happens in experiments. One way to measure what is happening in this experiment is to count the number of bubbles that appear. Put the bottle with the elodea in bright sunlight, and count the number of bubbles that appear in one minute. Then move the bottle out of the direct sun. Again count the number of bubbles that appear in one minute. How are the two measurements different? **Infer** why they are different.

Process Skill Tip

When you **infer,** you use what you have **observed** to form an opinion. That opinion is called an inference.

How Plants Make Food

FIND OUT

- how plants make their own food
- why plants need chlorophyll to make their food

VOCABULARY

photosynthesis
chlorophyll

Making Food

Like other animals, you cannot make food in your body. You must get your food by eating. Plants, however, can make their own food. This food-making process is called **photosynthesis** (foht•oh•SIN•thuh•sis). A process is a way of doing something.

The leaves of most plants are green. Plants get their green color from **chlorophyll** (KLAWR•uh•fil). Chlorophyll helps the plant use energy from the sun to make food. Plants need light to make food. They also need water and carbon dioxide. Carbon dioxide is a gas in the air.

◀ A plant that gets enough light (and soil and water) grows into a healthy plant.

The sun provides light energy to plants.

▲ A plant that does not get enough light does not grow well, even though it has soil and water. It may die.

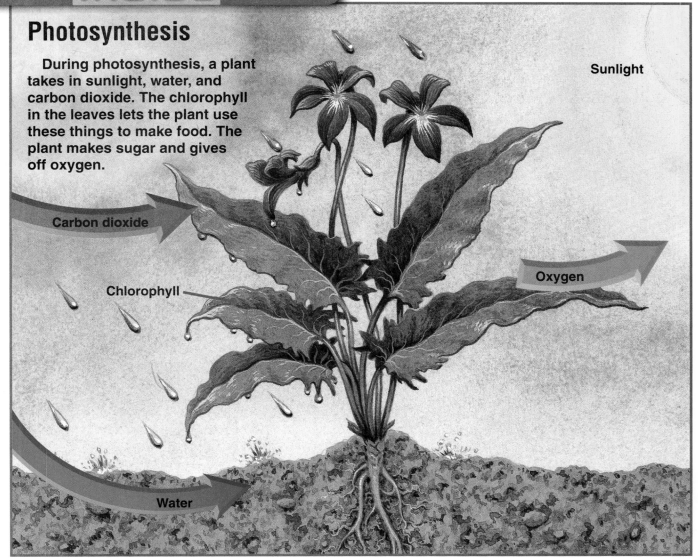

Photosynthesis

During photosynthesis, a plant takes in sunlight, water, and carbon dioxide. The chlorophyll in the leaves lets the plant use these things to make food. The plant makes sugar and gives off oxygen.

Sunlight

Carbon dioxide

Chlorophyll

Oxygen

Water

During photosynthesis, water and carbon dioxide combine inside a plant to make food. Sunlight provides the energy needed for this to happen. The food the plant makes is a kind of sugar. The plant uses some of the sugar right away and stores the rest.

During photosynthesis, plants also make oxygen. The oxygen is given off into the air through the plant's leaves. The bubbles you observed in the investigation were oxygen given off by the leaves into the water.

✔ **Name four things plants need for photosynthesis.**

How Plants Use Food

Plants use some of the food they make to grow larger. They also use it to make seeds. Some plants store food in their stems and roots so they can use it later. Other plants store sugar in fruits. This makes the fruit tasty to animals, who eat it and spread the seeds.

The stems, leaves, roots, seeds, fruits, and even flowers of plants are used as food by people and other animals.

✓ **What are three ways plants use the food they make?**

▲ Bananas grow in bunches called hands.

◄ The stalks of celery plants contain fiber and water.

◄ People eat the red fruit of the strawberry plant.

A potato is an underground stem that stores food made by the potato plant. ▼

▲ When you break open a pea pod you can see the pea seeds inside.

Summary

Photosynthesis is the process plants use to make their own food. Plants need chlorophyll, light, carbon dioxide, and water for photosynthesis. The sun provides the light energy that plants need to make food. Plants use the food they make to grow bigger and to make seeds. They store some of their food in roots, stems, and fruits. People and other animals eat many different plant parts.

Review

1. Describe what happens during photosynthesis.
2. Why are plants green?
3. How does chlorophyll help in photosynthesis?
4. **Critical Thinking** How does photosynthesis help make the food people and other animals eat?
5. **Test Prep** What do plants give off during photosynthesis?
   A carbon dioxide
   B water
   C oxygen
   D light

LINKS

MATH LINK

Plant Parts and Food Make a list of 20 foods you eat that come from plants. Identify how many of these foods come from roots, stems, leaves, fruits, seeds, and flowers. Make a bar graph from your list.

WRITING LINK

Informative Writing— Explanation Use what you know about photosynthesis to write a paragraph for your teacher that explains how a plant is like a food factory.

LANGUAGE ARTS LINK

Putting It Together The word *photosynthesis* is made up of the words *photo* and *synthesis*. Use a dictionary to find out what these words mean.

TECHNOLOGY LINK

To learn more about how people use the food that plants store, watch *Grocery Garden* on **Harcourt Science Newsroom Video** in your classroom video library.

Drought-Resistant Plants

Different kinds of plants live in different kinds of places. Water plants need lots of water. Plants that live in the desert need very little water. Plants that need little water are called drought-resistant plants.

What Makes Plants Drought Resistant?

Drought-resistant plants have traits that allow them to live successfully with little water. One trait is gray or white leaves or bark. Their light color reflects the heat of the sun rather than absorbing it. This keeps the plant cooler, so it doesn't dry out as much. Another trait these plants have is narrow leaves, which help the plant keep moisture in.

Many drought-resistant plants bloom early in the spring, when there is plenty of water. They develop seeds before the hot, dry months.

Some plants have underground bulbs or enlarged root systems that store food. When dry weather arrives, the plant has plenty of food it can use.

Who Needs Drought-Resistant Plants?

Some parts of the United States get little rain. Many of these places are warm and get lots of sun. More and more people are deciding to live in these warm, sunny places. These people often try to grow gardens with the kinds of plants they had where they came from. These plants need more water than they get naturally in dry areas, so people have to water them a lot. But this uses water that is needed for other things, such as farms, animals, and people.

One way to have pretty plants without using much water is to use a process called Xeriscaping (ZIR•uh•skayp•ing). Xeriscaping is the use of water-saving methods and drought-resistant plants in gardens and yards.

How Does Xeriscaping Work?

First the gardener analyzes the soil and the amount of water in the garden area. Then the gardener chooses plants that can grow well in those conditions. Often the gardener chooses plants that are native to the area because they have adapted to the local climate. The gardener puts a layer of mulch, such as leaves or wood chips, around each plant to help hold water in the ground. Xeriscaping saves water costs for the gardener and conserves water for the whole community.

Think About It

1. How can planting drought-resistant plants help the environment?
2. What are some native plants in your area?

WEB LINK:
For Science and Technology updates, visit the Harcourt Internet site.
www.harcourtschool.com/ca

Careers | Agricultural Extension Agent

What They Do Extension agents often work for state or local governments. These people offer help and information to farmers, gardeners, and teachers. They often travel to different areas to teach and train people in new technology used in agriculture.

Education and Training An extension agent must study agriculture and animal science. Training in computers and agricultural technology will be required for the agents of the future.

George Washington Carver

AGRICULTURAL CHEMIST

"I literally lived in the woods. I wanted to know every strange stone, flower, insect, bird, or beast."

How many ways can you think of to use a peanut? George Washington Carver found more than 300!

After completing college, Carver was invited to teach at the Tuskegee Institute in Alabama. For almost 50 years, he taught there and conducted experiments with plants. He experimented to solve many problems of farming. The problems included poor soil, amounts of sunlight and moisture, plant diseases, and ways of reproducing plants.

Carver persuaded farmers to rotate their crops so the soil would not lose all its nutrients. One year the farmers could plant cotton or tobacco, but the next year they planted peanuts or sweet potatoes. The land produced so many crops that Carver had to find new uses for them. Besides his work with peanuts, he found more than 100 uses for sweet potatoes and 75 for pecans.

Think About It

1. George Washington Carver was interested in plants from his boyhood. Think about the things that interest you now. Which ones do you think will interest you when you grow up?
2. What qualities do you think a plant scientist ought to have?

Some of the plants that Carver worked with ▼

What Stems Do

How does water move through a stem?

Materials

- 3 1-L plastic bottles
- water
- food coloring
- 3 freshly cut white carnations
- scissors

Procedure

1. Fill the plastic bottles with water. Add a few drops of food coloring. Put a different color in each bottle.

2. Trim the end off the stem of each flower. Place one flower in each bottle.

3. Keep the flowers in the bottles overnight. Then observe the flowers.

Draw Conclusions

Explain your observations. Did each flower show the same results? How could you change the procedure to change the results?

Growing Plants

Can plant parts be used to grow a new plant?

Materials

- 1 plant with many stems and leaves
- scissors
- 1-L plastic bottle
- water
- ruler

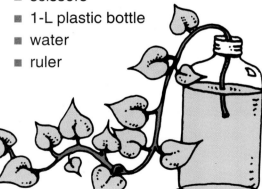

Procedure

1. Cut off a 15-cm piece of the plant.

2. Fill the plastic bottle with water. Place the cut part of the plant in the bottle.

3. Place the plant in bright sunlight. Predict what will happen.

Draw Conclusions

Observe the plant for ten days. Record any changes you observe. Compare your prediction with the actual results.

Vocabulary Review

Use the terms below to complete the sentences 1 through 7. The page numbers in ( ) tell you where to look in the chapter if you need help.

roots (A7) **germinate** (A13)
stem (A7) **photosynthesis** (A20)
leaves (A7) **chlorophyll** (A20)
seeds (A12)

1. Many new plants grow from ____.

2. The plant parts that grow out of stems are ____.

3. ____ gives plants their green color.

4. A seed needs water to ____.

5. The underground parts of a plant that take in water from the soil are the ____.

6. The food-making process of plants is ____.

7. A ____ connects the roots and leaves of a plant.

Connect Concepts

Use the terms from the Word Bank to complete the concept map.

wind chlorophyll water oxygen animals

How Plants Grow		
What Plants Need	**What Seeds Do**	**How Plants Make Food**
Roots help a plant take in water from the soil.	Many plants can form seeds. Seeds need air and water to sprout. Seeds are spread in many ways.	Plants make their own food by a process called photosynthesis.
Leaves take in carbon dioxide from the air. They give off **8.** ____.	Three ways seeds are spread are by **9.** ____, **10.** ____, and **11.** ____.	**12.** ____ in plants helps take in light.

Check Understanding

Write the letter of the best choice.

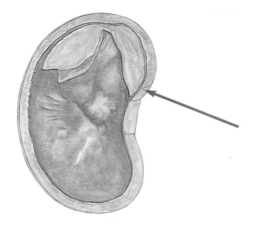

13. Look at the picture. Which part of the seed is the arrow pointing to?

    A stored food   **C** seed coat

    B young plant   **D** stem

14. Some plants are grown from bulbs. A bulb is a part of the —

    F root   **H** stem

    G seed   **J** leaf

Critical Thinking

15. What would happen to a farmer's crop if there were little or no rain for a long period of time?

16. How can a dandelion growing in the schoolyard be a parent to young dandelion plants growing miles from school?

17. If a plant reproduces by bulbs, does it make seeds, too? Explain.

Process Skills Review

18. You are growing two plants. You want to test one plant to find out how sunlight affects its growth. You will provide the other plant with everything it needs for growth. Explain how you will **observe** the plants and **compare** your results.

19. What can **observing** tree leaves help you learn?

Performance Assessment

Design a Garden

With a partner, design a garden to grow your favorite kinds of plants. Make a list of all the things you will need for your garden.

Chapter 2

Vocabulary Preview

inherit
trait
mammal
bird
amphibian
gills
fish
scale
reptile

Types of Animals

How many different kinds of animals can you name? You probably listed animals such as cats, dogs, cows, and fish. But there are many more. Even though there are many kinds of animals, they all need the same types of things to live and grow.

FAST FACT

It's a trick! These butterfly fish have spots on their tails that look like eyes. The "eyes" scare away larger fish that might eat them.

FAST FACT

Types of Animals on Earth

75% insects

25% all other animals

Swat! Slap! Mosquitoes bite. Bees sting. Of every 100 types of animals in the world, 75 are insects.

What Is an Animal?

In this lesson, you can . . .

 INVESTIGATE animal homes.

 LEARN ABOUT how animals meet their needs.

 LINK to math, writing, literature, and technology.

◀ **Ladybugs get food from this bluebonnet.**

 **INVESTIGATE**

Animal Homes

Activity Purpose Everyone needs a place to live—including animals. Animals live in many kinds of places that give them the things they need. In this investigation you will **observe** animal homes and use the homes to **classify** the animals.

Materials
- Animal Picture Cards

Activity Procedure

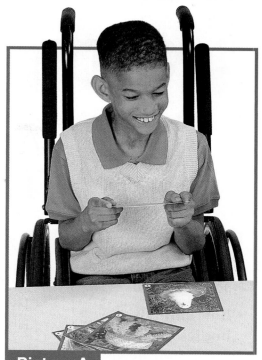

Picture A

1 Select six Animal Picture Cards or use the pictures on page A32. As you **observe** the cards, pay close attention to the types of homes the animals live in. (Picture A)

2 Describe each animal home you **observe**. **Record** your descriptions.

3 With a partner, discuss the different types of animal homes shown. Talk about the ways the animal homes are alike and the ways they are different. Then **classify** the animals by the types of homes they live in.

Draw Conclusions

1. **Compare** two of the animal homes you observed. Tell how each home helps protect the animal that lives there.

2. What did you **observe** about the home of a Canada goose and the home of an albatross?

3. **Scientists at Work** Scientists **classify** animals into groups based on what the animals have in common. How many groups did you classify the animals into? What were the groups?

Investigate Further Study the Animal Picture Cards again. This time, look at the body covering of each animal. Describe each covering. How can you use body coverings to **classify** the animals?

> **Process Skill Tip**
>
> When you **classify** things, you put them into groups. You put things into a group because they have something in common. For example, you could put into one group the animals that build nests.

Animals and Their Needs

FIND OUT

- what animals need so they can live
- how animals' bodies help them meet their needs
- how animals get their traits

VOCABULARY

inherit
trait

What Animals Need

Have you ever cared for a pet? If so, you know that a pet needs food and water. A pet also needs shelter, or a place to live. Wild animals have the same needs as pets. The difference is that wild animals must meet their needs on their own.

As you learned in the investigation, different animals make their homes in different surroundings. From their surroundings, they get all the things they need. This is something all animals have in common.

✔ **Name three things animals need.**

This reef is made up of tiny living animals called corals. Other animals, such as the dolphin shown here, look for food in the reef and use the reef for shelter. ▼

Animals Need Air

Have you ever thought about the air around you? Air contains a gas called oxygen. Animals need oxygen to live.

Animals that live on land, such as giraffes, have lungs that get oxygen from the air. Insects get oxygen from the air through tiny holes in their bodies. Many water animals, such as fish, get their oxygen from water. Other water animals, such as whales, must come to the surface and breathe air to get oxygen.

✔ **Name two ways animals get oxygen.**

▲ **An alligator comes to the water's surface to breathe the air it needs.**

Animals Need Water

The bodies of all animals contain water. Every day some of this water leaves the animals' bodies. For example, when an animal pants or sweats, it loses some water from its body. The animal must replace this water to stay alive.

Most animals get the water they need by drinking. The water they drink may come from puddles, streams, rivers, ponds, or lakes. Other animals get most of their water in the foods they eat.

✔ **How do animals get the water they need?**

At this water hole on the African plains, animals drink the water they need. ▼

Animals Need Food

All animals need food. Food gives animals the materials they need so they can grow and stay healthy. Animals also get energy from food.

Unlike plants, animals cannot make their own food. Instead, they get their food by eating plants or other animals. Some animals eat only plants. Some eat only animals. Some eat both.

How do animals get the food they need? Many of them have body parts that help them get their food. For example, an elephant uses its trunk to grab leaves from trees. A hawk can use its sharp claws to catch a mouse.

✔ **What do animals eat?**

▲ **This chameleon uses its tongue to catch insects.**

A panda eats only bamboo plants. ▼

Brown bears live in forests, where they eat many kinds of plants and animals. They often eat fish they catch in streams. They also eat grass and other plants.

Beavers Build Shelters

1

2

3

4

Animals Need Shelter

Most animals need shelter, or a place to live. Shelters protect animals from other animals and from the weather. Some birds build shelters called nests high in tree branches. They build their nests out of twigs, grass, and mud. Other animals, such as deer mice, build their homes in hollow logs or in spaces under rocks. Turtles use their own hard shells as their homes. Many other animals dig tunnels and make their homes in the ground.

✓ **Why do animals need shelter?**

1 **Beavers cut down trees to build a dam in a stream.**

2 **The dam makes a pond. In the pond, the beavers build their home, called a lodge.**

3 **To build their lodges, beavers use trees they have cut down and rocks that they cover with mud.**

4 **Young beavers, called kits, stay warm and dry inside the lodge.**

Animal Traits

Jellyfish, polar bears, and snakes don't look much alike, but they are all animals. Different animals have many different shapes and sizes. They also have many different body parts. For example, a bird has wings and feathers. A lion has paws and fur. All these features are important to the way an animal lives.

How do animals get their features? Young animals inherit their features from their parents. **Inherit** (in•HAIR•it) means "to receive from parents." The body features an animal inherits are called **traits**. Traits also include some things that animals do.

✔ **What are traits?**

▲ **A sea horse is a type of fish. This male sea horse has the trait of carrying its young inside a pouch.**

These young cheetah cubs will grow to look like their parents. They will stay with their mother for several years and will learn to hunt for their food. ▼

▲ **A mother duck watches her young ducklings carefully.**

▲ These young snakes will grow to look very much like the adult snake.

Summary

Animals need air, water, food, and shelter. Different animals have many different shapes and sizes and many different body parts. These traits help the animals get the things they need. All animals inherit their traits from their parents.

Review

1. How do animals that live in water get air?

2. Describe how beavers change their surroundings to meet their needs.

3. What are four things that animals need?

4. **Critical Thinking** Why will a young lion cub grow to look like an adult lion and not like a sea horse?

5. **Test Prep** Which of the following is **NOT** a need of all animals?

    A food   C air

    B water   D soil

LINKS

MATH LINK

How Many? Suppose that there are 15 duck families that live at a pond. If each of the families has 8 ducklings, how many ducks would live at the pond?

WRITING LINK

Informative Writing—Compare and Contrast Birds make many sounds. Listen to birds that live in your area. If possible, record their sounds with a sound recorder. Write a paragraph for your teacher that compares and contrasts the bird songs.

LITERATURE LINK

A Wolf Pup Diary You can learn about the life of a young wolf by reading *Look to the North: A Wolf Pup Diary* by Jean Craighead George.

TECHNOLOGY LINK

Learn more about animals by visiting the Smithsonian Internet Site.

www.si.edu/harcourt/science

What Are Mammals and Birds?

In this lesson, you can . . .

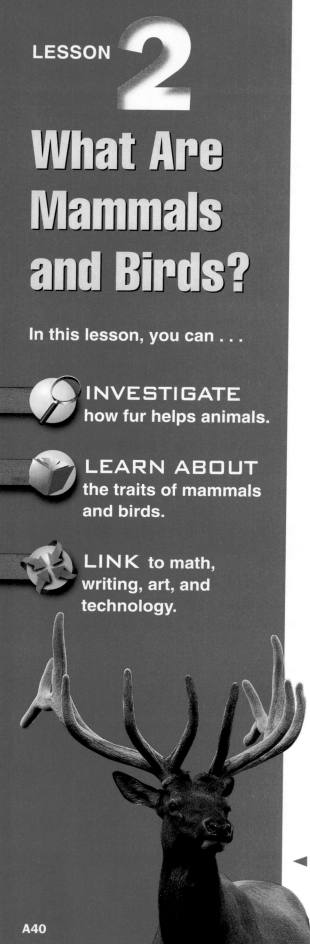

INVESTIGATE how fur helps animals.

LEARN ABOUT the traits of mammals and birds.

LINK to math, writing, art, and technology.

◄ The fur on this deer keeps him warm all winter long.

INVESTIGATE

Fur Helps Animals

Activity Purpose When it's cold outside, you might put on a jacket or a sweater to keep warm. Animals can't do that. In this investigation you will **use a model** to find out how fur helps keep animals warm.

Materials

- glue
- 2 metal cans
- cotton batting
- hot water
- 2 thermometers
- classroom clock

CAUTION

Activity Procedure

1 Make a chart like the one shown.

2 Spread glue around the outside of one can. Then put a thick layer of cotton around the can. Wait for the glue to dry. Then use your fingers to fluff the cotton. (Picture A)

Time	Water Temperature in Can with Cotton	Water Temperature in Can Without Cotton
Start		
10 min		
20 min		
30 min		

3 CAUTION Be careful with the hot water. **It can burn you.** Your teacher will fill both cans with hot water.

4 Place a thermometer in each can, and **record** the temperature of the water. (Picture B)

5 **Predict** what will happen to the temperature. Check the temperature of the water in each can every 10 minutes for a period of 30 minutes. **Record** the temperatures on the chart.

Picture A

Draw Conclusions

1. In which can did the water stay hot longer? Why?

2. How did your prediction compare to the actual result?

3. **Scientists at Work** Scientists often **use a model** to study things they can't observe easily. In this investigation, you made a model of an animal with fur. Why was using a model easier than observing an animal?

Picture B

Process Skill Tip

It would be hard to measure the temperature of a real animal to find out how fur helps it stay warm. **Using a model** helps you learn about animal fur.

A41

Mammals and Birds

FIND OUT

- four traits of mammals
- five traits of birds

VOCABULARY

mammal
bird

Mammals

In the investigation you learned that fur can help an animal stay warm. Animals that have fur or hair are called **mammals** (MAM•uhlz). Horses, cows, and dogs are all mammals.

Mammals use lungs to breathe. Mammals that live in water, such as whales, also breathe with lungs. But these mammals must come to the surface of the water to breathe the air they need.

Most mammals give birth to live young. A cat gives birth to many kittens at one time. Before the kittens

THE INSIDE STORY

Keeping Warm

A polar bear's fur looks white, but it is really clear. The fur looks white because it reflects sunlight.

hair

fat

The skin of a polar bear is black. The black skin takes in the heat from the sun. Polar bears have a thick layer of fat under their skin. This fat helps keep a polar bear warm.

are born, the mother cat carries them inside her. After the kittens are born, they feed on milk made by their mother's body. Feeding their young with milk from the mother's body is another trait of all mammals.

When a mammal is born, it cannot care for itself. It must be sheltered and fed by its mother. The milk gives them what they need to grow and stay healthy.

Most mammals learn from their parents how to care for themselves. The parents often teach their young how to find food. In time a young mammal learns what it needs to know to live on its own.

▲ These puppies drink milk from their mother to get the food they need.

✔ **What are four traits mammals inherit from their parents?**

◀ Gorillas often live in large families. All the adults help care for the young.

Types of Mammals

There are many types of mammals. Most of them have the four traits you read about. Some also have other traits, such as trunks, pouches, or wings. Mammals are often placed into groups based on traits they share. Some of these groups and their traits are shown on this page.

✔ **Name three traits used to place mammals in groups.**

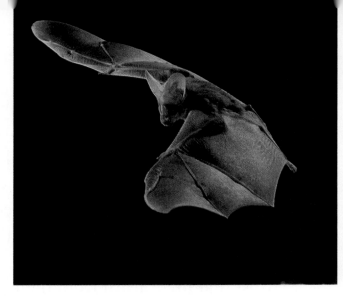

▲ Bats are the only mammals that fly.

A koala is one of a few mammals that carry their young in a pouch. ▼

▲ This spiny echidna (ee•KID•nuh), an anteater, has fur and lungs. It is a mammal, but it does not give birth to live young. It lays eggs.

This orangutan (oh•RANG•oo•tan) is a primate. Primates are mammals that can use their hands to grasp objects. ▼

Whales are mammals that live in water. They have very little hair. This helps them glide easily through the water. ▶

Birds

Birds are animals that have feathers, two legs, and wings. Most birds use their wings for flying. Some birds, such as penguins, cannot fly. But like other birds, they still have feathers and wings.

Like mammals, birds have lungs for breathing air. Many birds also care for their young for a while after the young are born. Unlike most young mammals, young birds hatch from eggs.

Feathers cover most of a bird's body. But not all feathers are the same. Some feathers help keep a bird warm. Other feathers help birds fly. For example, the wing feathers of many birds have a shape that helps them fly.

✔ **What are five traits of birds?**

▲
A weaverbird uses leaves to make a hanging nest. The mother bird lays her eggs on soft grass placed inside the nest.

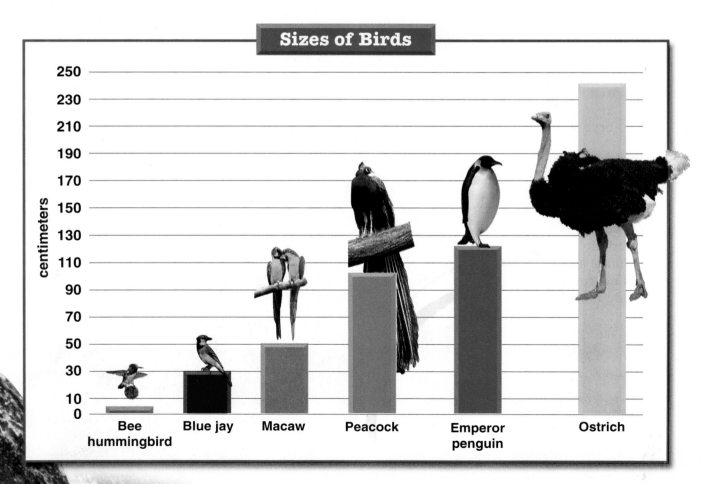

Sizes of Birds

(centimeters: 0, 10, 30, 50, 70, 90, 110, 130, 150, 170, 190, 210, 230, 250)

Bee hummingbird | Blue jay | Macaw | Peacock | Emperor penguin | Ostrich

Types of Birds

There are many types of birds. Like mammals, birds are grouped together because of traits they share. The most common traits used for grouping birds are beak shape and foot shape.

Beak shape can be used to tell what kind of food a bird eats. For example, wading birds have long beaks that help them catch fish and dig small animals from the mud.

Foot shape can be used to tell where a bird lives. For example, wading birds have long toes that keep them from sinking into the mud. For some birds foot shape is also important in getting food.

✓ **What can you tell about a bird from the shape of its beak or feet?**

A barn owl catches other animals for food. The feet of a barn owl are useful for catching animals such as mice.

A cardinal uses its beak to eat seeds. It uses its feet to hold on to branches. ▶

The purple gallinule (GAL·ih·nool) lives in marshes and swamps. It has long, thin toes that help it walk on lily pads and other plants in the water. ▼

The great blue heron is a wading bird. Its beak has a shape that is useful for catching fish. ▶

Summary

Mammals are animals that have fur or hair and breathe with lungs. Most mammals also give birth to live young and feed their young with milk from the mother's body. Birds are animals that have feathers, two legs, and wings. Like mammals, birds breathe with lungs. Unlike most mammals, birds lay eggs from which their young are hatched.

Review

1. Name a mammal that lives in the water. How does it breathe?
2. How does the spiny echidna differ from most other mammals?
3. What two features of birds are most often used to classify them? Why?
4. **Critical Thinking** A bat can fly, but a bat is a mammal. What traits do you think bats have that make them mammals instead of birds?
5. **Test Prep** Which trait is shared by birds and mammals?
   - A have feathers
   - B have fur
   - C breathe with lungs
   - D give birth to live young

LINKS

MATH LINK

Interpret Graphs Look at the graph on page A45. Which birds have the longest tails? If the length of the tails were added to the length of the bodies in the graph, which bird would be the longest?

WRITING LINK

Informative Writing— Classification Go bird-watching in your schoolyard, a park, or in your back yard. If possible, use binoculars. Write a description of each bird to share with your classmates. Identify as many birds as you can.

ART LINK

Animal Tracks You can identify many animals by the tracks they make with their feet. Make a collage of tracks. Label each track with the animal's name.

TECHNOLOGY LINK

Learn more about mammals and birds by investigating *Whose Tracks Are These?* on **Harcourt Science Explorations CD-ROM.**

What Are Amphibians, Fish, and Reptiles?

In this lesson, you can . . .

INVESTIGATE how frogs change as they grow.

LEARN ABOUT amphibians, fish, and reptiles.

LINK to math, writing, technology, and other areas.

INVESTIGATE

From Egg to Frog

Activity Purpose Frogs lay eggs in the water. When a young frog hatches, it can live only in water. But as the young frog grows, its body changes. The changes get it ready to live on land. In this investigation you will **observe** these changes in real frogs.

Materials

- gravel
- aquarium
- water
- ruler
- water plants
- rock
- tadpoles
- dried fish food

Activity Procedure

1. Put a layer of gravel on the bottom of the aquarium. Add 12 cm to 15 cm of water.

◄ Unlike frogs you may know about, this red-eyed tree frog makes its home in trees.

2 Float some water plants on top of the water, and stick others into the gravel. Add the rock. It should be big enough so that frogs can sit on it later and be out of the water. (Picture A)

Picture A

3 Put two or three tadpoles, or young frogs, in the water. Put the aquarium where there is some light but no direct sunlight.

4 Feed the tadpoles a small amount of dried fish food once a day. Add fresh water to the aquarium once a week.

5 **Observe** the tadpoles every day. Once a week, make a drawing of what they look like.

Draw Conclusions

1. What changes did you see as the tadpoles grew?

2. When the tadpoles began to climb out of the water, what did their bodies look like?

3. **Scientists at Work** Scientists often repeat investigations to check the accuracy of their results. Often the results will be different because of uncertainty in the observations that were made. If you did the tadpole investigation again, do you think the results would be the same? Explain your answer. What could you do to collect better data?

Process Skill Tip

When you **observe,** you use your senses of sight, hearing, smell, and touch. Then you **record,** or write down, your observations.

Amphibians, Fish, and Reptiles

FIND OUT

• four traits of amphibians

• four traits of fish

• three traits of reptiles

VOCABULARY

amphibian
gills
fish
scales
reptile

Amphibians

In the investigation, you observed that a tadpole lives in water. But as the tadpole grows into a frog, it spends more time out of the water. Frogs are amphibians. **Amphibians** (am•FIB•ee•uhnz) are animals that have thin, moist skin with no scales.

Many amphibians lay eggs in the water. The eggs stay there until they hatch. The young amphibians live in the water, just as tadpoles do. Most adult amphibians live on land.

✔ **Name three traits of an amphibian.**

◄ A salamander moves its body from side to side to help its legs move forward.

Newts live in water for part of the year. Then they live on land. ▼

▲ Toads live most of their adult lives on land. Unlike some other amphibians, toads have rough, bumpy skin.

Frog Metamorphosis

A frog changes as it grows from an egg to an adult. The changes it goes through are called *metamorphosis* (met·uh·MAWR·fuh·sis).

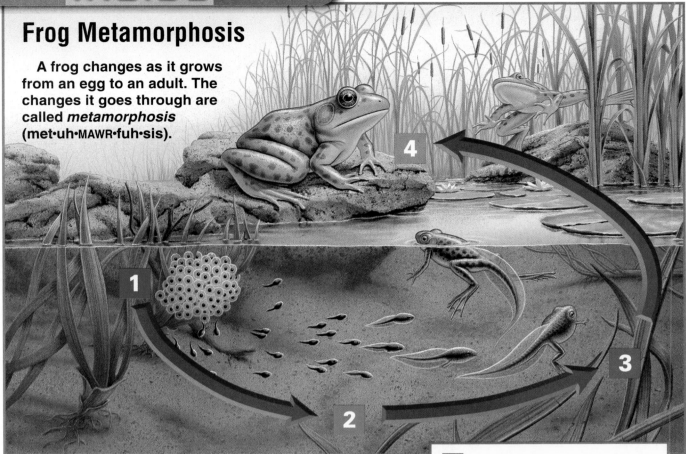

Frogs Grow and Change

As you saw in the investigation, young frogs look very different from adult frogs. Young frogs hatch from eggs and begin life in the water. They breathe with gills. **Gills** are body parts that take in oxygen from the water.

As they grow, young frogs change. In time, they form lungs. Once they have lungs, their gills begin to disappear. Then they develop other body parts that help them live on land. Adult frogs spend most of the year on land near water.

✔ **What body parts do young frogs have that adult frogs do not have?**

1 A frog lays many eggs at one time. The eggs are covered by a jellylike coating.

2 Newborn tadpoles have gills for breathing in water. They also have a tail but no legs.

3 As a tadpole grows, lungs begin to form. Back and front legs begin to grow. These parts allow an adult frog to live on land.

4 Once the lungs work, the gills and the tail disappear. The adult frog is now ready to live on land.

Fish

Fish are animals that live their whole lives in water. Like young amphibians, fish have gills. The gills are on the sides of a fish's head. The gills take in oxygen as water moves over them.

Most fish are covered with scales. **Scales** are small, thin, flat plates that help protect the fish.

Different fish have many different shapes and sizes. Like other animals, some fish eat plants and others eat animals. Most fish lay eggs, but some fish give birth to live young.

✔ **What are two traits of fish?**

▲ **This Guadeloupe bass has a skeleton made of bone.**

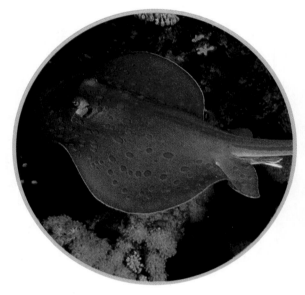

▲ **This ray has a cartilage skeleton just like a shark, but its body is flat.**

Sharks do not have bones. Instead, their skeletons are made of a softer material called cartilage (KAR•tuh•lij). ▼

The Bodies of Fish

A fish's body is just right for its life in water. Most fish have body shapes that allow them to move easily in water. The smooth scales that cover fish also help them glide through water.

Fish have fins. They use their fins to move forward and backward. The tail fin moves from side to side and helps a fish move forward. Other fins help the fish turn in different directions.

✔ **What are three ways a fish's body is just right for life in water?**

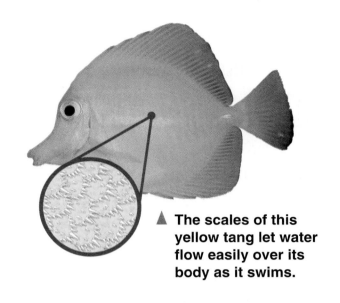

▲ **The scales of this yellow tang let water flow easily over its body as it swims.**

▲ **This rainbow trout has gills that take in oxygen from water.**

▲ **The fins on this goldfish help it swim and turn its body through the water.**

Fish Young

Young fish are hatched from eggs. Some fish carry their eggs inside their bodies until the eggs hatch. But most fish lay their eggs in water. They lay many eggs at a time.

Some fish care for their eggs by guarding them. But most fish leave their eggs alone after they are laid. Other animals eat many of the eggs. The young fish that do hatch are very small. But they must find food and avoid enemies without help from their parents.

✓ **What are two ways fish produce young?**

▲ **This stickleback fish builds a nest to lay its eggs in.**

This cardinal fish carries its eggs in its mouth until they are ready to be hatched. ▼

Reptiles

Reptiles (REP•tylz) are land animals that have dry skin covered by scales. Because they live mostly on land, reptiles use lungs to breathe air. Reptiles that spend a lot of time in water must come to the surface to breathe air. A crocodile, for instance, often stays in water. But it stays near the surface so its nose and eyes are above the water. This allows the crocodile to breathe and see.

Many reptiles hatch from eggs laid on land. The eggs have a tough, leathery shell. Other reptiles are born live. Either way, most of the young are able to meet their needs as soon as they are born.

Reptiles are found almost everywhere on Earth except for the coldest places. Many live in warm, wet tropical rain forests or in hot, dry deserts.

✔ **What are three traits of reptiles?**

▲ **The Eastern box turtle hatches from eggs laid on land.**

The turtle has a hard shell that protects most of its body. The turtle has scales on its legs and tail. ▼

A55

Types of Reptiles

There are three main groups of reptiles. Lizards and snakes are in one group. Their bodies have rows of scales that overlap. Many lizards live in very warm places. They have four legs and long tails. Snakes don't have legs. They move by pushing their bodies against the ground.

Alligators and crocodiles are another reptile group. They live in water a lot of the time. They come out of the water to sun themselves.

Tortoises and turtles make up the third group of reptiles. They are the only reptiles that have shells. Tortoises live on land. Turtles live in water.

✔ **What are the three groups of reptiles?**

▲ The boa is a large snake. Like other snakes, it sheds its scaly skin and grows new skin.

▲ The Australian frilled lizard uses a fan-shaped body part to scare away enemies.

This is an American crocodile. A crocodile can lie very still in the water, with only its eyes and nose above the water. This helps the crocodile catch animals that can't see it. ▼

▲ This is a Galápagos tortoise. Like turtles, tortoises have hard shells that protect them from enemies.

Summary

Amphibians are animals that begin life in water, change in form, and then live on land. Fish live in the water, use gills for breathing, and have body parts that help them swim. Reptiles are animals that are covered with scales.

Review

1. What happens during the metamorphosis of a frog?
2. List three features that help fish live and move in water.
3. What do gills do?
4. **Critical Thinking** Why do many amphibians stay near the water for their whole lives?
5. **Test Prep** Which trait is shared by most fish, amphibians, and reptiles?

   A fins   C eggs
   B scales   D legs

LINKS

MATH LINK

Using Graphs Take a survey of the kinds of amphibians, fish, and reptiles that people keep as pets. Use a computer graphing program such as *Graph Links* to make a bar graph to show your results.

WRITING LINK

Narrative Writing—Story What if you were a frog? Write a story for a younger child telling how you change as you grow.

LITERATURE LINK

Verdi To learn more about a snake called a python, read *Verdi* by Janell Cannon.

ART LINK

Collage Make a collage that shows adult animals with their young.

TECHNOLOGY LINK

Learn about endangered reptiles by watching *Endangered Animals* on the **Harcourt Science Newsroom Video** in your classroom video library.

LESSON 4

What Is Extinction?

In this lesson, you can . . .

 INVESTIGATE endangered animals.

 LEARN ABOUT living things that are threatened, endangered, or extinct.

 LINK to math, writing, social studies, and technology.

Endangered Animals

Activity Purpose Over time, the numbers of some animals can become so low that they are in danger of disappearing forever. These animals are called endangered. In this investigation, you will **use numbers** to **predict** what might happen to some endangered animals.

Materials
- reference books
- graph paper
- ruler

Activity Procedure

1 Find lists of endangered species in reference books or on the Internet. (Picture A)

◀ Zebras are one type of endangered animal.

Picture A

2 Choose five endangered animals from the lists. Look for information about how the numbers of these animals have changed over time. Find out how many of each animal are living now.

3 Make a bar graph for your animals. For each animal, draw one bar to show how many were alive 10 years ago. Use a second bar to show how many are alive now. (Picture B)

4 **Infer** what will happen in the future to the animals on your graph. Explain your inferences, and share them with the class.

Draw Conclusions

1. How did **using numbers** help you **organize your data** in this activity?

2. What could happen that would change your prediction? **Record** your ideas.

Picture B

3. **Scientists at Work** Scientists **use numbers** to help them **organize their data**. They then use their data to make inferences. How did making a bar graph help you make your prediction about the future of the animals?

Investigate Further Animals are not the only kinds of organisms that can become endangered. Find information on five kinds of plants that are endangered, and make a bar graph as you did for the animals.

Process Skill Tip

When you **infer**, you are using what you have observed to explain something that has happened. You can **use numbers** to help you organize data that supports your inference.

Extinction

FIND OUT

- **how different species are threatened with extinction**
- **why animals become extinct**
- **how some living animals look like extinct animals**

VOCABULARY

extinct
species
endangered
threatened
fossil

Threatened, Endangered, Extinct

Last time you were outside, did you see any robins or ladybugs? How about oak trees or grass? These animals and plants may be easy to find. Other kinds of organisms are less common.

Although there are billions of ladybugs in the world, some kinds of organisms have only a few hundred members left. When there are only a few hundred individuals of one kind of organism, there is a chance that all of the individuals will die and the organism will become **extinct**. When a plant or animal becomes extinct, it is gone forever.

Each living organism that scientists have identified has its own name. This name identifies a **species** (SPEE•sheez) of organism. The desert tortoise is a species of animal. The prickly pear cactus is a species of plant. Species that are in danger of becoming extinct are called **endangered**. Scientists add the names of these species to the endangered species list.

◀ The desert tortoise lives in Mexico and the southern United States. It is listed as a threatened species.

Before an organism becomes endangered, there may be a reduction in its numbers. When scientists notice that the number of organisms is steadily going down, they say that the organism is **threatened**. A threatened organism is on its way to becoming endangered or extinct.

The desert tortoise is a threatened species. To protect the tortoise, scientists have put it on the threatened species list.

The whooping crane is a bird that lives in wet, swampy areas where it eats snakes and frogs. It is on the endangered species list because only about 150 of the birds are left in the world.

The saber-toothed cat roamed the forests of the world more than a million years ago. It hunted mastodons—giant elephant-like animals. When the mastodons died out, the saber-toothed cat had nothing to eat. Eventually, they

▲ **The bald eagle was once an endangered species. In many places, it has been taken off the endangered species list.**

became extinct. We know they existed because scientists have found their bones buried in the ground. Evidence of an animal or plant that lived a long time ago on Earth is called a **fossil**.

✔ **What does *endangered* mean?**

Saber-toothed cats have been extinct for thousands of years. ▶

How Animals Become Extinct

Many kinds of animals that once lived on Earth have become extinct. Extinction is a natural process. Over time, some species live while others die out.

Suppose a certain species' environment suddenly changes. Maybe it becomes colder or wetter. Or maybe a new predator moves in or the animal's main food source disappears. How does the species react? It adapts to the new environment, moves to a different environment, or dies.

Although extinction can be natural, often people cause a species to become extinct. Most animals today become extinct because their *habitat*, or the area they live in, is destroyed. When trees and grasslands are cut down to make room for houses and roads, animals that live on the land have to go somewhere else. Sometimes there is nowhere for them to go, and they die.

Most animals know how to avoid predators in their habitats. But when a new predator appears, the animals may not know how to avoid it. In this case, the predator can easily kill many of the animals and may cause their extinction.

◀ **The dusky seaside sparrow used to live along the Florida coast. As people started to build houses there, the sparrow's habitat was destroyed. The animal became extinct just a few years ago when the last bird died.**

This is exactly what happened in Africa's Lake Victoria. People took a large fish from another part of the continent and put it in the lake. Soon most of the smaller species of fish had been eaten by the new predator. In total, over 200 species of local fish became extinct.

Many animals in the wild are hunted for food or sport. Today, we have laws that tell us which animals can be hunted and which cannot be hunted. But a few hundred years ago, these laws didn't exist and people hunted some animals until they were extinct or nearly extinct.

The Caribbean monk seal is an animal that became extinct this way. Because the seals ate fish, fishers saw them as competition. So they killed thousands of the seals. The last monk seal was killed near the coast of Florida in 1922.

Some species become extinct for only one reason. But usually extinction has more than one cause. For example, loss of habitat might reduce a population to very few individuals. This small population could then be easily wiped out by a new predator.

✔ **What are the causes of extinction today?**

Some Animals Today Look Like Extinct Animals

When animals die, sometimes their bodies are buried and over millions of years become fossils. Scientists use fossils to make models of animals that lived long ago. Even if a fossil is not complete, scientists can put together the pieces they have and then infer to complete the model.

After scientists put together models of some of the animals that are now extinct, they found something very interesting. Some of the models looked like animals that are alive today. For example, the woolly mammoth became extinct many thousands of years ago. But the woolly mammoth looked a lot like an elephant—an animal that lives today.

✔ **How do scientists know what extinct animals from long ago looked like?**

◀ Like today's elephant the woolly mammoth had a long trunk, big ears, and tusks. Because the mammoth lived in a very cold environment, it was much hairier than today's elephant, which lives in a hot climate.

The Tasmanian tiger-wolf (left) became extinct in 1936. Hunting by local farmers angry with the tiger-wolves for eating their livestock reduced the tiger-wolf population to very low numbers. An unknown disease killed the last few animals. The tiger-wolf looked a lot like today's wolf (above).

Moas (left) were giant, flightless birds found only on the islands of New Zealand. Overhunting and new predators, such as the dogs and rats that were brought onto the islands by humans, led to the moa's extinction more than 200 years ago. The African ostrich (right) looks much like a moa. ▶

Species Watch

Animals on the endangered and threatened species lists are protected by different laws. Some of the laws prevent the animals from being hunted. Others protect the habitats they live in from being used by humans.

In some cases, the animals do better under the protection of these laws. They are able to reproduce, and their numbers increase until they are no longer endangered.

✔ **How do laws protect endangered animals?**

▲ The Key deer is the smallest deer in North America. It lives on the southern islands of Florida, known as the Keys. As more people move to the Keys, less habitat is available for the deer. Key deer were put on the Endangered Species list in 1967. The deer cannot be hunted and they have land set aside for them to live on.

The grizzly bear is on the threatened species list. The bears live mostly in Canada and Alaska now, where there are fewer people to disturb them. Because of the bears' enormous size, people used to hunt them as trophies. Today, loss of habitat is the main reason for their decline. ▼

▲ Red wolves were killed by people who were afraid of them and by people who didn't want the wolves to eat their sheep. Later, more and more of the wolves' habitat was cleared in order to make room for houses. The wolves were put on the Endangered Species list in 1967. Then scientists began breeding them and then releasing the young wolves into their natural habitat again.

Summary

Sometimes species of animals go extinct. Fossils show us that animals that are not on Earth today existed thousands or even millions of years ago. Extinction is sometimes caused by natural changes in habitat. Other times it is caused by people. Many animals alive today look like animals that went extinct long ago. Some species living today are in danger of becoming extinct. These animals are protected by laws and watched by scientists.

Review

1. How are threatened species different from endangered species?
2. How can people cause animals to go extinct?
3. What can we learn about animals living today by looking at fossils of extinct animals?
4. **Critical Thinking** How can we better protect animals that are threatened or endangered?
5. **Test Prep** What is the main cause of animal extinction today?
   A fossils
   B hunting
   C habitat loss
   D weather

LINKS

MATH LINK

How Tall? Moas grew to a height of about 4 meters. Today's ostriches are about $2\frac{1}{2}$ meters tall. How much taller was the moa than the ostrich? How much taller is the ostrich than you are?

WRITING LINK

Informative Writing—Report
Find out about an endangered or threatened species that interests you. Write a report for your teacher explaining the factors that are causing its numbers to decline. What laws has the government set up to protect the animal?

SOCIAL STUDIES LINK

The Law Use your media center to find out when the Endangered Species Act became a law.

TECHNOLOGY LINK

To learn more about endangered animals, watch *Endangered Animals* on the **Harcourt Science Newsroom Video** in your classroom video library.

DISCOVERING Animals

No one knows how many kinds of animals there are. New kinds are found every year. There are more than one and one-half million kinds of animals! More than one million kinds of animals are insects. Some scientists think there could be as many as 50 million kinds of animals!

Grouping Animals

People have been observing animals for centuries. New animals are discovered as scientists and explorers go to new places. One of the first people to observe animals and to write about them was Aristotle. He lived about 350 B.C. He divided animals into two groups. One was made up of animals with backbones and red blood. This group

The History of Animal Discovery

350 B.C.
Aristotle develops a classification system for animals.

1600s
John Ray discovers that whales are mammals.

350 B.C.   1400   1500   1600

1400–1600
Age of exploration— many animals are discovered.

1590
The microscope is invented.

included horses, cats, dogs, and oxen. The other group did not have backbones or red blood.

Since then, scientists have discovered that most animals do not have backbones. Clams, spiders, ants, sponges, worms, jellyfish, and squids are all part of this group.

Your senses can mislead you when you study animals. A whale looks like a fish, and it lives in the water. Not until the 1600s did an English scientist, John Ray, observe whales closely. He learned that they are mammals, just as humans are.

Discovering New Animals

The microscope was invented during the late 1500s. Using this tool, scientists began to discover living things made up of only one cell. In 1665 Robert Hooke published a book of drawings of biological specimens viewed through a

1665
Robert Hooke publishes a collection of his drawings.

1700 ❯ 1900 2000

1977
Animals are discovered living near thermal vents deep in the ocean.

microscope. Scientists today use microscopes to study all kinds of cells. These studies help scientists understand how animals are related to one another.

When explorers during the 1500s and 1600s traveled to new places, they returned home with animals that had never been seen before. They brought parrots and other brightly colored birds from tropical areas such as South America. They also brought many different kinds of monkeys from those areas. A giraffe from East Africa was sent to China. All of these animals were studied carefully by scientists.

People continue to find and study new animals. Modern explorers search the oceans for unknown species. We still know very little about animals living at the bottom of the ocean. Thermal vents are places where heat comes from the ocean floor. Many strange creatures live near these thermal vents.

Scientists will continue to explore unfamiliar places, such as rain forests, ocean floors, and volcanoes. Each new place will probably have animals we have never seen before.

Think About It

• How have microscopes helped scientists learn about animals?

Rodolfo Dirzo

TROPICAL ECOLOGIST

"I am interested in . . . the loss of animals in tropical ecosystems."

Growing up in Mexico, Rodolfo Dirzo used to watch bugs. That early interest led him to study snails and slugs far away in Wales. After completing his education, he returned to Mexico. He has taught for many years at the Organization for Tropical Studies. He does research on tropical forests. Teaching is one of Dirzo's main interests. He especially wants to interest Latin American students in ecology.

Besides teaching, Dirzo studies two different forests in Mexico. In one, the forest has not been disturbed. There are many kinds of plants and animals. In the other, some of the forest has been cut down. As a result, many of the animals that would be expected to live there are no longer there. Dirzo compares the two places. He uses his imagination and his training in science to describe what happens to a habitat that has changed. Without animals to help spread seeds and to trample down the vegetation, the forest plants may change. Dirzo expects that there will be fewer kinds of trees without the animals to help provide places for many different plants to grow.

Think About It

1. What might cause animals to leave a forest?
2. How does comparing the two forests help Dirzo analyze his data?

Rain forest

Shell Study

Why is a spiral shell larger at one end?

Materials

- safety goggles
- gloves
- spiral shell from an animal such as a whelk, conch, or sea snail
- coarse sandpaper
- hand lens

Procedure

1 **CAUTION** **Put on the safety goggles and gloves.** Observe the outside of the shell. Rub the tip of the shell with sandpaper until you have a hole about 5 millimeters (about $\frac{1}{4}$ in.) wide.

2 Use the hand lens to observe the inside of the shell. What do you see?

Draw Conclusions

Animals that live in spiral shells usually keep their shells for their whole lives. When they begin their lives, they are very small. Their shells are very small too.

Think about the shell you observed. Why do you think the spiral is small at one end and gets bigger at the other end?

Feather Study

What are the parts of feathers?

Materials

- 1 or 2 types of feathers from a bird
- hand lens

Procedure

1 Study the feathers. Use the hand lens to look at their parts. Record what you observe.

2 Touch the feathers as you look at them. Record what you feel.

Draw Conclusions

Discuss what you know about birds. Think of ways the feathers help birds fly.

Buying Endangered Species

What can you do to protect endangered species?

Materials

- newspaper and magazine ads
- large sheet of paper
- markers

Procedure

1 Choose a category from the following list.

clothes	household
food	pets
furniture	plants

2 Look for newspaper and magazine ads in the category you selected. Make a list of products that might be made from an endangered species. Include the name of the endangered species next to the product.

3 Look for information about the products on your list. You may use reference books or the Internet in your search.

4 Make a table like the one shown to display your findings. Use the "Not Recommended" column to list things that a person might not use because the product might harm an endangered species. Use the "Recommended" column to list things that a person might recommend using because the product would not endanger a species. In the Substitute column, list alternatives that would not endanger a species.

5 Communicate your findings with your classmates.

Draw Conclusions

What would make you think about adding, removing, or changing things in your table?

Not Recommended	Recommended	Substitute
teak desk	maple desk	oak desk

Inside an Egg

What is inside an egg?

Materials

- uncooked egg
- plastic disposable gloves
- clear plastic bowl
- paper towel
- hand lens

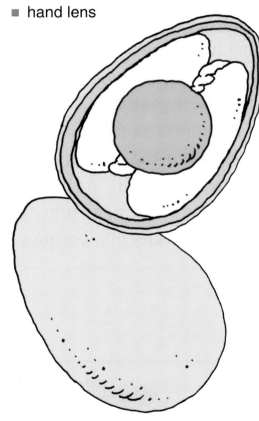

Procedure

1 **CAUTION** **Put on the plastic gloves. Do not touch the egg with your fingers. Wash your hands after you complete this activity.** Break the egg into the bowl. Place the shell on the paper towel.

2 Use the hand lens to observe the parts of the egg. Identify the egg white and the yolk. Look carefully for the small white spot on the yolk. A young chick would grow from this spot.

3 Find the twisted strands in the egg white. Predict what you think they might do.

4 Use the hand lens to observe the shell and the thin lining inside the shell. How do you think the tiny holes in the eggshell help the growing chick? What might the lining do?

Draw Conclusions

How does the hard shell protect the egg? Would a soft shell work as well? Explain your ideas.

Chapter 2 Review and Test Preparation

Vocabulary Review

Use the terms below to complete the sentences 1 through 14. The page numbers in ( ) tell you where to look in the chapter if you need help.

inherit (A38)
traits (A38)
mammals (A42)
birds (A45)
amphibians (A50)
gills (A51)
fish (A52)

scales (A52)
reptiles (A55)
extinct (A60)
species (A60)
endangered (A60)
threatened (A61)
fossil (A61)

1. One trait of ___ is a body covering called fur.
2. The features a young animal gets from its parents are called ___.
3. Animals ___ their traits from their parents.
4. Animals that begin life in water and later live on land are ___.
5. ___ have bodies covered with feathers.
6. Reptiles and fish have ___.
7. Scales make it easy for ___ to glide through the water.
8. Young amphibians and fish use ___ to take in oxygen.
9. ___ have dry, scaly skin.
10. Evidence of a plant or animal that lived long ago is a ___.
11. When all of one kind of organism dies, the organism is ___.
12. If the numbers of an organism are going down, the organism is ___.
13. A specific scientific name identifies a ___ of an organism.
14. An ___ species may become extinct.

Connect Concepts

Write the terms that belong in the concept map.

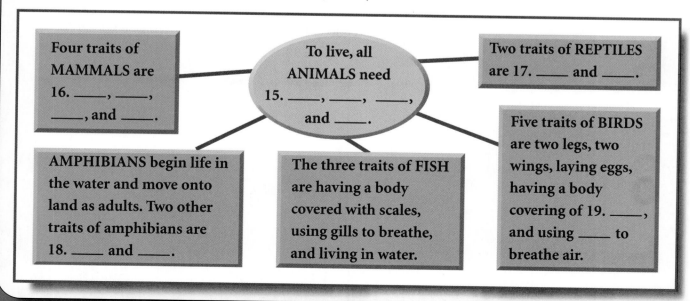

Four traits of MAMMALS are 16. ___, ___, ___, and ___.

To live, all ANIMALS need 15. ___, ___, ___, and ___.

Two traits of REPTILES are 17. ___ and ___.

AMPHIBIANS begin life in the water and move onto land as adults. Two other traits of amphibians are 18. ___ and ___.

The three traits of FISH are having a body covered with scales, using gills to breathe, and living in water.

Five traits of BIRDS are two legs, two wings, laying eggs, having a body covering of 19. ___, and using ___ to breathe air.

Check Understanding

Write the letter of the best choice.

20. If all the individuals of a species are dead, the species is —
A endangered C thriving
B threatened D extinct

21. What kind of shelter do beavers build?
F dam H den
G lodge J nest

22. Which kind of animal feeds its young with milk from its body?
A fish C amphibian
B mammal D bird

23. Young reptiles —
F can meet their needs as soon as they are born
G can swim
H are carried in a pouch
J begin life in the water

Critical Thinking

24. What are the differences between the terms *threatened, endangered,* and *extinct*?

25. Describe how the body parts of a shark help it survive.

26. How are polar bears and bats alike?

Process Skills Review

27. Use what you have learned about animals to **classify** these animals into groups: snake, robin, dog, lizard, cow, goose, whale. Explain why you grouped the animals as you did.

28. Explain how making and **using a model** of a bird's nest can help you learn about birds.

29. How can you use your senses to **observe** birds?

Performance Assessment

Grouping Animals

Use the picture cards from the Investigate in Lesson 1. Group them by using what you have learned about animals. Are there any animals that don't belong in a group? What traits do these animals have?

Chapter 3

Where Living Things Are Found

Living things are all around us—in the air, on the land, and in the water. In this chapter you'll explore where living things are found and how their bodies and behaviors help them live in their environments.

Vocabulary Preview

environment	deciduous forest
ecosystem	tropical rain forest
population	coastal forest
community	coniferous forest
habitat	desert
forest	fresh water
salt water	

FAST FACT

One of the most unusual wildflowers of the southwest United States is the ground cone. It looks like a pine cone sitting on the ground. Since most animals don't eat pine cones, this is a great way of hiding!

FAST FACT

There are about 2,500 black rhinoceroses left in the wild. Because of their small numbers, they are endangered.

Endangered Animals	
Animal	**Number Alive**
Giant Pandas	1,000
Manatees	1,900
Black Rhinoceroses	2,500
Cheetahs	11,000

LESSON 1

What Are Ecosystems?

In this lesson, you can . . .

INVESTIGATE what makes up an environment.

LEARN ABOUT parts of an environment.

LINK to math, writing, literature, and technology.

Observing an Environment

Activity Purpose You may have seen trees, insects, and mammals near your home. You may also have seen grass, flowers, worms, and birds. All these things get what they need to live from their *environment,* or everything around them.

In this investigation you will **observe** an environment to find out what kinds of things live there. You will also observe the nonliving things that are part of the environment.

Materials
- wire clothes hanger

Activity Procedure

1 Bend your hanger to make a square. Go outside and place the hanger on the ground. Inside this square is the environment you will **observe.** (Picture A)

◄ These bees live and raise their young in the hive. They make honey to feed the young.

2 Make a list of all the things you **observe.** Next to each thing on your list, **record** whether it is living or nonliving. Write *L* for living and *N* for nonliving.

3 Ask a classmate to share his or her list with you. **Compare** the environments each of you observed.

4 Choose a living thing you **observed** in your hanger environment. Talk with a classmate about which things in the environment help the living thing survive.

Picture A

Draw Conclusions

1. Describe the environment you **observed**.

2. How can you use **observation** to find out how an animal lives?

3. **Scientists at Work** Scientists learn by **observing** and by **gathering data.** They also learn from the data gathered by others. What did you learn about an environment from your classmate's data?

Investigate Further **Observe** a sample of soil in which an earthworm lives. Describe the environment.

Process Skill Tip

When you **observe** living things in their environments, you can **gather data** about the organisms and the environment. The data can help you learn about the environment and about the things that live there.

Living Things and Their Environments

FIND OUT

- **how an environment affects a living thing**
- **what makes up an ecosystem**

VOCABULARY

environment
ecosystem
population
community
habitat

Where Things Live

Think about where different kinds of plants and animals live. Some kinds of plants and animals live in hot, dry places. Others live in cool, shady forests. Fish live in water. Some insects live in the ground. Others live on plants. In the investigation you observed an environment. An **environment** (en•VY•ruhn•muhnt) is everything around a living thing.

Living things get what they need to live from their environments. They need things such as air, water, food, and shelter. When many kinds of living things share an environment, they must also share the things they need. For example, the plants and animals in a pond all use the air, water, and food from that pond.

✔ **What do living things get from an environment?**

A raccoon in a city may find food in trash cans. Many animals can live in more than one environment. ▼

A raccoon in a forest may catch fish to eat. ▶

The Parts of an Ecosystem

In an environment the living and nonliving things that affect each other, or interact, form an **ecosystem** (EK•oh•sis•tuhm). An ecosystem, such as the pond shown on this page, has many parts.

Frogs live in the pond. All of the frogs, as a group, are called a population. A **population** (pahp•yoo•LAY•shuhn) is a group of the same kind of living things that live in the same place at the same time.

Populations of insects, waterlilies, and cattails live in the pond, too. Together these populations form a community. A **community** (kuh•MYOO•nuh•tee) is all the populations that live in an ecosystem.

Within the pond ecosystem, each population lives in a **habitat** (HAB•ih•tat). A habitat provides a population with all its needs and includes nonliving things and living things. There are many habitats in an ecosystem. For example, the cattails live on the edge of the pond. That is their habitat.

✔ **What makes up an ecosystem?**

The frog population, the cattail population, and all the other populations in this pond form a community.

The pond is the habitat, or home, of all the living things that make up the community.

Nonliving things, such as air, sunlight, water, rocks, and soil, are also part of an ecosystem. The community of living things needs the nonliving things to survive.

The ecosystem of this pond is made up of all the living and nonliving things that interact in and around the pond.

Fires in 1988 destroyed the large trees of this ecosystem. Before 1988 these large trees in Yellowstone National Park were the habitat of many living things.

Ten years after the fire, these wildflowers show that life has returned to Yellowstone.

How Ecosystems Change

Ecosystems can change. Some changes to ecosystems are caused by nature. For example, floods or fires can kill many living things and destroy habitats. But some living things survive when an ecosystem is damaged. A fire doesn't destroy all the seeds in the ground. The seeds that survive grow into new plants. As the plants grow, animals that feed on them return to the area.

A flood can also harm an ecosystem. But a flood brings a new layer of rich soil to a riverbank. New plants grow in the soil.

Ecosystems are also changed by living things. Some changes help the living things meet their needs. For example, people cut down trees and use the wood to build homes and make other products. Beavers cut down trees to build dams and lodges in streams. The other animals that lived in the trees must find new homes.

Many spiders spin webs to use as homes and to help capture food. ▼

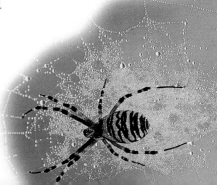

When an ecosystem changes, the animals in it sometimes move to a nearby part of the ecosystem. But sometimes the ecosystem is changed so much that the plants and animals can no longer live there.

✓ **Why do ecosystems change?**

Summary

An environment is everything that surrounds a living thing. The living and nonliving things that interact in an environment make up an ecosystem. An ecosystem is made up of smaller parts that include populations, communities, and habitats, as well as nonliving things, such as air, sunlight, and soil. Nature and living things can change ecosystems.

Review

1. What is an environment?
2. What nonliving things are found in an ecosystem?
3. What is a population?
4. **Critical Thinking** How can building a new road change an ecosystem?
5. **Test Prep** A pond that contains waterlilies, frogs, fish, insects, and cattails is an example of —

   A a population   C a habitat

   B an ecosystem   D a community

LINKS

MATH LINK

Summing Populations
Suppose an ecosystem has 54 squirrels, 12 rabbits, 15 trees, and 100 grasshoppers. How many animals are in the community? How many populations are there?

WRITING LINK

Informative Writing—Report
What if a flood destroyed part of an ecosystem near your home? Write a newspaper report for your class telling what happened to an animal because of the flood.

LITERATURE LINK

Read About Fire To learn more about fires and ecosystems, read *Wildfires* by Ann Armbruster.

TECHNOLOGY LINK

Learn more about how changes in an ecosystem can affect the living things there by watching *Tainted Water* on the **Harcourt Science Newsroom Video** in your classroom video library.

LESSON 2

What Are Forest Ecosystems?

In this lesson, you can . . .

INVESTIGATE
trees in forests.

LEARN ABOUT
different types of forests.

LINK to math, writing, art, and technology.

Variety in Forests

Activity Purpose
Forests have trees. But did you know that there are several types of forests? In this investigation you will **use numbers** to **interpret data** about trees in two kinds of forests.

Materials
- tray of beans, labeled *Tray 1*
- tray of beans, labeled *Tray 2*
- 2 paper cups

Activity Procedure

1 Make a data table like the one shown. Tray 1 stands for the trees in a tropical rain forest. Tray 2 stands for the trees in a deciduous forest. Each kind of bean stands for a different kind of tree.

2 Scoop a cupful of beans from each tray. Carefully pour each cup of beans into its own pile.

◄ **Moose like this one live in coniferous forests.**

Tropical Rain Forest (Tray 1)		Deciduous Forest (Tray 2)	
Kind of Bean	Number of Beans	Kind of Bean	Number of Beans

3 Work with a partner. One partner should work with the beans from Tray 1. The other partner should work with the beans from Tray 2. (Picture A)

4 Sort the beans into groups so that each group contains only one kind of bean.

5 **Record** a description of each type of bean in the data table. Count the number of beans in each small pile. Record these numbers in the data table.

Picture A

Draw Conclusions

1. How many kinds of "trees" were in each "forest"?

2. Which forest had the most trees of one kind? Why do you think this was so?

3. **Scientists at Work** Scientists learn by **gathering, recording,** and **interpreting data.** What did you learn from your data about variety in forests?

Investigate Further Suppose you want to find out what kinds of trees are most common in your community. Explain how you could **use numbers** to find out.

Process Skill Tip

Using numbers is one way to **record data** from an investigation. When you **interpret data,** you **draw a conclusion** based on the data you have collected.

Forest Ecosystems

FIND OUT

- about four kinds of forests
- about living things in different kinds of forests

VOCABULARY

forest
deciduous forest
tropical rain forest
coastal forest
coniferous forest

Types of Forests

You probably know that a **forest** is an area in which the main plants are trees. But many other kinds of plants and animals also live in forests.

Forests grow in many parts of the world. Some forests are named for the types of trees that grow in them. Other forests are named for the area in which they grow.

Each type of forest needs a certain amount of rainfall and sunshine. Each also has certain temperatures that let it grow best. If any of these things change, the kinds of plants that grow in the forest may also change.

✔ **What is a forest?**

This graph shows how much rain falls each year in each kind of forest. ▼

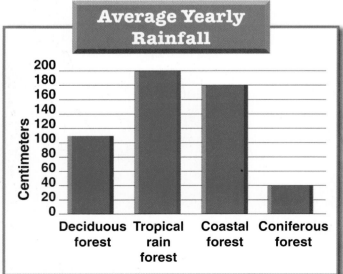

This graph shows the average yearly temperature in each kind of forest. ▼

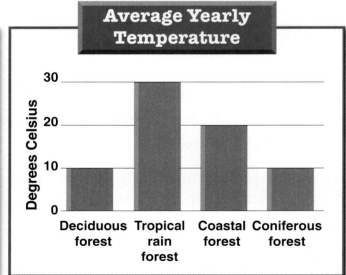

Deciduous Forests

Some trees, such as maples and oaks, have large, flat leaves that drop off each fall. New leaves grow back in the spring. Trees that lose and regrow their leaves each year are called deciduous (dee•SIJ•oo•uhs) trees. Forests made up mostly of these trees are **deciduous forests**. They grow in places that have warm, wet summers and cold winters.

Deciduous leaves change color before they drop in the fall. When a deciduous tree drops its leaves, it needs less water. This helps the tree live through the winter, when water may be frozen.

The deciduous forest is a habitat for many kinds of living things, such as ferns, shrubs, and mosses. Animals such as insects, spiders, snakes, frogs, birds, rabbits, deer, and bears also live here.

✔ **Where do deciduous forests grow?**

The leaves of deciduous trees change color just before they drop from the trees in the fall. ▼

▲ During the winter deciduous trees have no leaves.

Deciduous trees grow new leaves in the spring. ▼

In the summer a deciduous forest looks healthy and green. ▼

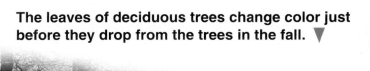

A87

Tropical Rain Forests

Tropical rain forests grow in places such as Hawai'i and Costa Rica. These places are hot and wet all year. The trees grow very tall, and their leaves stay green all year.

More types of living things live in rain forests than anywhere else on Earth. Plants and animals make their homes in all the layers of the forest, from the tops of the trees to the ground.

✔ **Where do tropical rain forests grow?**

◄ This moth lives in the tropical rain forest. It feeds on the plants that grow beneath the trees.

THE INSIDE STORY

Layers of the Rain Forest

A tropical rain forest has three main layers. The top layer is called the *canopy.* It is formed by the branches and leaves of the tallest trees. Below the canopy is the *understory.* The understory is formed by plants that don't grow as tall as trees. The *forest floor* is the lowest layer. Many kinds of plants and animals make their homes in each layer of a tropical rain forest.

Coastal Forests

Coastal forests grow where there is a lot of rain. Unlike a tropical rain forest, a coastal forest grows where it does not get too warm or too cold. But like tropical rain forests, coastal forests are thick with many kinds of tall trees. Coastal forests have the same kinds of layers as tropical rain forests.

✓ **Describe a coastal forest environment.**

▲ The northern spotted owl thrives in the moist, cool environment of the coastal forest.

Canopy

Understory

Forest Floor

1 The leaves of the canopy get lots of water and sunlight. Many animals drink water that collects on the leaves.

2 Plants of the understory get less sunlight and water than those in the canopy. Orchids, mosses, and ferns grow on the trunks of the tall trees.

3 Little sunlight reaches the rain-forest floor, and few nutrients are found in the soil. Plants that grow here must find other ways to get nutrients.

Coniferous Forests

What kind of trees would you find where there are very cold winters and cool summers? Mostly, you would find *conifers* (KAHN•uh•ferz)—trees that form seeds in cones. Conifers have needle-like leaves. Pines, spruces, and firs are common conifers. Conifers don't lose their needles in the fall. They stay green all year. This is why conifers are often called *evergreens*. Forests that contain mostly these kinds of trees are coniferous (koh•NIF•er•uhs) forests.

Conifers grow in areas that get less rain than other types of forests. The needle-shaped leaves of these trees help keep the trees from losing too much water.

Many conifers are shaped like triangles. This shape helps keep heavy snow from piling up on a tree's larger branches in winter, which might cause them to break.

Coniferous forests often have many lakes and streams. The trees, lakes, and streams provide habitats for many animals. Squirrels, moose, and wolves are common. Insects such as mosquitoes and flies also live in coniferous forests.

✔ **What kinds of trees grow in a coniferous forest?**

Coniferous forests are homes for animals such as moose, bears, and wolves. ▼

Summary

There are different types of forest ecosystems. The main types of forests are deciduous forests, tropical rain forests, coastal forests, and coniferous forests. These forests provide habitats for many kinds of plants and animals.

Review

1. What is a forest?
2. Which kind of forest has trees that lose their leaves in the fall?
3. What are the layers of a tropical rain forest?
4. **Critical Thinking** What is the main difference between a tropical rain forest and a coastal forest?
5. **Test Prep** A deciduous forest has —

    A cool summers and warm winters

    B warm, wet summers and dry winters

    C warm, wet summers and cold winters

    D warm, dry summers and dry winters

LINKS

MATH LINK

Interpret a Graph Look back at the first graph on page A86. What is the difference in yearly rainfall between the tropical rain forest and the deciduous forest? Which gets more rain each year?

WRITING LINK

Expressive Writing—Friendly Letter Pick a forest from this lesson. Imagine that you live there. Write a letter to a classmate telling what you like most about your forest.

ART LINK

Leaf Prints Gather leaves from the trees that grow in your area. Dip the leaves into paint, and make leaf prints on paper. Label each print.

TECHNOLOGY LINK

Explore forests as you complete the activity *Backpacking Through Forests* on **Harcourt Science Explorations CD-ROM.**

LESSON **3**

What Is a Desert Ecosystem?

In this lesson, you can . . .

INVESTIGATE a desert ecosystem.

LEARN ABOUT desert ecosystems.

LINK to math, writing, health, and technology.

◄ **This scorpion is one type of animal that lives in the desert.**

INVESTIGATE

Make a Desert Ecosystem

Activity Purpose A desert is a very dry place. But this ecosystem is home to many kinds of living things. In this investigation you will **make a model** of a desert ecosystem.

Materials
- shoe box
- plastic wrap
- sandy soil
- 2 or 3 desert plants
- small rocks

Activity Procedure

1 **Make a model** of a desert ecosystem. Start by lining the shoe box with plastic wrap. Place sandy soil in the shoe box. Make sure the soil is deep enough for the plants.

2 Place the plants in the soil, and place the rocks around them. Lightly sprinkle the soil with water. (Picture A)

3 Place your desert ecosystem in a sunny location. (Picture B)

4 Every two or three days, use your finger to **observe** how dry the soil is. If the soil is *very* dry, add a small amount of water. If the soil is damp, do not add water. Be careful not to water the plants too much.

5 Continue to **observe** and care for your desert ecosystem. **Record** what you observe.

Picture A

Draw Conclusions

1. What kind of environment does your desert ecosystem model?

2. How does **making a model** help you learn about a desert?

3. **Scientists at Work** Scientists often learn by **making models**. What other types of ecosystems can you make models of?

Picture B

Investigate Further How would getting rain every day change a desert ecosystem? **Plan an experiment** in which you could **use a model** to find out.

Process Skill Tip

Observing a desert is difficult to do in the classroom. To learn more about the real thing, you can **make a model** of a desert.

Desert Ecosystems

Types of Deserts

FIND OUT

- **about two kinds of deserts**
- **how plants and animals get what they need in a desert ecosystem**

VOCABULARY

desert

A **desert** is an ecosystem found where there is very little rainfall. Most deserts get less than 25 centimeters (about 10 in.) of rain each year. Desert plants and animals need very little water to live.

In the investigation you made a model of a hot desert. In summer, hot deserts can have temperatures over 43°C (about 110°F) during the day. At night, the temperatures drop to around 7°C (about 45°F). Most hot deserts have mild winters in which the temperature usually stays above freezing.

Besides the hot deserts you probably know about, there are cold deserts. These deserts have freezing temperatures and blizzards in the winter. But in the hottest months, they are as hot as hot deserts.

✔ **What are the two kinds of deserts?**

The Taklimakan Desert is a cold desert located in western China. ▼

This hot desert is located in the southwestern part of the United States. ▼

CALIFORNIA

Anza-Borrego Desert State Park

Taklimakan Desert
CHINA

Parts of a Cactus

The parts of the barrel cactus allow it to live in hot deserts. These parts are common to many other desert plants.

1 A barrel cactus has a thick stem that stores water taken in by the roots. The water is stored in the center part of the stem.

2 Like most cacti, the barrel cactus has a thick skin that is covered with spines. The skin and spines help keep the plant from losing water. The spines also protect the plant from being eaten by animals.

3 The barrel cactus has shallow roots that spread out near the soil's surface. When it rains, these roots quickly soak up the water.

Desert Plants

Deserts are dry places. Plants that grow in deserts have parts that help them save water. Many desert plants grow low to the ground, where it is coolest. Most desert plants have long, shallow roots that spread out near the top of the soil. Here the roots can easily soak up water when it does rain.

Many desert plants have thick stems that store water. Some animals eat these stems to get the water they need to live.

Some desert plants, such as the barrel cactus, have spiny leaves. Spiny leaves help keep the plant from losing water.

✔ **How do desert plants get water?**

Desert Animals

Many animals live in the desert. Desert animals get most of their water by eating plants that store water or by eating other animals.

Reptiles such as snakes and lizards live well in the desert. They stay in the shade during the hot days. During the cold nights they keep warm near rocks, which the sun made hot during the day.

Small mammals such as bats, rabbits, and squirrels also live in deserts. These animals are active at night, when it is cooler. During the day they sleep in their shelters, which shade them from the sun. Some animals burrow into the soil to stay out of the sun.

Scorpions and insects are other desert animals. These animals have hard body coverings that keep them from losing much water.

✔ **How do desert animals get water?**

This sidewinder has dry, scaly skin that helps keep water inside its body. ▼

The shape of this bird's beak helps it get water from the stems of the saguaro cactus. It also uses the saguaro as a home. ▼

◀ Saguaro cactus

Summary

A desert ecosystem has a dry environment. Some deserts are hot, while other deserts are cold. Plants and animals that live in deserts have parts that help them get what they need to live.

Review

1. What is a desert?
2. Where do plants of the hot desert store water?
3. Other than by eating plants, how do desert animals get water?
4. **Critical Thinking** More kinds of animals and plants live in hot deserts than in cold deserts. Why do you think this is so?
5. **Test Prep** The average amount of rain a desert gets in one year is about —
   A 25 mm
   B 25 cm
   C 250 cm
   D 25 m

The large ears of this jackrabbit help it hear enemies. The jackrabbit also gets rid of extra heat from its body through the thin skin on its ears. ▶

LINKS

MATH LINK

Water from Plants Desert plants store water. To get an idea of how much water a plant can store, squeeze a piece of fruit over a bowl. Measure the amount of juice that comes out.

WRITING LINK

Informative Writing— Compare and Contrast Find out about one desert plant. For your teacher, write a paragraph to compare it to a plant that grows in another ecosystem.

HEALTH LINK

Water and Health Your body needs plenty of water when it is hot outside. With a partner, make a list of 10 things you can do to increase the amount of water you give your body on a hot day.

TECHNOLOGY LINK

Learn more about desert plants and animals by visiting this Internet Site.
www.scilinks.org/harcourt

LESSON 4

What Are Water Ecosystems?

In this lesson, you can . . .

INVESTIGATE freshwater ecosystems.

LEARN ABOUT two types of water ecosystems.

LINK to math, writing, social studies, and technology.

INVESTIGATE

Make a Freshwater Ecosystem

Activity Purpose If you have ever visited a lake, you may know that many kinds of plants and animals live there. Lakes and ponds are freshwater ecosystems. In this investigation you will **make a model** of a freshwater ecosystem.

Materials

- aquarium or other large, clear plastic container
- gravel
- sand
- sheet of paper
- fresh water
- freshwater plants
- rocks
- fish and snails

Activity Procedure

1 Put a layer of gravel at the bottom of the tank. Add a layer of sand on top of the gravel.

◄ Dolphins live, swim, and play in saltwater ecosystems.

2 Set the aquarium in a place where it isn't too sunny. Place a sheet of paper over the sand. Slowly add the water to the tank. Make sure you pour the water onto the paper so the sand will stay in place. (Picture A)

Picture A

3 Remove the paper, and put the plants and rocks into the tank. Let the tank sit for about one week. After one week, add the fish and snails. (Picture B)

4 **Observe** and care for your freshwater ecosystem.

Draw Conclusions

1. What are some things you **observed** in your freshwater ecosystem?

2. Why do you think you waited to add the fish to the tank?

Picture B

3. **Scientists at Work** Scientists often **make a model** of an ecosystem so they can **observe** it in a laboratory. How did making a model help you observe a freshwater ecosystem? How is your model different from a real pond?

Investigate Further What other kinds of plants and animals might live in a freshwater ecosystem? To find out, visit a pet shop that sells fish. Make a list of the freshwater plants and animals you find there.

Process Skill Tip

It can be difficult to **observe** all the living things in a freshwater pond or lake. You can learn about the real thing by **making a model** of a freshwater ecosystem.

A99

Water Ecosystems

FIND OUT

- about freshwater and saltwater ecosystems
- what plants and animals live in water ecosystems

VOCABULARY

salt water
fresh water

The blue parts of this map show the major water ecosystems of the world. ▼

Types of Water Ecosystems

Water covers more than 70 percent of Earth's surface. When you look at a globe, you can see that most of this water is in oceans and seas. Oceans and seas contain **salt water**, or water that has a lot of salt in it. Marshes and a few lakes also have salt water in them. These ecosystems are called *saltwater ecosystems.*

In the investigation you made a model of a freshwater ecosystem. **Fresh water** is water that has very little salt in it. Lakes, rivers, ponds, streams, and some marshes are *freshwater ecosystems.*

✔ **What are two types of water ecosystems?**

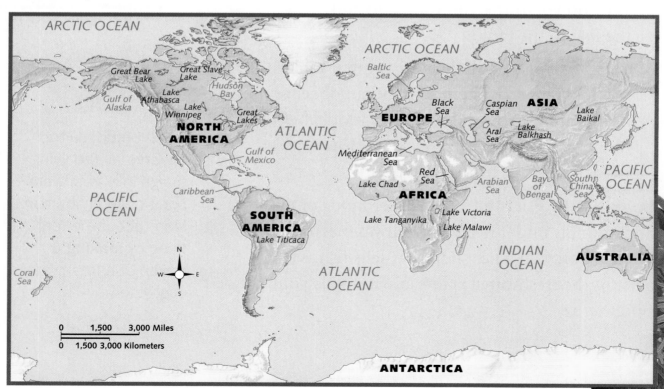

Saltwater Ecosystems

There are many different saltwater ecosystems because salt water is not the same everywhere. The amount of salt in ocean water is different in different places. Near the surface, rain can make the water less salty. Water is also less salty near shores where fresh water from rivers and streams flows into oceans. But no matter where you are in the ocean, the water has more salt in it than fresh water has.

Ocean water that is near shore or at the surface is often warmer than water deep in the ocean. This is because the sun warms the water in these areas. At the shoreline, salt water may collect in tide pools. Many plants and animals live in this warm, shallow water.

✔ **Why might salt water be less salty near shore?**

Barnacles (BAR•nuh•kulz) are small animals that live out their lives stuck to rocks and other objects. ▼

A tide pool is a saltwater ecosystem that forms at a shoreline. ▼

◀ Some anemones (uh•NEM•uh•neez) live in the warm, shallow waters of tide pools.

Ocean Ecosystems

The oceans are Earth's largest ecosystems. Because they are so large, many kinds of plants and animals live in them. All these living things are suited to life in salt water.

Not all parts of the ocean are the same. The saltiness of the water can be different. Water is deeper in some places than in others. The water temperature also changes from place to place. All these differences, along with how deep into the water the sunlight can reach, affect the kinds of living things that are found in different parts of the ocean.

✓ **What do all ocean plants and animals have in common?**

Ocean Zones

The ocean can be divided into zones. Each zone is defined by how much sunlight it gets. Areas that get the most sunlight usually have the warmest temperatures and more plant and animal life. Areas that receive little sunlight are dark and have few animals and very few plants. They also have very cold water.

This underwater kelp forest grows in shallow water. It provides food and shelter for many different fish and other ocean animals.

◀ These tropical fish live in areas of warm water.

Where water is shallow, sunlight reaches the ocean bottom. The sunlight allows many plants to grow in this zone. Animals that feed on these plants also live here.

Farther from shore, sunlight cannot reach the ocean bottom. Plants in this part of the ocean float near the surface, where they can get sunlight. Many swimming animals come to the surface to feed. Others feed on the animals that eat the plants.

This angler fish lives in the deep part of the ocean. ▼

Sunlight cannot reach the floor of the deep ocean. This part of the ocean has almost no plants. Water is very cold here. Because there are very few plants (if there are any at all), the deep ocean also has the fewest animals.

Freshwater Ecosystems

Not all freshwater ecosystems are the same. The main kinds of freshwater ecosystems include rivers, streams, lakes, and ponds.

Many plants and animals live in or around rivers and streams. Rivers and streams have moving fresh water. The water may move quickly or slowly. How fast the water moves helps determine what living things can survive in the water.

The water in lakes and ponds is still. Lakes are usually larger and have deeper water than ponds. Water temperature depends on where the lake or pond is and how deep the water is.

As in an ocean, most plants and animals in a lake or pond live in the shallow water. The fewest plants and animals live where the water is too deep for sunlight to reach the bottom.

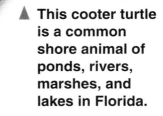

▲ This cooter turtle is a common shore animal of ponds, rivers, marshes, and lakes in Florida.

✔ **What are two kinds of freshwater ecosystems?**

The American egret is a wading bird that lives near freshwater ecosystems such as lakes. ▼

A young mayfly can stick to a rock or a plant so fast-moving water won't wash it away. ▼

The bullhead catfish makes its home in a lake. ▼

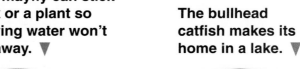

Summary

Water ecosystems may have salt water or fresh water. An ocean is a saltwater ecosystem. Rivers, streams, lakes, and ponds are freshwater ecosystems. Different kinds of plants and animals live in and around these water ecosystems.

Review

1. What are the two kinds of water ecosystems? Name two ways they are different.

2. In a pond, where do most of the animals live?

3. Which zone of the ocean gets the least amount of sunlight?

4. **Critical Thinking** What would happen to the animals and plants in a saltwater ecosystem if it were flooded by fresh water? Explain your answer.

5. **Test Prep** Which is **NOT** a freshwater ecosystem?

    A river   **C** pond
    B lake   **D** tide pool

LINKS

MATH LINK

Using Graphs Use a computer graphing program such as **Graph Links** to make a bar graph of the following water depths: river, 1 meter; lake, 6 meters; ocean, 122 meters. How much deeper is the ocean than the lake?

WRITING LINK

Informative Writing— Narration Suppose you are a tour guide on a submarine in the deep ocean. Write a narration that describes to your passengers the kinds of plants and animals you would expect to find living there.

SOCIAL STUDIES LINK

Mapping Water Ecosystems Make an outline map of your state. Draw the major bodies of water. Label them as fresh or salt water.

TECHNOLOGY LINK

Visit the Harcourt Learning Site for related links, activities, and resources.

www.harcourtschool.com/ca

WELCOME TO THE LEARNING SITE

USING COMPUTERS TO DESCRIBE THE ENVIRONMENT

Do you know what kind of environment you live in? Students all over the world are using computers to help them learn more about the plants, the animals, and other things in their environments.

Ecosystem Movies

Students at Gilliland Elementary School in Blue Mound, Texas, have been using computers to create a multimedia field guide for their hometown. They take careful notes during field trips into the Blackland Prairie near their school. They take photographs and make audio and video recordings. Afterward, the students combine everything on a computer to make the field guide.

The GLOBE Program

-60 -40 -20 0 20 40 60
Maximum Temperature (C)

March 27, 1995
24 Hour Average Forecast
National Meteorological Center

People who use the field guide can see photographs of the wildflowers in the area. They can also watch videos of the class and hear students talk about the history of the prairie.

A World of Information

Students at many schools belong to a program called GLOBE, or Global Learning and Observations to Benefit the Environment. The GLOBE program includes students, teachers, and scientists from all over the world.

First, GLOBE scientists teach teachers how to take samples and make measurements. Then the teachers teach their students how to do it. The teachers and students regularly collect data from their own environments. They measure and record information about soil, water, air, and plants in their area. They enter all their data onto the main GLOBE Web site.

Mapmaking on the Internet

The scientists at GLOBE put together the data from all of the schools. They use the data to learn about specific areas and about patterns occurring all over the world. Because so many schools are sending in data, the scientists can learn much more than they would if they were working on their own. One of the things they do with the data is make environmental maps of the world. Students and teachers can log onto the GLOBE Web site to see these maps.

Think About It

1. What would you include in a field guide for your environment?
2. What kinds of maps could GLOBE scientists make from students' information?

WEB LINK:
For Science and Technology updates, visit the Harcourt Internet site.
www.harcourtschool.com/ca

Careers Teacher

What They Do
Teachers work with children or adults to help them learn. They often use computers and other tools to make learning new ideas fun.

Education and Training Almost all teachers have college degrees. Most colleges offer courses that help students learn how to teach. Teachers specialize in the subject or the grade level they want to teach.

Margaret Morse Nice

ORNITHOLOGIST

"It was an unknown world and each day I made fresh discoveries."

Ornithologists are people who study birds. Perhaps, like Margaret Morse Nice, you have watched birds in your back yard. By the age of 12, she was recording her observations about birds. What began as fun became her lifework.

After college, Morse married Leonard Nice, whom she had met there. Each time the family moved, Margaret Nice studied the birds around her home.

Nice was one of the first to use colored bands to identify birds. To follow birds over time, she would first capture a bird. Then she would place a colored band of plastic on the bird's leg and let the bird go. In this way, Nice studied how birds mated, built nests, and raised their young.

Nice and her husband wrote a book together on the birds of Oklahoma. Nice later published a two-part study of song sparrows. She wrote more than 250 articles for magazines during her lifetime. She also translated into English many of the articles that people from other countries had written about birds.

Think About It

1. Why is it helpful to have someone translate articles written by scientists in other countries?

2. What birds can you observe from your home?

Earthworm Habitat

What is the habitat of an earthworm?

Materials

- clear plastic container
- garden soil (not potting soil)
- 2 to 3 earthworms
- small rocks, sticks, and leaves
- wax paper
- water

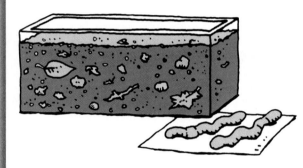

Procedure

1 Loosely spread the soil on the wax paper. Add the rocks, sticks, and leaves. Add a small amount of water so the soil is moist but not wet. Mix these materials together.

2 Add the soil mixture to the plastic container. Carefully add the earthworms to the loose soil. Place your earthworm habitat in a warm, dark place. Keep the soil moist.

Draw Conclusions

After observing your earthworm habitat for a week, make a list of the things you think the habitat you provided gave your earthworms that they needed to live.

Salt Water and Fresh Water

How are salt water and fresh water different?

Materials

- small jar
- water
- egg in the shell
- small spoon
- salt

Procedure

1 Half fill the jar with water. Put the egg in the jar. Record what happens to the egg.

2 Remove the egg, and stir a spoonful of salt into the water. Put the egg back into the water, and record what happens to the egg.

3 Continue adding salt to the water until you observe a change.

Draw Conclusions

How do you think salt in the water affects the animals living in the ocean?

Chapter 3 Review and Test Preparation

Vocabulary Review

Use the terms below to complete the sentences 1 through 12. The page numbers in ( ) tell you where to look in the chapter if you need help.

environment (A80)
ecosystem (A81)
population (A81)
community (A81)
habitat (A81)
forest (A86)
deciduous forest (A87)
tropical rain forest (A88)
coastal forest (A89)
coniferous forest (A90)
desert (A94)
salt water (A100)
fresh water (A100)

1. An area where the main plants are trees is called a ___.

2. All the living things of the same kind that live in the same area at the same time make up a ___.

3. The populations that live together in the same place make up a ___.

4. An ecosystem that is very dry is a ___.

5. The interactions between the living and nonliving parts of the environment make up an ___.

6. To a population of frogs living near a pond, the pond is its ___.

7. Rivers and most lakes are ___ ecosystems.

8. A ___ has warm summers and cool winters. The trees drop their leaves in the fall.

9. Two types of forests that get a lot of rain are a ___ and a ___.

10. An ___ is everything that surrounds a living thing.

11. The winters are cold in a ___, and the trees have needle-shaped leaves.

12. The water in the ocean is ___.

Connect Concepts

Write the terms from the Word Bank where they belong in the concept map.

tropical rain   **coastal**   **forests**
coniferous   **deciduous**

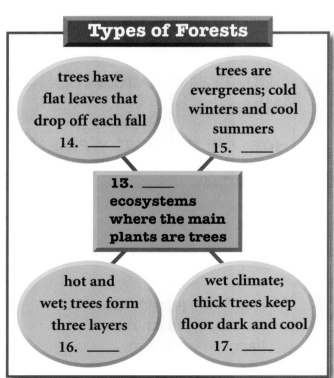

Types of Forests

trees have flat leaves that drop off each fall
14. ___

trees are evergreens; cold winters and cool summers
15. ___

13. ___ ecosystems where the main plants are trees

hot and wet; trees form three layers
16. ___

wet climate; thick trees keep floor dark and cool
17. ___

Check Understanding

Write the letter of the best choice.

18. What might happen to a forest that is damaged by fire?

    A It will grow back.

    B It is destroyed forever.

    C It will stay the same.

    D It will fill up with water and become a marsh.

19. Which characteristic of conifers helps keep them from losing water?

    F broad, flat leaves

    G thick, fleshy leaves

    H triangular shape

    J needle-shaped leaves

20. What are the two types of desert?

    A dry and wet

    B hot and cold

    C fresh and salt

    D tropical and coastal

21. What are the two types of water ecosystems?

    F fresh and salt

    G hot and cold

    H hot and dry

    J deciduous and coniferous

Critical Thinking

22. Why might a raccoon hunt for food in a trash can instead of in a forest?

23. How can the building of new homes and roads by humans affect the plants and animals in an area?

Process Skills Review

24. In Lesson 1 you used your **observations** to **gather data** about organisms in their environment. What are some of the ways that you gathered data?

25. Find three examples in the chapter where you could **use numbers** to **record data**. Why is this a good way to **interpret data**?

26. In Lessons 3 and 4 you **made a model** of two ecosystems—a desert and a pond. How did either model help you learn about the features of these ecosystems?

Performance Assessment

Diagram a Rain Forest

Work with two or three other students. On a large sheet of paper, draw a rain-forest ecosystem. Show the three layers, and label each. Then draw or describe two or more animals that live in each layer.

Unit Project Wrap Up

Here are some ideas for ways to wrap up your unit project.

Take Photographs

Use a camera to take photographs to illustrate your handbook. Label each photograph with the time and date it was taken, and identify the subject.

Draw a Map

Draw a map of the area in which you made your observations. Show features like streams and forests. Draw on the map the plants and animals you found in the places you found them. See what conclusions you can draw about the needs of plants and animals based on where they live.

Make a Graph

Find a way to sort the living and nonliving things you found. Then make a bar graph to organize your data. You may want to use a computer graphing program.

Investigate Further

How could you make your project better? What other questions do you have about plants and animals? Plan ways to find answers to your questions. Use the Science Handbook on pages R2-R9 for help.

The Solar System

UNIT B

EARTH SCIENCE

The Solar System

Unit Project   ## Game Show

Write game show questions about the solar system.
Use the chapter titles in this unit for question categories.
Write ten questions and answers for each category. Make
plans to produce the game show during the unit.

Vocabulary Preview

phase
lunar eclipse
solar eclipse
rotation
axis
revolution

Earth, the Water Planet

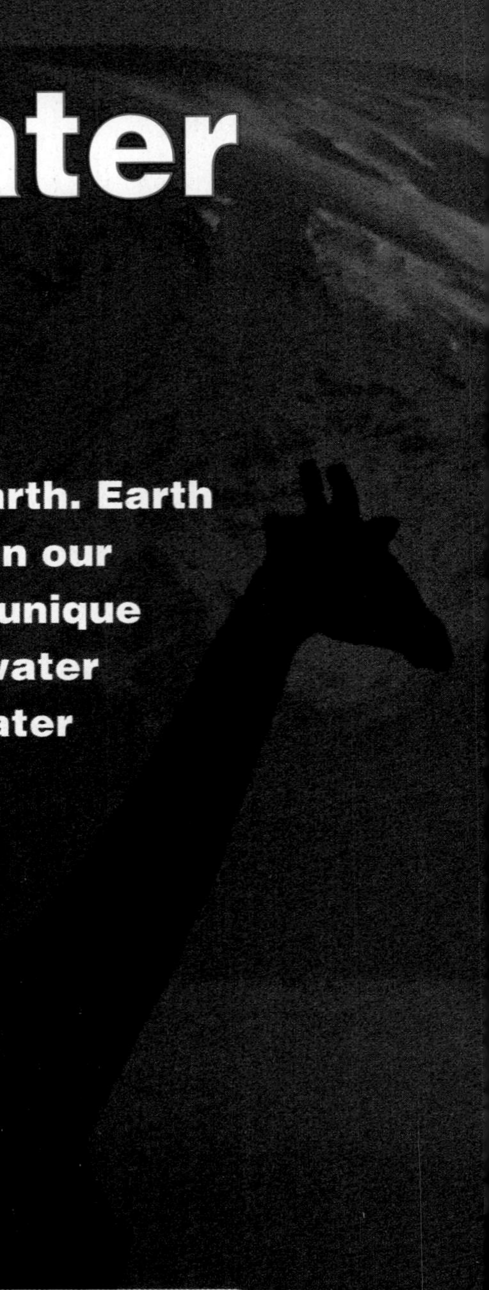

We live on planet Earth. Earth is one of nine planets in our solar system. Earth is unique because it has liquid water on the surface. It is water that makes Earth able to sustain life.

≡ FAST FACT

You may have heard the saying "Once in a blue moon." What is a blue moon? Sometimes we see two full moons in one month. The second full moon is called a blue moon. The saying has nothing to do with the moon's color.

LESSON 1

What Is Earth Like?

In this lesson, you can . . .

INVESTIGATE how much water covers Earth.

LEARN ABOUT water on Earth.

LINK to math, writing, social studies, and technology.

Land or Water

Activity Purpose Does Earth's surface have more land or more water? In this investigation you will play a game to **collect data** about Earth's surface. Then you will **use numbers** to estimate the amount of water on Earth's surface.

Materials
- plastic inflatable globe

Activity Procedure

1 Work in groups of five. Choose one person to be the recorder. The other four people will toss the ball.

2 Have the four ball tossers stand in a circle. The recorder hands the ball to the first person, who gently tosses the ball to another person in the circle. (Picture A)

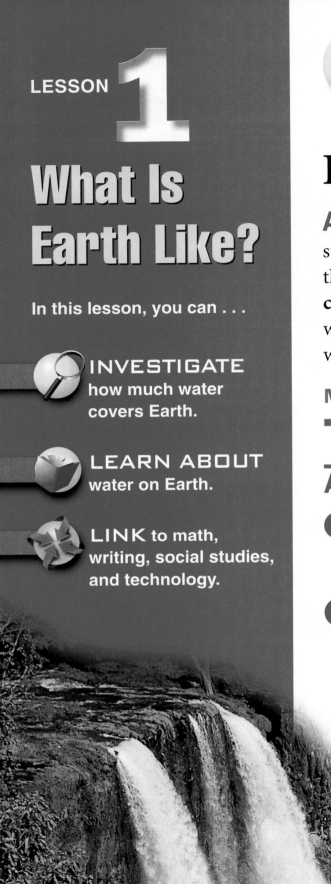

◀ Earth's water makes our planet different from all the others.

B4

3 The catcher should catch the ball with open hands. Check to see if the tip of the catcher's right index finger is on land or water. The recorder should **record** this data.

Picture A

4 Continue tossing and recording until the ball has been tossed 20 times.

5 Repeat Steps 3 and 4 two more times.

Draw Conclusions

1. Total your counts. How many times did the catcher's right index finger touch water? Touch land?

2. Where did the catchers' fingers land more often? Why do you think so?

3. **Scientists at Work** Scientists **use numbers** to **collect data.** Using your data, estimate how much of Earth's surface is covered by water.

Investigate Further You repeated this investigation 3 times. The more data you collect, the better your data becomes. How would doing the investigation 10 times change your data? Try it to find out.

Process Skill Tip

Collecting data by **using numbers** can help you answer questions. By doing the activity several times, you increase the amount of data you collect. Then you can **interpret the data** to find an answer to your question.

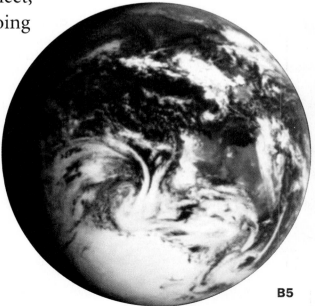

This view of Earth from space makes it easy to see why Earth is sometimes called the water planet. ▶

Water on Earth

FIND OUT

- why water is important
- about the two forms of water on Earth

The Water Planet

What makes Earth different from other planets? Water.

From space, Earth looks like a blue marble. The water that covers most of the planet makes it look blue. Earth's lands are really small islands in the middle of huge oceans and seas.

Water makes life on Earth possible. All organisms need water to live. Scientists hypothesize that planets that do not have water probably could not have life.

All animals need water to stay alive. ▼

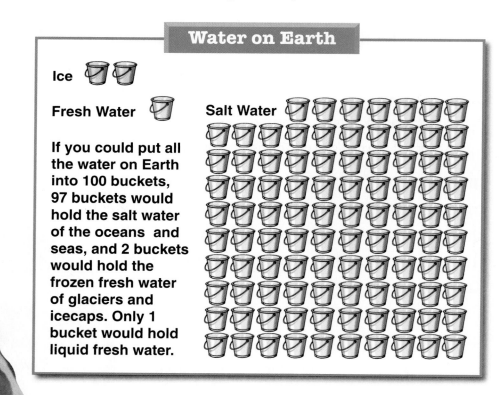

Water on Earth

Ice

Fresh Water

Salt Water

If you could put all the water on Earth into 100 buckets, 97 buckets would hold the salt water of the oceans and seas, and 2 buckets would hold the frozen fresh water of glaciers and icecaps. Only 1 bucket would hold liquid fresh water.

The water on Earth is found in two forms, salt water and fresh water. Salt water is found in the oceans and large seas. Fresh water is found in lakes, ponds, and rivers. Fresh water is also found frozen in glaciers and icecaps.

✔ **Why is water important?**

Summary

Water makes Earth different from other planets. Much of Earth is covered with water. Without water no life would be possible on Earth.

Review

1. How is Earth different from other planets?
2. Why does Earth look blue from space?
3. On Earth, is there more fresh water or more salt water?
4. **Critical Thinking** Could life exist on Earth if there were no fresh water?
5. **Test Prep** Which of the following contain salt water?
   - **A** ponds
   - **B** glaciers
   - **C** seas
   - **D** rivers

LINKS

MATH LINK

Water Study the chart on page B6. Use a computer graphing program such as **Graph Links** to make a bar graph of the data.

WRITING LINK

Narrative Writing—Story Write a story for a younger child that tells about water on Earth.

SOCIAL STUDIES LINK

Salt Lakes Throughout the world there are several lakes that contain salt water. One of these lakes is in the United States. Find out where it is, and draw a map to show its location.

TECHNOLOGY LINK

To learn more about water on Earth, visit the National Air and Space Museum Internet Site. **www.si.edu/harcourt/science**

LESSON 2

How Do the Moon and Earth Interact?

In this lesson, you can . . .

 INVESTIGATE the phases of the moon.

 LEARN ABOUT why the moon seems to change.

 LINK to math, writing, literature, and technology.

The Moon's Phases

Activity Purpose Like several other planets, Earth has a moon. If you look at the moon each night, you will see that its shape seems to change. These shapes are called *phases*. In this investigation you will **observe** how a light shining on a ball looks different as you move around the ball.

Materials
- lamp with no shade
- softball

Activity Procedure

1 Work with a partner. Turn on the lamp. Your teacher will darken the room.

2 Have Person 1 hold the ball and stand with his or her back to the lighted bulb. Hold the ball as shown. Continue holding the ball this way until the end of the procedure. (Picture A)

◄ You see the moon rise from Earth. But if you were on the moon, you would see Earth rise!

3 Have Person 2 stand in position 1 in Picture A. **Observe** the ball. Make a drawing of the ball's lighted side.

4 Person 2 now moves to position 2. Turn toward the ball. Make a drawing of the lighted part of the ball.

5 Have Person 2 move to position 3. Make a drawing of the lighted part of the ball.

6 Person 2 again moves, this time to position 4. Turn toward the ball. Make a drawing of the lighted part of the ball.

Picture A

7 Switch roles and repeat the procedure so Person 1 can observe the patterns of light on the ball.

Draw Conclusions

1. What part of the ball was lighted at each position?

2. The ball represents the moon. What does the light bulb represent? What represents a person viewing the moon from Earth?

3. **Scientists at Work** Scientists **use models** to make **inferences** to explain how things work. If the ball represents the moon, what can you infer that the different parts of the lighted ball represent?

Process Skill Tip

When you **observe** something, you use your senses to get information about it. When you **infer**, you use your observations to form an opinion.

How the Moon and Earth Interact

The Phases of the Moon

FIND OUT

• what the moon's phases are

• what causes eclipses

VOCABULARY

phase
lunar eclipse
solar eclipse

If you watch the moon for a month, its shape seems to change. Sometimes it looks like a big round ball. At other times you see a thin sliver. Why do these changes happen?

The half of the moon that faces the sun is always lighted. As the moon moves around Earth, different amounts of its lighted and dark sides face Earth. The moon's phase depends on the part of the lighted half you can see. **Phases** are the different shapes the moon seems to have in the sky.

It takes about one month for the moon to revolve around Earth. It takes the same amount of time for the moon to rotate. This causes the same side of the moon to always face Earth. ▶

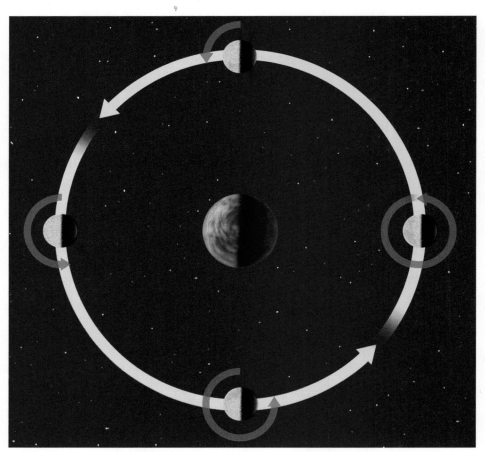

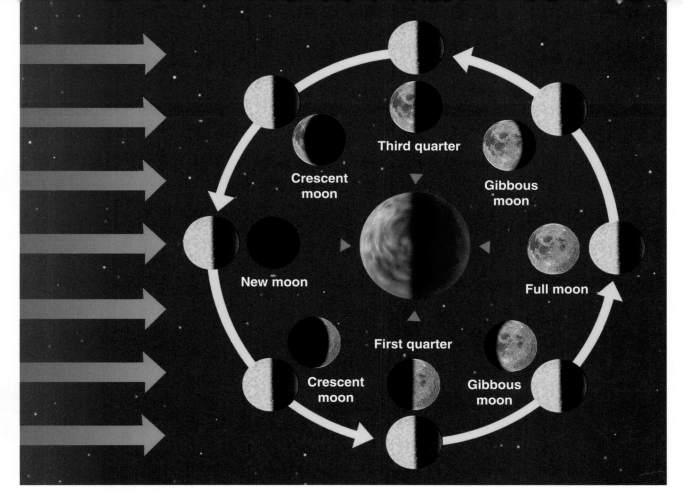

▲ The photographs show what the moon
looks like from Earth. The drawings show
what the moon would look like from space.

The moon goes through all of its phases every $29\frac{1}{2}$ days. During the phase called the new moon, the lighted half faces away from Earth. You can't see the moon at all. After the new moon, the moon seems to get bigger.

As the moon continues in its orbit around Earth, one lighted edge comes into view. This is a crescent moon. About one week after the new moon, half of the moon's lighted face can be seen. This is the first quarter. The next phase is the gibbous moon.

It shows a little less than $\frac{3}{4}$ of the moon's lighted side.

About two weeks after the new moon, you see the full moon. At full moon you can see the whole face of the moon. The moon has completed half of its orbit around Earth.

After the full moon, the phases reverse. The lighted part you see gets smaller. First you see the gibbous moon again. Then you see the third quarter. The last phase is another crescent moon.

✔ **What are the moon's phases?**

Eclipses of the Moon

Everything the sun shines on casts a shadow. Earth and the moon cast shadows, too. Most of the time these shadows fall on empty space. But sometimes these shadows can be seen from Earth's surface.

You know the moon revolves around Earth. At times the Earth is between the sun and moon. If the sun, Earth, and moon are in a straight line, Earth blocks some of the sun's light from falling on the moon. Although you should see a full moon, the moon gets dark for a time. This is called a lunar eclipse. A **lunar eclipse** happens when Earth's shadow falls on the moon.

✔ **What causes a lunar eclipse?**

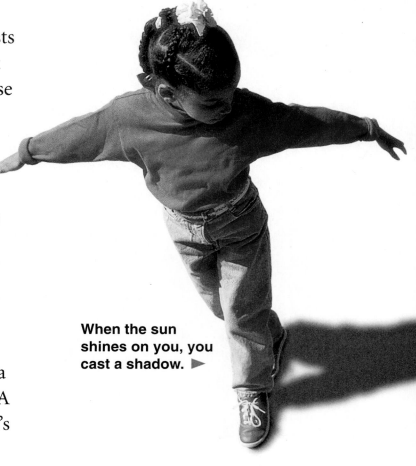

When the sun shines on you, you cast a shadow. ►

Sun

◀ A total lunar eclipse causes all of the moon's face to look dark red. Total lunar eclipses do not happen as often as partial eclipses. This is because the sun, the Earth, and the moon need to be in a straight line for Earth's shadow to completely cover the moon.

A partial lunar eclipse blocks only part of the sun's light. Watching partial eclipses helped early scientists figure out that Earth is round. Why would eclipses help them see that Earth is round? ▼

The sun shines on objects in space. They cast shadows, too. Sometimes Earth's shadow falls on the moon. This causes a lunar eclipse. ▼

Earth

Moon

Eclipses of the Sun

A shadow slowly covers the sun. The whole sky turns dark in the middle of the day. Ancient peoples thought this was the end of the world. Today we know it's a solar eclipse. A **solar eclipse** happens when the moon's shadow falls on Earth. This happens when the moon moves between the Earth and the sun.

During a total solar eclipse, the moon blocks out the sun. Only a halo of sunlight remains around the moon. The areas where a total eclipse can be seen is small. Outside this area only part of the sun is covered.

✔ **What causes a solar eclipse?**

A total solar eclipse happens when the moon moves between Earth and the sun. These photos show what the sun looks like as a total solar eclipse takes place. Total solar eclipses are rare. ▶

People in the small shadow area see the total eclipse. Those outside the shadow see a partial eclipse. ▼

Sun

Summary

Phases are the different shapes the moon seems to have in the sky. The moon goes through its phases every $29\frac{1}{2}$ days. Eclipses happen when one object in space moves into the shadow of another. There are lunar eclipses and solar eclipses.

Review

1. Describe a new moon.
2. Compare and contrast a lunar and a solar eclipse.
3. What do you see from Earth during a total solar eclipse?
4. **Critical Thinking** Tell what phase the moon is in during a lunar eclipse. Explain your answer.
5. **Test Prep** Which of these is **NOT** a phase of the moon?

   A new   C crescent
   B full   D eclipse

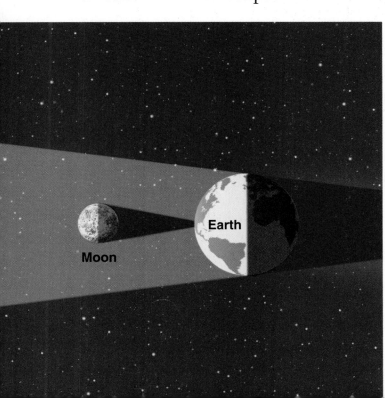

Moon   Earth

LINKS

MATH LINK

Sketch It Sketch the shape of the moon each night for one month. Start with the new moon. How much time does it take for all eight phases to take place? Predict the date of the next new moon. Compare your prediction to the actual results.

WRITING LINK

Narrative Writing—Personal Story When the sun got dark in ancient times, people were frightened. Suppose that you lived then. You are seeing a solar eclipse. Write a story for a friend to explain what you think is happening.

LITERATURE LINK

Find Out More Find out more about the sun, the moon, and eclipses by reading *The Sun and the Moon* by Patrick Moore.

TECHNOLOGY LINK

Learn more about interactions in space by investigating *Blast Off into Orbit* on **Harcourt Science Explorations CD-ROM.**

What Causes Earth's Seasons?

In this lesson, you can . . .

 INVESTIGATE how Earth's tilt causes seasons.

 LEARN ABOUT the seasons.

 LINK to math, writing, art, and technology.

 **INVESTIGATE**

How the Sun Strikes Earth

Activity Purpose Many places on Earth are hot in summer and cold in winter. In this investigation you will find out why. You will **compare** the way light rays strike a surface. Then you will **infer** how this affects Earth's temperatures.

Materials

- clear tape
- graph paper
- large book
- flashlight
- meterstick
- black marker
- wooden block
- red marker

Activity Procedure

1 Tape the graph paper to the book.

2 Hold the flashlight about 50 cm above the book. Shine the light straight down. The beam will make a circle on the paper. If the circle is bigger than the paper, bring the light closer.

◄ **The leaves of some trees turn red, orange, and gold in the fall.**

3 Have a partner use the black marker to draw around the light beam on the paper. (Picture A)

4 **Observe** the brightness of the light on the squares. **Record** your observations.

5 Keep the flashlight in the same position. Have a partner put the block under one end of the book and use the red marker to draw around the light on the paper. (Picture B)

6 **Observe** the brightness on the squares again. **Record** your observations.

Picture A

Draw Conclusions

1. How many squares are inside the black line? How many squares are inside the red line?

2. Inside which line was the light brighter?

3. **Scientists at Work** Scientists **compare** things to find out how they are the same and how they are different. Compare the results of Steps 3 and 5 of the investigation. Do straight light rays or tilted light rays give stronger light? Suppose the paper is Earth's surface. The light is the sun. Which area would have warmer weather? Explain.

Investigate Further **Predict** what will happen if the book is tilted even more. Test your prediction.

Picture B

Process Skill Tip

When you **compare**, you **observe** the properties of two or more things to see how they are alike and how they are different.

The Seasons

FIND OUT

- why there are seasons
- what causes day and night

VOCABULARY

rotation
axis
revolution

How Earth Moves in Space

You are sitting reading this book. It seems like you are still. But you're not. Earth is traveling through space at almost 107,800 kilometers (67,000 mi) per hour. You are moving with Earth. You are also flying around the solar system as Earth orbits the sun.

Earth moves in two ways. First, Earth spins like a top. This is called rotation. **Rotation** (roh•TAY•shuhn) is the spinning of an object on its axis. Earth's **axis** (AK•sis) is an imaginary line that goes through the North Pole and the South Pole. Earth rotates on its axis once every 24 hours. One rotation takes one day.

Earth also circles the sun. This is called revolution. A **revolution** (rev•uh•LOO•shuhn) is the movement of one object around another object. Earth makes one revolution around the sun every $365\frac{1}{4}$ days. One revolution takes one year.

Earth rotates on its axis as it revolves around the sun. ▶

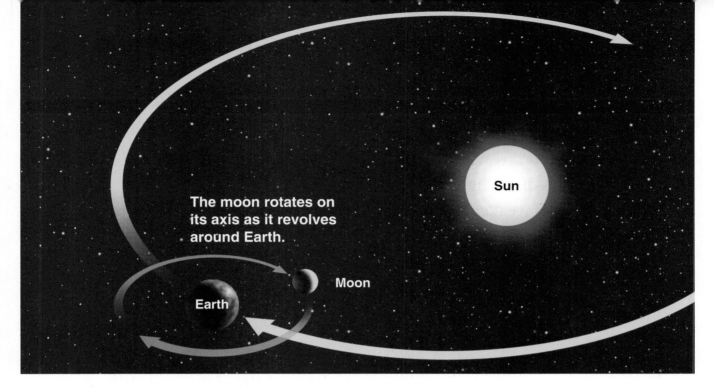

The moon rotates on its axis as it revolves around Earth.

Sun

Moon

Earth

▲ Both Earth and the moon rotate. The Earth rotates once a day. The moon rotates about once a month.

The moon also rotates and revolves. It rotates on its axis. It revolves around Earth. A day on the moon, or one rotation, is about 29 Earth days long. The moon takes this same amount of time to revolve around Earth.

Objects on Earth cast shadows. Shadows can help us observe Earth's rotation. As Earth rotates, the sun's position seems to change in the sky. But it is really the Earth that is moving.

In the morning the sun seems low in the sky. Objects cast long shadows. As the Earth rotates, the sun seems to move higher in the sky. Shadows get shorter. At noon, the sun is overhead. Objects cast short shadows—or no shadows at all. As Earth continues to rotate, the sun looks lower in the sky again. Shadows get longer until the sun sets.

✔ **What is rotation?**

Shadows are short at noon. They're longer at 2:00 P.M. because the sun is lower in the sky. ▼

What Causes Seasons

In most places on Earth, summer and winter are different. Summer is hot. There are many hours of daylight. Sunlight is strong. Winter is cold. The hours of daylight are shorter. Sunlight is weaker. Summer and winter are two seasons.

Earth has seasons because its axis is tilted. This means Earth is tipped to one side, like the book in the investigation was tilted. The tilt changes the way sunlight hits Earth at different times of the year. Sometimes the sun's rays are almost straight when they hit Earth's surface. At other times the sun's rays are slanted. This changes the amount of light and heat the surface gets.

Earth's axis is always pointing the same way in space. But because Earth is moving, the axis changes position compared with the position of the sun.

For part of the year the top of the axis (the North Pole) points in the direction of the sun. When Earth is in this position, it is summer in the northern half. During that time the bottom of the axis (the South Pole) points away from the sun. When Earth is in this position, it is winter in the southern half.

Earth has a curved surface. Some sunlight hits the surface straight on. Some sunlight hits the surface on a slant. ▼

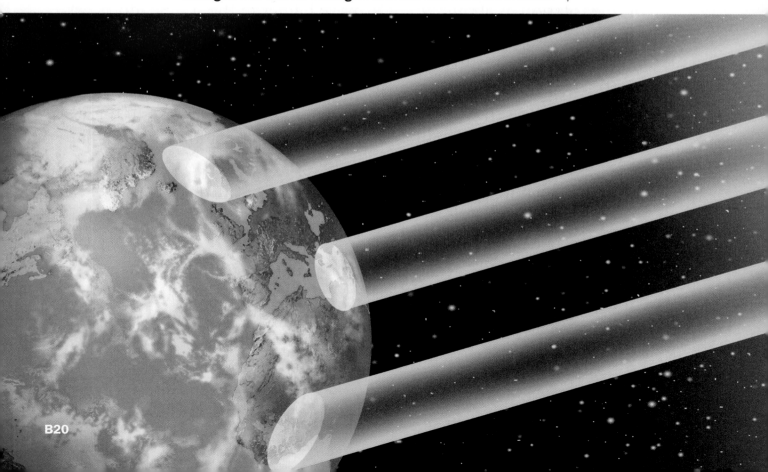

Spring

Summer

Winter

Fall

Whichever end of Earth's axis points in the direction of the sun, the sun shines more directly on that part of Earth. This direct sunlight heats the ground and the air. It is summer.

Earth is always moving around the sun. Three months after summer starts, the top of the axis is not pointing in the direction of the sun anymore. Neither is the bottom of the axis. Days and nights are of equal length. Both the top half and the bottom half of the Earth get the same amount of light. Temperatures are cooler than in summer and warmer than in winter. It is fall in the northern half.

Three months later the northern half of the Earth points away from the sun. The sun shines less directly on its surface. Rays are slanted. Slanted rays cover a larger area, so the ground and the air are heated less. This makes the northern half of the Earth colder. It is winter.

Another three months pass. Again neither axis points in the direction of the sun. Days and nights are almost equal in length. Now it is spring. A full year has passed. Then the cycle starts again with summer.

Seasons in the northern and southern halves of Earth are reversed. When the northern half of Earth has spring, the southern half has fall. When the northern half has winter, the southern half has summer. Australia is on the southern half of Earth. So in Australia December is in the middle of summer. July is in the middle of winter.

✔ **Why are there seasons?**

What Causes Day and Night

It's 4:00 P.M. Your family decides to call a friend in Asia. When your dad makes the call, he wakes up your Asian friend. He was sleeping. It's the middle of the night there.

As you move from place to place on Earth, time changes. When you are eating dinner, people on the other side of the world might be having breakfast.

▲ When it is day in Chicago, Illinois, . . .

. . . it is night in Hong Kong, China. Hong Kong is on the other side of Earth from Chicago. ▼

Sunlight always shines on half of Earth. The other half is in darkness. ▼

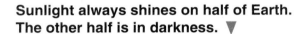

Sun

Earth's rotation causes this difference in time. At any one time, half of Earth is in sunlight. The other half is in darkness. The half in sunlight has day. The half in darkness has night.

✔ **How much of Earth's surface is in sunlight at one time?**

Summary

Earth rotates on its axis and revolves around the sun. Earth has seasons because its axis is tilted. The sun heats Earth's surface differently at different times of the year. Night and day happen as Earth rotates. Places on Earth's surface move from sunlight into darkness and back.

Review

1. What is a revolution?
2. When it is winter in the northern half of Earth, what season is it in the southern half?
3. Why are many places warmer in summer than in winter?
4. **Critical Thinking** How would day and night be different if Earth did not rotate?
5. **Test Prep** The tilt of Earth's axis causes —

   A rotation
   B day and night
   C seasons
   D sunlight

LINKS

MATH LINK

Measuring Shadows Put a stick in the ground. Measure the length of its shadow each hour. How does the shadow change? How could you use this shadow as a clock?

WRITING LINK

Persuasive Writing—Opinion Which is your favorite season? Write a paragraph for your family about why you like that season. Try to persuade them to agree with you.

ART LINK

Season Mobile Make a mobile about your favorite season. Include pictures or objects to show both things you see and activities you enjoy during that season.

TECHNOLOGY LINK

Learn more about seasons and other chapter topics by visiting this Internet Site.
www.scilinks.org/harcourt

Red Sprites, Blue Jets, and ELVES

Suppose you saw something completely new. How would you describe it? That was the challenge facing some airplane pilots and scientists. They tried to name unusual flashes they saw in the sky by calling them "upward lightning," "flames," and even "giant glowing doughnuts"!

Sprites, Jets, and ELVES

In 1989 scientists began trying to show that these light flashes are real. A videotape showed the unusual flashes during a thunderstorm. Nearly 20 were photographed during the early 1990s using video cameras that could work with very little light.

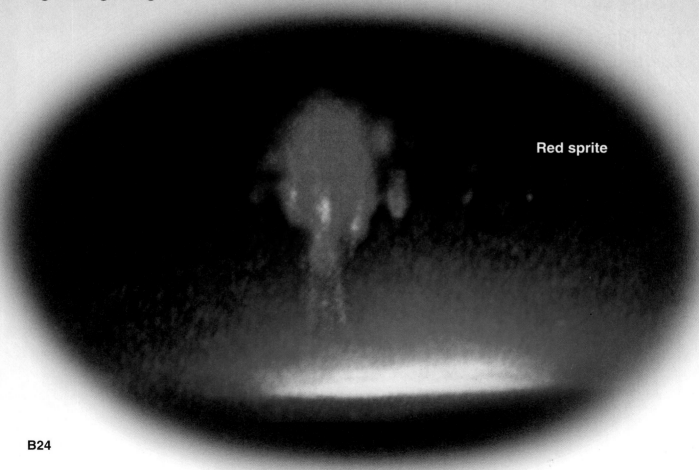

Red sprite

At least three types of flashes were identified. The scientists finally decided to name them sprites, jets, and ELVES.

ELVES stands for "*e*missions of *l*ight and *v*ery-low-frequency perturbations from *e*lectromagnetic-pulse *s*ources." ELVES are very dim, quick red flashes. They move outward like ripples on a pond.

Sprites are red and seem to move in groups. They appear above thunderstorm systems, 65–75 kilometers (about 40–47 mi) above the ground. They have a "head" and strands coming down from the head.

Blue jets were once described as rocket lightning. In 1994 a color video showed that these glowing streaks are blue. Blue jets occur lower in the atmosphere than red sprites do.

People in airplanes could see blue jets and red sprites because the people were above storms. No one had ever seen ELVES.

Finding Sprites, Jets, and ELVES

There are several reasons why it took so long to discover these unusual lights:

- They are dim and can be seen only after the eyes have adjusted to the dark.
- Sprites last only about 3 ten-thousandths of a second.
- Only about 1 in 100 lightning strikes produces these lights.

Think About It

- What do you think scientists thought of the early reports of sprites and jets, before the videotapes?

WEB LINK:
For Science and Technology updates, visit the Harcourt Internet site.
www.harcourtschool.com/ca

Careers — Meteorologist

What They Do Meteorologists study the atmosphere and weather. They may also research new uses for computer programs in the study of weather.

Education and Training Someone who wants to be a meteorologist must study science in college. Many meteorologists also get training in weather research and technology.

Clyde Tombaugh
ASTRONOMER, INVENTOR

"I think the driving thing was curiosity about the universe. That fascinated me."

Working on a farm in Kansas taught Clyde Tombaugh to be persistent and creative with materials at hand. He was always interested in astronomy. His uncle and father had a telescope, which they gave him when he was 9 years old. By the time Tombaugh was 20, he decided to build his own telescope. He used part of a dairy machine for the base and part of his father's 1910 Buick.

Later, Tombaugh's uncle asked Tombaugh to build a telescope for him. Tombaugh also built a better telescope for himself. With that homemade telescope, he observed Mars and Jupiter. He drew what he saw and sent his sketches to the Lowell Observatory in Flagstaff, Arizona. The scientists at the

Tombaugh in 1995 with his first telescope

observatory invited him to come and work there.

On February 18, 1930, Tombaugh discovered the planet Pluto. Other scientists had predicted its existence, but he was the first to locate it in the sky.

Think About It

1. What have you read about Tombaugh that leads you to think he is resourceful?
2. How was Tombaugh's discovery of Pluto related to work by other scientists?

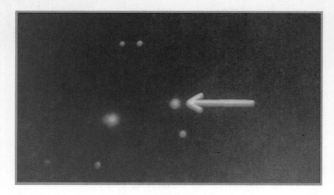

Telescope photo of Pluto, 1930

Earth Model

Why do we have seasons?

Materials
- Styrofoam ball
- flashlight
- two pencils

Procedure

1. Stick a pencil through the middle of the ball. This represents Earth's axis.

2. With the other pencil, draw a line around the middle of the ball. This is the equator. Put the Earth on a table. The axis should lean to the right.

3. Shine the flashlight on the left side of the Earth. The light represents the sun. Place the light about 13 cm away. Observe where the light rays hit the ball.

4. Shine the light on the right side of the Earth. Where do the light rays hit the ball? Compare how the light hits the ball each time.

Draw Conclusions
How does this explain seasons in the northern half of the Earth?

A Look at Rotation

How does day become night?

Materials
- a small self-stick note
- spinning Earth globe
- flashlight

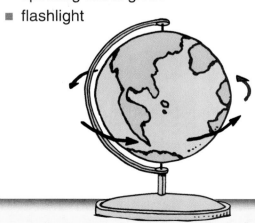

Procedure

1. Write where you live on the self-stick note. Place the note on your state on the globe.

2. Shine the flashlight on the globe. Your teacher will then turn off the lights.

3. Slowly spin the globe counterclockwise.

Draw Conclusions
What happens to the place where you put your note? What does this represent?

Vocabulary Review

Use the terms below to complete the sentences. The page numbers in ( ) tell you where to look in the chapter if you need help.

phases (B10)
lunar eclipse (B12)
solar eclipse (B14)
rotation (B18)
axis (B18)
revolution (B18)

1. When the moon's shadow falls on Earth, we see a ____.

2. The spinning of an object on its axis is called ____.

3. The moon has ____ that make it seem to change shape.

4. Earth has an imaginary line, or ____, that runs through the North Pole and the South Pole.

5. The movement of one object around another object is called ____.

6. When Earth's shadow falls on the moon, we see a ____.

Connect Concepts

Use the terms below to complete the concept map.

oceans   lakes   glaciers
fresh water   salt water   forms

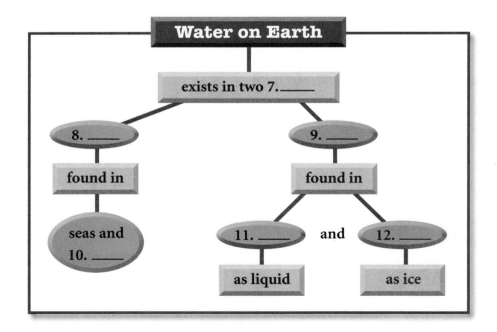

Water on Earth

exists in two 7. ____

8. ____

found in

seas and
10. ____

9. ____

found in

11. ____   and   12. ____

as liquid   as ice

Check Understanding

Write the letter of the best choice.

13. Fresh water is **NOT** found —
A under Earth's surface
B in lakes
C in oceans
D in rivers

14. Two revolutions of Earth take —
F two days
G two weeks
H two months
J two years

15. When the moon looks like a lighted circle in the sky, it is in the ___ phase.
A full-moon
B new-moon
C crescent-moon
D gibbous-moon

16. Earth has seasons because its
F moon has phases
G rotation is short
H axis is tilted
J surface is smooth

17. It takes how long for the moon to go through its phases?
A 10 days
B $29\frac{1}{2}$ days
C $6\frac{1}{2}$ months
D 2 years

Critical Thinking

18. Why do we always see the same side of the moon from Earth?

19. How would Earth be different if its axis were not tilted?

Process Skills Review

20. Why is **using numbers** a good way to **collect data**?

21. **Compare** the revolutions of the moon and Earth. How are they alike? How are they different?

22. It is always cold at the North Pole. What can you **infer** about the way the sun's rays hit the North Pole?

23. Look at the pictures on pages B14 and B15. Use what you **observe** in the pictures to make a statement about solar eclipses.

Performance Assessment

Going Through a Phase

Work with a partner to make a model or a poster that shows the phases of the moon. Include the name and a description of each phase.

Chapter 2

The Solar System and Beyond

Vocabulary Preview

- solar system
- orbit
- planet
- asteroid
- comet
- star
- constellation
- telescope

Looking up at a clear night sky, you will see tiny points of light. If you could leave Earth and travel through space to get closer to those lights, you would see that they are other worlds and other suns, but not like the Earth and the sun that we know.

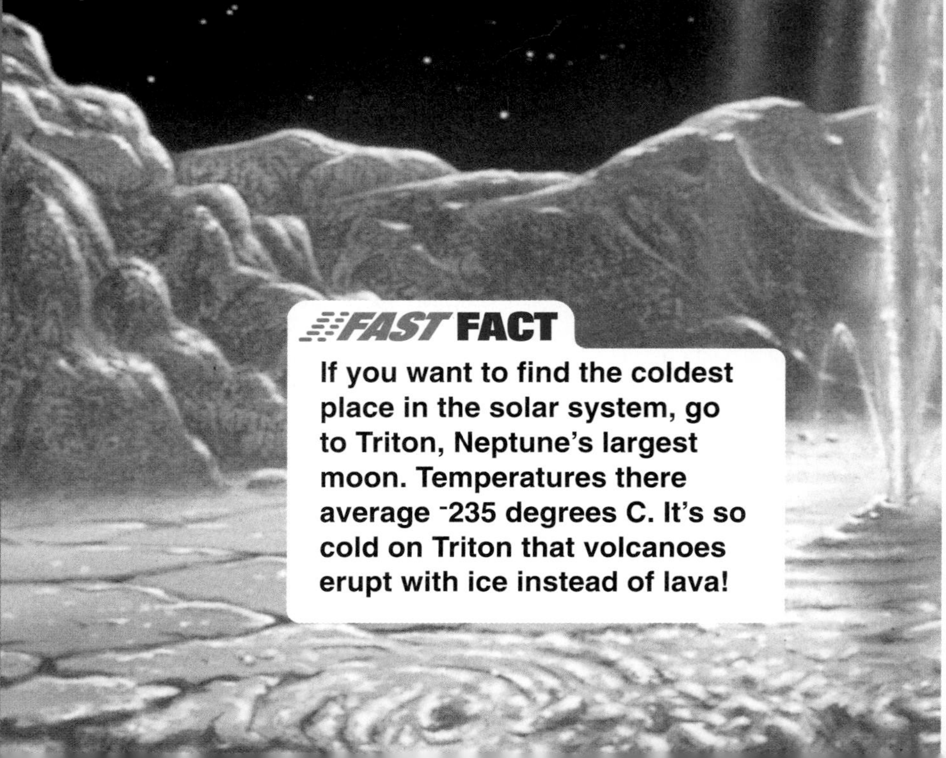

FAST FACT

If you want to find the coldest place in the solar system, go to Triton, Neptune's largest moon. Temperatures there average $^{-}235$ degrees C. It's so cold on Triton that volcanoes erupt with ice instead of lava!

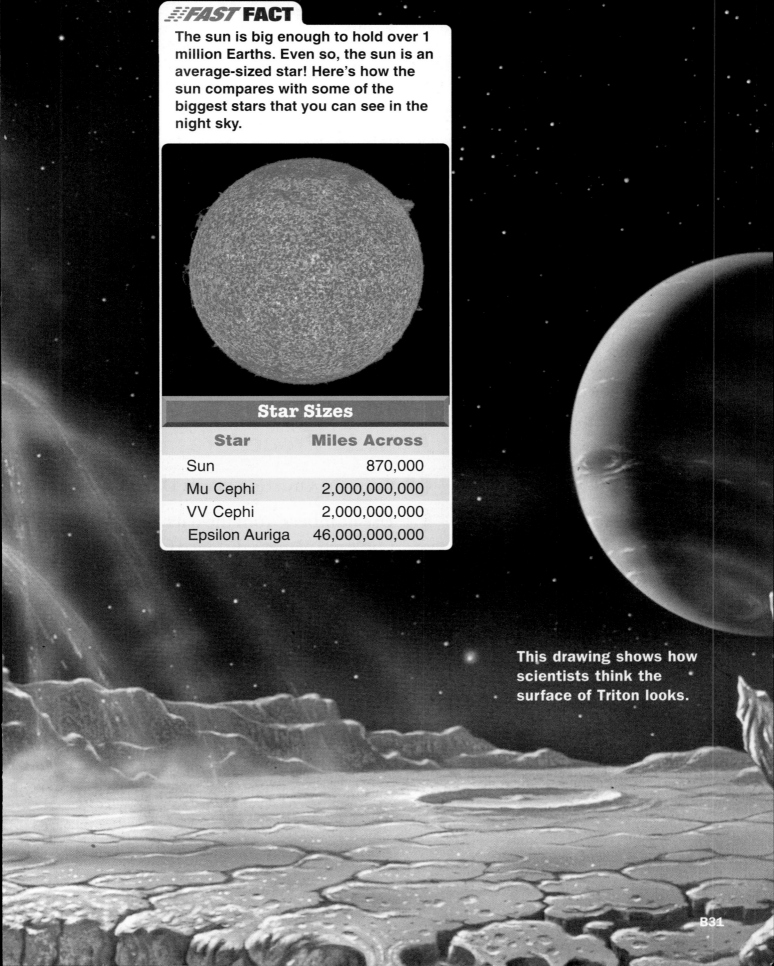

The sun is big enough to hold over 1 million Earths. Even so, the sun is an average-sized star! Here's how the sun compares with some of the biggest stars that you can see in the night sky.

Star Sizes	
Star	Miles Across
Sun	870,000
Mu Cephi	2,000,000,000
VV Cephi	2,000,000,000
Epsilon Auriga	46,000,000,000

This drawing shows how scientists think the surface of Triton looks.

What Is the Solar System?

In this lesson, you can . . .

INVESTIGATE the planets.

LEARN ABOUT objects in the solar system.

LINK to math, writing, health, and technology.

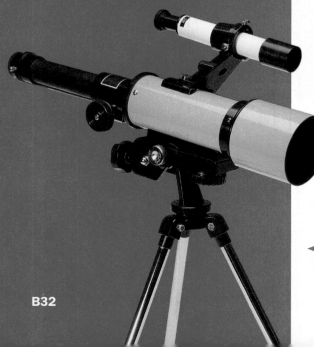

INVESTIGATE

The Planets

Activity Purpose
Nine planets circle the sun. They are not all alike. In this investigation you will use some of the planets' properties to **order** them. Then you will **classify** the planets by using the data you have organized.

Materials
- pencil
- paper

Activity Procedure

1. Copy the Ordering Planet Data chart.

2. **Use numbers** from the data table to find each planet's distance from the sun. **Record** in your table the names of the planets, beginning with the one closest to the sun.

3. **Use numbers** from the data table to find the distance across each planet. The planet with the shortest distance across is the smallest planet. Use numbers to **order** the planets by size. **Record** the names of the planets in order, beginning with the smallest planet.

◀ Telescopes help us see things that are far away.

Ordering Planet Data

Closest to the Sun to Farthest from the Sun	Smallest to Largest	Shortest Year to Longest Year

Planet Data

Planet	Distance from Sun (in millions of kilometers)	Distance Across (in kilometers)	Length of Year (y=Earth year d=Earth day)
Earth	150	12,750	365 d
Jupiter	778	143,000	12 y
Mars	228	6,800	2 y
Mercury	58	4,900	88 d
Neptune	4,505	49,000	165 y
Pluto	5,890	2,300	248 y
Saturn	1,427	120,000	29 y
Uranus	2,869	51,000	84 y
Venus	108	12,000	225 d

Draw Conclusions

1. Which planet is closest to the sun? Farthest from the sun?

2. Which is the largest planet? The smallest?

3. **Scientists at Work** Scientists sometimes **use numbers** to put things in **order**. Scientists have studied the same data you used in this investigation. How did using numbers help you realize the **space relationships** between the planets?

Process Skill Tip

You can **use numbers to order** objects. Putting objects in order allows you to **use space relationships** to describe the positions of objects.

The Solar System

FIND OUT

- the names of the planets
- about other bodies in the solar system

VOCABULARY

solar system
orbit
planet
asteroid
comet

The Structure of the Solar System

The **solar system** is the sun and the objects that orbit around it. An **orbit** is the path an object takes as it moves around another object in space. All the planets you studied in the investigation, including Earth, orbit the sun.

You learned about some parts of the solar system in the investigation. The solar system has nine planets, including Earth. A **planet** is a large body of rock or gas that orbits the sun. The solar system also has many moons. Moons are large, rocky objects that orbit planets. Earth has one moon. Other planets have no moons or many moons. Comets and asteroids are also parts of the solar system.

✔ **What is the solar system?**

THE INSIDE STORY

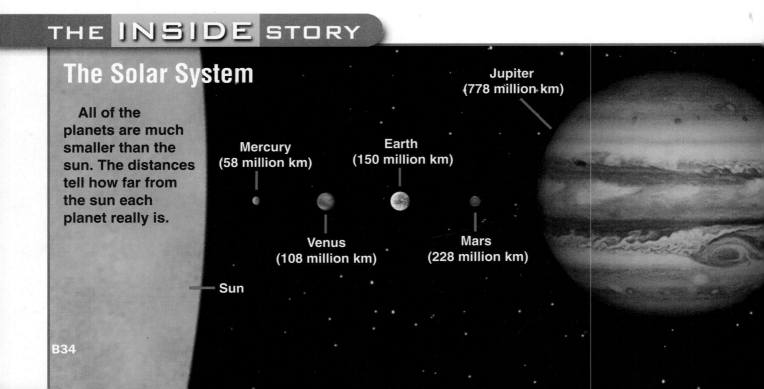

The Solar System

All of the planets are much smaller than the sun. The distances tell how far from the sun each planet really is.

Jupiter
(778 million km)

Mercury
(58 million km)

Earth
(150 million km)

Venus
(108 million km)

Mars
(228 million km)

Sun

The Sun

The sun is the center of the solar system. It is a *star*—a hot ball of glowing gases. It looks different to us from other stars because it is closer to us than other stars are.

The sun is very hot and bright. The sun is also big. All of the planets and moons of the solar system could fit inside it.

Gravity on the sun is very strong. That's because of its great size. *Gravity* is the force of one object's pull on another. The sun's gravity helps hold the objects in the solar system in orbit.

✔ **What is the sun?**

The sun is 1.35 million kilometers (about 838,900 mi) across. The Earth is tiny compared with the sun. The sun could hold more than one million Earths inside it. ▶

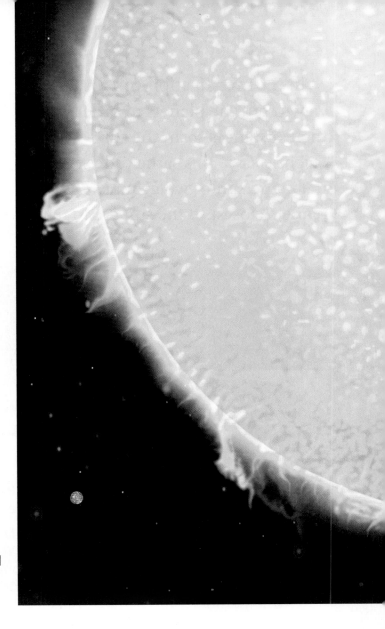

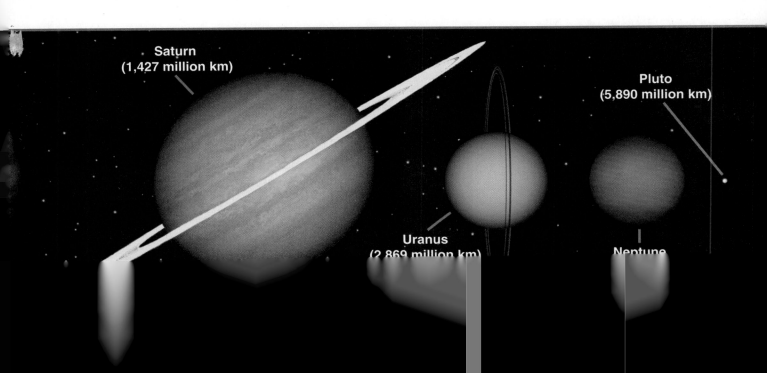

Saturn
(1,427 million km)

Pluto
(5,890 million km)

Uranus
(2,869 million km)

Neptune

The Inner Planets

In the investigation you found a way to put the planets in order by their distances from the sun. Scientists use this same order to put the planets into two groups. The four planets closest to the sun are in one group. They are called the *inner planets*. The five other planets are the *outer planets*.

The inner planets are Mercury, Venus, Earth, and Mars. They are alike in many ways. They all have rocky surfaces. Because they are

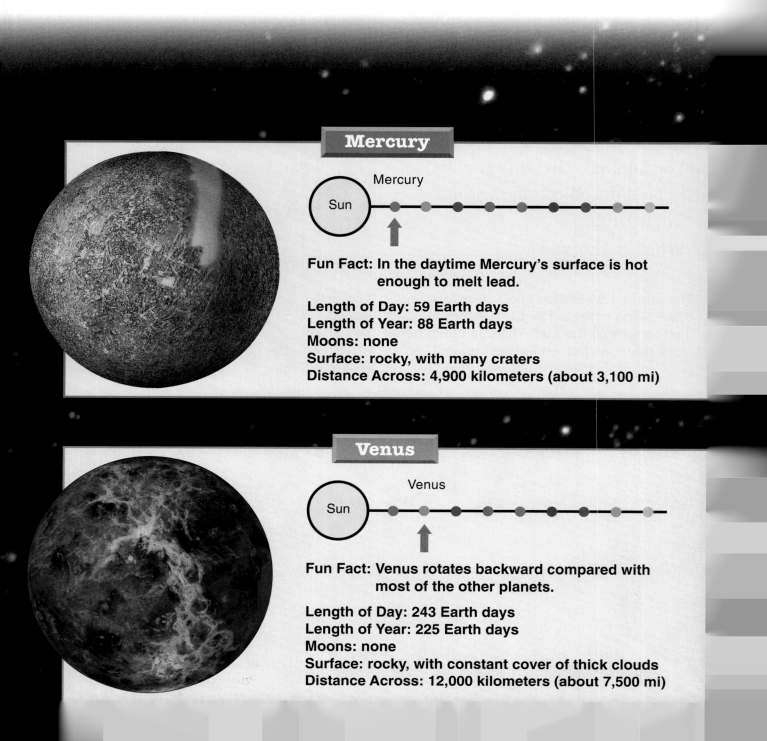

Mercury

Mercury

Sun

Fun Fact: In the daytime Mercury's surface is hot enough to melt lead.

Length of Day: 59 Earth days
Length of Year: 88 Earth days
Moons: none
Surface: rocky, with many craters
Distance Across: 4,900 kilometers (about 3,100 mi)

Venus

Venus

Sun

Fun Fact: Venus rotates backward compared with most of the other planets.

Length of Day: 243 Earth days
Length of Year: 225 Earth days
Moons: none
Surface: rocky, with constant cover of thick clouds
Distance Across: 12,000 kilometers (about 7,500 mi)

closer to the sun, they are warmer than the outer planets. The inner planets are also smaller than most of the outer planets. None of them has more than two moons.

Earth is different from the other inner planets. It has a watery surface. It is the only planet with a lot of oxygen in its atmosphere. Earth also has plant life and animal life.

✔ **List the inner planets in order from the sun.**

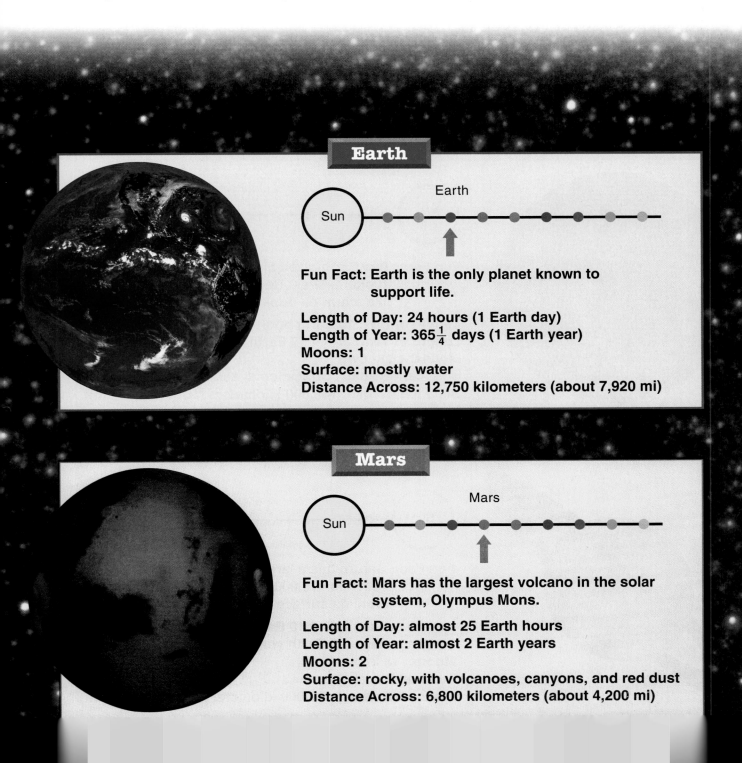

Earth

Fun Fact: Earth is the only planet known to support life.

Length of Day: 24 hours (1 Earth day)
Length of Year: $365\frac{1}{4}$ days (1 Earth year)
Moons: 1
Surface: mostly water
Distance Across: 12,750 kilometers (about 7,920 mi)

Mars

Fun Fact: Mars has the largest volcano in the solar system, Olympus Mons.

Length of Day: almost 25 Earth hours
Length of Year: almost 2 Earth years
Moons: 2
Surface: rocky, with volcanoes, canyons, and red dust
Distance Across: 6,800 kilometers (about 4,200 mi)

The Outer Planets

The five planets farthest from the sun are called the outer planets. The outer planets are Jupiter, Saturn, Uranus, Neptune, and Pluto.

The outer planets are alike in many ways. They are made mostly of frozen gases. They are very far from the sun, so their surfaces are much colder than the inner planets. All but Pluto are much larger than the inner planets. Jupiter is the solar system's largest planet. It is more than 1,000 times larger than Earth. Most of the outer planets have many moons. Many also have rings of dust and ice around them.

Pluto is different from the other outer planets. It is the smallest planet in the solar system. It is smaller than Earth's moon.

✔ **List the outer planets in order from the sun.**

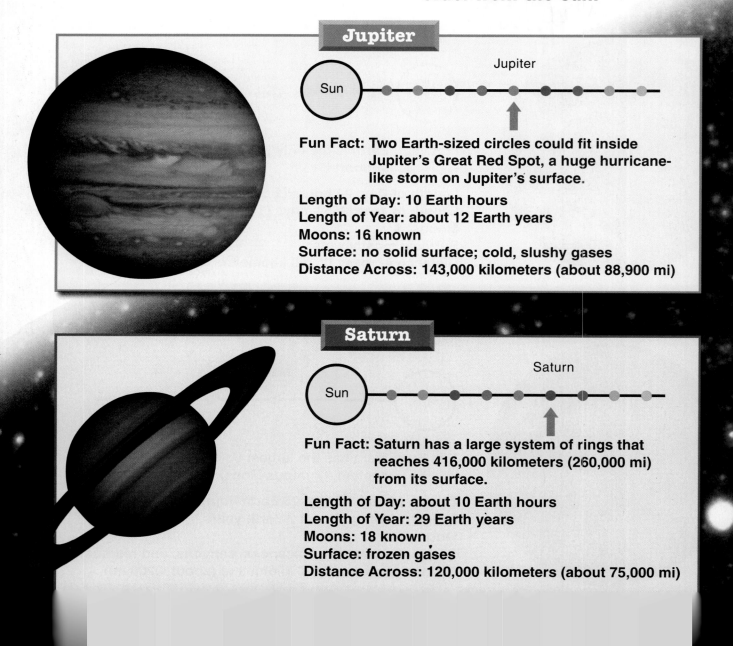

Jupiter

Jupiter

Sun

Fun Fact: Two Earth-sized circles could fit inside Jupiter's Great Red Spot, a huge hurricane-like storm on Jupiter's surface.

Length of Day: 10 Earth hours
Length of Year: about 12 Earth years
Moons: 16 known
Surface: no solid surface; cold, slushy gases
Distance Across: 143,000 kilometers (about 88,900 mi)

Saturn

Saturn

Sun

Fun Fact: Saturn has a large system of rings that reaches 416,000 kilometers (260,000 mi) from its surface.

Length of Day: about 10 Earth hours
Length of Year: 29 Earth years
Moons: 18 known
Surface: frozen gases
Distance Across: 120,000 kilometers (about 75,000 mi)

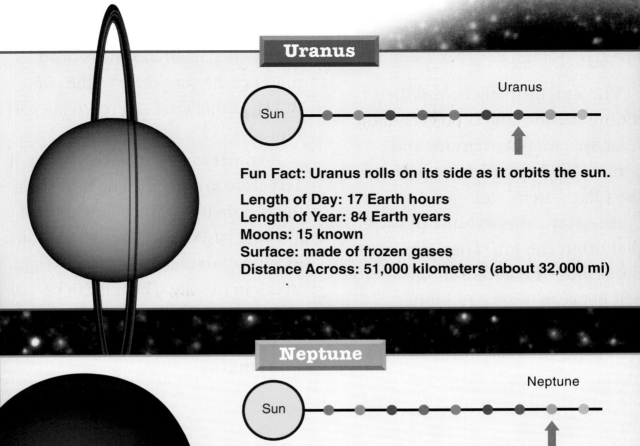

Uranus

Uranus

Fun Fact: Uranus rolls on its side as it orbits the sun.

Length of Day: 17 Earth hours
Length of Year: 84 Earth years
Moons: 15 known
Surface: made of frozen gases
Distance Across: 51,000 kilometers (about 32,000 mi)

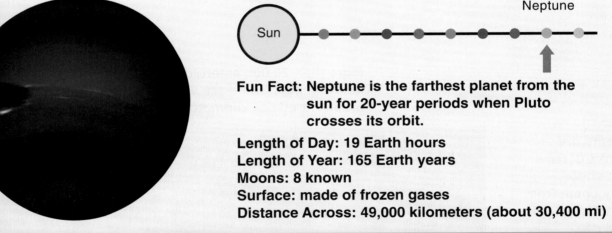

Neptune

Neptune

**Fun Fact: Neptune is the farthest planet from the
sun for 20-year periods when Pluto
crosses its orbit.**

Length of Day: 19 Earth hours
Length of Year: 165 Earth years
Moons: 8 known
Surface: made of frozen gases
Distance Across: 49,000 kilometers (about 30,400 mi)

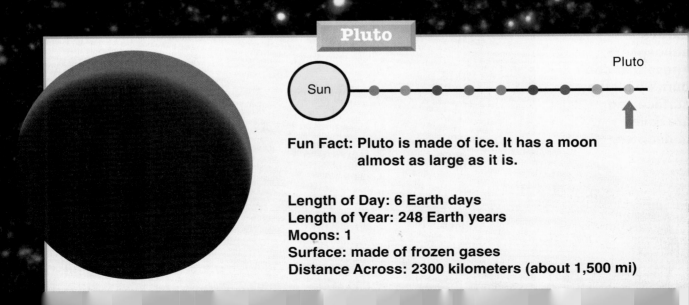

Pluto

Pluto

**Fun Fact: Pluto is made of ice. It has a moon
almost as large as it is.**

Length of Day: 6 Earth days
Length of Year: 248 Earth years
Moons: 1
Surface: made of frozen gases
Distance Across: 2300 kilometers (about 1,500 mi)

Other Bodies in the Solar System

The sun, the planets, and their moons are the largest objects in the solar system. But asteroids and comets, while smaller, are parts of the solar system, too.

An **asteroid** is a chunk of rock that orbits the sun. There are thousands of asteroids in the asteroid belt between Mars and Jupiter.

A **comet** is a large ball of ice and dust that orbits the sun. The orbit of a comet is shaped like a large, flat oval. One part of a comet's orbit might come very close to the sun. But the other part can reach far past Pluto.

A comet can be seen only when it gets close to the sun. The heat from the sun melts a comet's ice to form glowing gases. The gases stream out in a long tail that looks like a bright streak in the sky. The tail can be millions of kilometers long.

✔ **What are asteroids and comets?**

More than 20,000 asteroids are in the asteroid belt. Some are small. Others are hundreds of kilometers wide. ▼

Meteors are chunks of rock from space. Many come from the asteroid belt. Each day, hundreds of meteors enter Earth's atmosphere. Those that don't burn up hit the surface and are called meteorites. ▼

Sun

◀ Comets orbit the sun, too. Halley's comet can be seen from Earth every 76 years.

Summary

The solar system has nine planets that orbit the sun. Earth is one of those planets. Asteroids and comets are also parts of the solar system.

Review

1. What is a planet?
2. List three ways the inner planets are alike.
3. List three ways the outer planets are alike.
4. **Critical Thinking** How are asteroids and meteorites alike? How are they different?
5. **Test Prep** A comet is visible in the sky only when it is close to —

   A the sun
   B Earth
   C Mars
   D Pluto

LINKS

MATH LINK

How Many Moons? Make a bar graph showing the number of moons each planet has. How does the number of Earth's moons compare with the number of moons of other planets?

WRITING LINK

Narrative Writing—Story Pick a planet. Write a story for your teacher that tells what life would be like on that planet. Describe what it might be like to visit there.

HEALTH LINK

Sun Safety The sun's rays can harm the skin. That's why people use sunscreen. Sunscreens have an SPF number. Find out what *SPF* means. What SPF number sunscreen should you wear every day to protect you from the sun?

TECHNOLOGY LINK

Learn more about Mars by viewing *Mars Pathfinder Discovery* on the **Harcourt Science Newsroom Video** in your classroom video library.

INVESTIGATE

Star Patterns

Activity Purpose

Can you see patterns in the stars? People saw star patterns in ancient times. They saw horses, bears, and dragons in the sky. In this investigation you will make your own star pattern. Then you will **compare** the pattern to objects you know about.

Materials

- gummed stars
- black construction paper
- white crayon or chalk

Activity Procedure

1 Take the stars in your hand. Hold your hand about a half meter above the paper. Drop the stars onto the black paper. Glue the stars where they fall on the paper. (Picture A)

◄ Telescopes were invented many years ago. This telescope was used by scientists around the year 1620.

LESSON 2

What Is Beyond the Solar System?

In this lesson, you can . . .

 INVESTIGATE star patterns.

 LEARN ABOUT the stars we see in the sky.

 LINK to math, writing, literature, and technology.

2 **Observe** the stars. Look for a picture that the stars make. Use the white crayon to connect the stars to show the picture or pattern. You can connect all of the stars or just some of them.

3 Trade star patterns with other people in your class. See if they can tell what your star pattern is.

Picture A

Draw Conclusions

1. People have looked at the stars for thousands of years. Different people have seen different pictures in the stars. Why do you think this is so?

2. Some people look at a star pattern and see different things. A star pattern that looks like a water dipper to one person might look like part of a bear to another person. Look again at the stars on your paper. What other patterns can you find in them?

3. **Scientists at Work** Scientists **compare** things to see how they are alike. In the investigation you compared your star pattern to objects you know about. What person, animal, or object does your star pattern look like?

Investigate Further **Observe** real star patterns. Choose a star pattern, and draw it as you see it with the unaided eye. Look at the star pattern again using binoculars or a telescope. Use another color to add anything to the pattern that you didn't see before. **Compare** what you saw in your two observations.

Process Skill Tip

When you **compare** things, you look for properties that are the same.

The Way We See Stars

Star Patterns

A **star** is a hot ball of glowing gases—like our sun. The stars you see at night are much like the sun, but they are farther away. This makes the stars look very small. It also makes the stars look like they are all the same distance from Earth. But they are not. Some stars are not too far from the solar system. Some are very, very far away.

Ursa Major Native Americans named the constellation shown here the Great Bear (Ursa Major). The seven stars highlighted inside the bear make up the Big Dipper. The people of ancient China thought the stars of the Big Dipper looked like a chariot. The chariot carried the king of the sky. ▼

Just as you did in the investigation, ancient people looked for patterns in the stars. Then they made up stories to explain the patterns. A group of stars that forms a pattern is a **constellation**. People all over the world looked at the same stars and saw different patterns.

✔ **What is a constellation?**

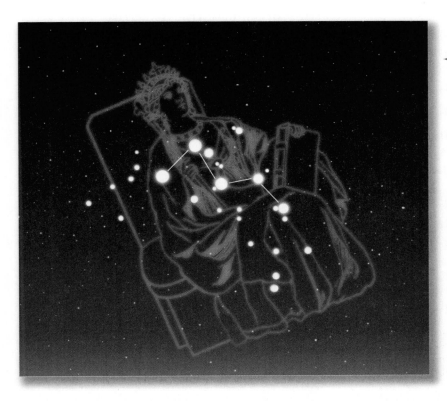

◀ **Cassiopeia** The people of ancient Greece called this constellation Cassiopeia. In the story they made up, Cassiopeia was the queen of part of Africa. She said that her daughter was more beautiful than anyone. Her bragging made one of the Greek gods angry. So he tried to take away Cassiopeia's daughter. A hero named Perseus saved the girl. But the angry god punished Cassiopeia. He turned her into a constellation.

◀ **Tayamni** This constellation was named by the Native American people called the Lakota. Tayamni means "the animal." The ancient Greeks had a different name for Tayamni. They called part of the same pattern Orion, the hunter. The three bright stars in the middle of Tayamni form the animal's back. The same stars form the belt of Orion.

Stars Seem to Move

Pick a constellation. Find it at the start of the evening and again later that night. You will see that it has moved. Stars don't really move around us. But they seem to move because Earth rotates. The spot where you are moves as Earth spins, so the stars above you change. Since Earth turns toward the east, the stars rise above the horizon in the east. As Earth keeps turning, the stars keep moving across the sky. When they finally get to the horizon in the west, they go below the horizon. They seem to disappear.

Stars and Seasons

This is the Big Dipper, part of the constellation Ursa Major. If you watch carefully, you can see how this constellation seems to move from place to place as the seasons change.

▲ In the spring, the Big Dipper is high in the sky. It looks upside down.

▲ In the summer, the Big Dipper has moved down in the sky. Its handle is pointing up.

You see different constellations at different times of the year. This is because Earth revolves around the sun. As Earth circles the sun, you see stars in different parts of space.

Polaris, or the North Star, is the only star that seems to stand still. The North Star is above Earth's axis.

The constellations near the North Star don't move across the sky. They just circle around the North Star. The Big Dipper is a constellation that circles the North Star.

✔ **Why do stars seem to move across the sky?**

▲ In the fall, the Big Dipper is low in the sky. It looks as if it could hold water.

▲ In the winter, the Big Dipper has moved up in the sky. Its handle is pointing down.

Observing Stars

People have looked at the stars for thousands of years. But many stars were not bright enough for people to see until the invention of the telescope. A **telescope** is an instrument that makes things that are far away look clearer and bigger. Many more stars can be seen with the telescope than with the unaided eye.

The astronomer Galileo used one of the first telescopes. He saw Saturn's rings through it in the early 1600s. Galileo's telescope made things look about 30 times as close as they are. Now telescopes can make things look thousands of times as close.

✔ **What does a telescope do?**

To see stars, you look through the eyepiece.

This piece helps you point the telescope to the right spot.

Light from the stars goes through this tube to the eyepiece.

Light enters the telescope here. It goes through a lens. The bigger this lens is, the larger the stars look.

The telescope stands on three legs. The legs are called a tripod. The tripod holds the telescope still while you use it.

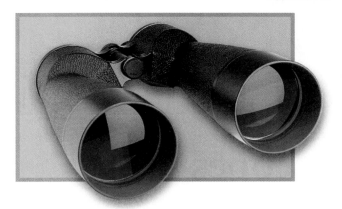

▲ Some binoculars are made to look at the stars. Like telescopes, they make faraway things look bigger. Most of them aren't as powerful as telescopes, but they are easier to use and carry.

Summary

Constellations are groups of stars that form patterns. A telescope is a tool that makes faraway things look clearer and bigger. More stars can be seen with a telescope than without one.

Review

1. What is a star?
2. In which direction do most constellations move in the sky?
3. How do the number of stars you can see without a telescope compare to the number you can see with a telescope?
4. **Critical Thinking** Why might different people see different patterns in the same stars?
5. **Test Prep** Stars seem to move across the sky each night because —
   A they orbit Earth
   B they are bright
   C Earth rotates
   D Earth is tilted

LINKS

MATH LINK

Star Track Pick a constellation. Find it in the night sky. Draw its position each week on a sheet of paper. After three months, look at your results. Use arrows to show the constellation's movement. How did it move?

WRITING LINK

Expressive Writing—Poem Write a poem about the night sky. What does it look like? How does it make you feel? Share your poem with classmates.

LITERATURE LINK

Studying Stars What are stars like? How did they form? How do they change? Find out in *The Stars: Light in the Night Sky* by Jeanne Bendick.

TECHNOLOGY LINK

Visit the Harcourt Learning Site for related links, activities, and resources.
www.harcourtschool.com/ca

How Do People Study the Solar System?

In this lesson, you can . . .

INVESTIGATE how to make a telescope.

LEARN ABOUT how people study objects in space.

LINK to math, writing, social studies, and technology.

INVESTIGATE

Telescopes

Activity Purpose Because distances in space are so great, scientists need to use instruments to study what is beyond Earth's atmosphere. In this investigation you will make a simple telescope and use it to observe some objects in space.

Materials
- small piece of modeling clay
- 1 thin (eyepiece) lens
- small-diameter cardboard tube
- 1 thick (objective) lens
- large-diameter cardboard tube

Activity Procedure

1 Press small pieces of clay to the outside of the thin lens. Then put the lens in one end of the small tube. Use enough clay to hold the lens in place, keeping the lens as straight as possible. Be careful not to smear the middle of the lens with clay. (Picture A)

2 Repeat Step 1 using the thick lens and large tube.

◀ **This vehicle is the moon rover. Astronauts used it to travel over the surface of the moon.**

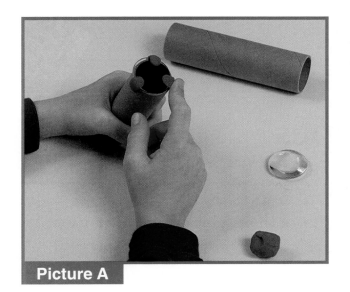

Picture A

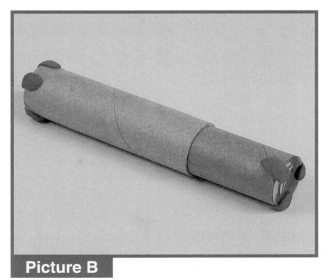

Picture B

3 Slide the open end of the small tube into the larger tube to make a telescope. (Picture B)

4 Hold your telescope, and look at an object through one lens. Then turn the telescope around, and look through the other lens. Slide the small tube in and out of the large tube until what you see is in focus, or not blurry. How do objects appear through each lens?

Draw Conclusions

1. What did you **observe** as you looked through each lens?

2. Using your observations, **infer** which lens you should look through to **observe** the stars. Explain your answer.

3. **Scientists at Work** Some scientists use telescopes to **observe** objects in space. How would your telescope make observing objects in the night sky easier?

Investigate Further Use your telescope to observe the moon at night. **Record** your observations.

Process Skill Tip

When you **observe** an object, you use your senses to notice details about it. Using a telescope helps you observe objects that are too far away to be seen clearly using only your eyes.

Telescopes

FIND OUT

- **about telescopes**
- **about missions into space**

Types of Telescopes

Using nothing more than your eyes, you can see most of the planets in the solar system. But what if you want to see them as more than just points of light in the sky? What if you want to see objects in space that are even farther away than the visible planets? Or what if you want to see smaller objects, such as moons? To do any of these things, you need to use a telescope.

◄ **This telescope is very old. It uses two lenses to magnify objects that are far away.**

B52

Two very different types of telescopes are used to observe objects in space: *radio telescopes,* which detect radio waves, and *optical telescopes*, which use light. There are two types of optical telescopes. A refracting telescope, which is what you made in the investigation, uses lenses to magnify an object, or make it appear larger. A reflecting telescope uses a curved mirror to magnify an object. Most large telescopes used today are reflecting telescopes.

✔ **What are two types of optical telescopes?**

▲ **Even without using a telescope, you can see dark areas, bright areas, and craters on the moon.**

Using a strong telescope lets you see more detail. Compare this photograph with the other one of the moon above. ▶

Observatories

Telescopes that scientists use are much larger than the one you made in the investigation. Besides being large, telescopes that are used to study space objects are powerful. Many of them have cameras that constantly take pictures of space. Computers keep the telescopes pointed at the same place in the sky. Astronomers then study the pictures to find out about space objects.

Earth's atmosphere limits what optical telescopes can "see." Moving air causes the "twinkling" of stars. It also blurs pictures taken using optical telescopes. This is why observatories that use optical telescopes are often located high on mountains, where the air is thinner.

The large mirror of the Keck telescope is made up of many smaller mirrors. They work together to gather light and magnify images of objects in space. ▼

This is a photograph of Keck Observatory in Hawai`i. An observatory is a building where scientists study the planets, the sun, and other distant objects in the sky. This observatory is at the top of an inactive volcano more than 4000 meters (about 13,130 ft) above sea level. ▼

▲ A radio telescope collects radio waves with a large, bowl-shaped antenna. Scientists study images formed by these waves to learn about the objects that gave them off. This radio telescope is in Arecibo (ar•uh•SEE•boh), Puerto Rico.

Scientists have found that stars and other objects in space give off more than just light. Radio telescopes work the way optical telescopes do. But instead of collecting and focusing light, they collect and focus invisible radio waves. Moving air, clouds, and poor weather don't affect radio waves. Computers process the data collected by radio telescopes. The computers then make pictures that astronomers can study.

✔ **What causes stars to twinkle?**

Space Telescopes

The telescopes you have seen so far in this chapter are located on Earth's surface. Scientists have also built telescopes for use in space.

These telescopes don't have any problems caused by the atmosphere.

✔ **Why are telescopes put in space?**

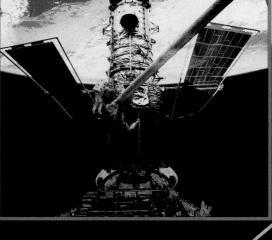

Hubble Space Telescope

The Hubble Space Telescope, or HST, is a reflecting telescope. Its mirror, which has a diameter of 240 cm (about 94 in.), can "see" details ten times as clearly as telescopes on Earth.

The HST uses sunlight as its energy source. The instrument's solar panels change sunlight into electricity. Each panel is about $2\frac{1}{2}$ meters (about 8 ft) wide and 13 meters (about 42 ft) long.

The main cover tube of the HST protects the telescope as well as other instruments used to study space.

The main mirror of the HST is located near the back of the main cover.

Summary

A telescope is a device that people use to observe distant objects. A refracting telescope uses lenses, and a reflecting telescope uses mirrors to magnify an object. Radio telescopes collect and focus radio waves. The Hubble Space Telescope is an optical telescope in orbit around Earth.

Review

1. What are two types of telescopes?
2. What limits the things an Earth-based optical telescope can "see"?
3. Why are observatories often built on mountaintops?
4. **Critical Thinking** What are some advantages of getting information from telescopes in space? What are some disadvantages?
5. **Test Prep** An instrument that uses lenses to magnify distant objects is a —

    A radio telescope
    B refracting telescope
    C reflecting telescope
    D space station

LINKS

MATH LINK

How Far? Earth and Jupiter are about 630 million km apart. Earth is about 28,000 km around in the middle. How many times would you have to go around the Earth to go as far as it is to Jupiter?

WRITING LINK

Informative Writing—Description Find out about a typical day on the space shuttle. Then write a composition for a friend describing a typical day of your mission.

SOCIAL STUDIES LINK

Galileo Galileo used one of the first telescopes to observe the sun. Use reference materials to find out what he saw and how it affected him.

TECHNOLOGY LINK

To learn more about pictures from space, watch *Hubble Images* on the **Harcourt Science Newsroom Video** in your classroom video library.

Sky Watchers

For centuries people around the world observed the night sky by using only their eyes. These sky watchers made detailed observations and charted what they saw. They used the information they gathered to decide when to plant their crops or to take journeys.

Early Observatories

The Anasazi of North America were one of the cultures that made early observatories. An Anasazi observatory has been found in New Mexico.

In England there is a group of huge stones called Stonehenge. The stones are set in a circle in a way that would allow risings and settings of the sun and the moon to be tracked. Scientists and historians hypothesize that Stonehenge is a giant calendar made of rocks.

The First Telescopes

With the use of lenses to make telescopes, people learned much more about the night sky. Galileo, a scientist in Italy, read about the telescope and made his own. It could magnify objects 20 or 30 times. From his observations, Galileo made inferences about the objects in the

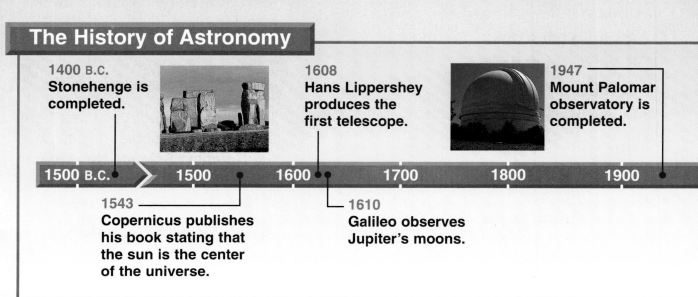

The History of Astronomy

1400 B.C.
Stonehenge is completed.

1608
Hans Lippershey produces the first telescope.

1947
Mount Palomar observatory is completed.

1500 B.C.   1500   1600   1700   1800   1900

1543
Copernicus publishes his book stating that the sun is the center of the universe.

1610
Galileo observes Jupiter's moons.

sky. He even saw moons orbiting Jupiter.

Modern Telescopes

During the twentieth century, bigger and bigger telescopes were designed. These telescopes use mirrors instead of lenses. The larger the mirror, the more detail in the image it produces. One of the newest

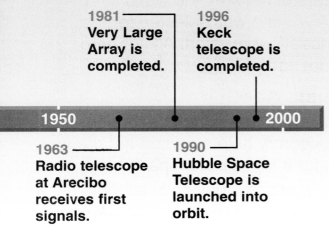

1981
Very Large Array is completed.

1996
Keck telescope is completed.

1950   2000

1963
Radio telescope at Arecibo receives first signals.

1990
Hubble Space Telescope is launched into orbit.

of these telescopes is at the Keck Observatory at the top of Mauna Kea, Hawai'i. At 10 meters (400 in.) across, the two Keck telescopes have the largest mirrors of any telescopes in the world.

Radio telescopes have made it possible to explore space day or night, rain or shine. That's because these telescopes pick up radio waves instead of light. The largest radio telescope is near Arecibo in Puerto Rico. In New Mexico, the Very Large Array is made up of 27 radio telescope antennas, each one measuring 25 meters (82 ft) across.

Scientists are always trying to find better ways of observing the night sky. They've even put a telescope in space. The Hubble Space Telescope orbits high above the atmosphere of Earth. Without the atmosphere to look through, it can make clearer pictures than ground-based telescopes.

Think About It

1. Why would people in ancient civilizations be interested in the stars and planets?

2. Why does the Hubble Space Telescope take clearer pictures than telescopes on Earth?

Mae Jemison

ASTRONAUT, PHYSICIAN, BIOMEDICAL ENGINEER

"I want to make sure we use all our talent, not just 25 percent."

Mae Jemison was the first African-American woman in space. She was a mission specialist on the 1992 *Endeavour* space shuttle flight. Before the flight, she helped check the shuttle, its computer software, and the tiles that protect the ship from burning up when returning to Earth.

For Jemison, becoming an astronaut was a childhood dream come true. She began her career by going to medical school. While a student, she traveled to Thailand, Cuba, and Kenya to offer medical help. She joined the Peace Corps after graduating from medical school. She spent two years in West Africa.

Jemison returned to the United States and became a doctor in Los Angeles. She applied to the National Aeronautics and Space Administration (NASA) to be an astronaut. She was not accepted the first time she applied. She applied again and was accepted. After five years of training and working at NASA, she was selected for the *Endeavour* mission. All her hard work had paid off!

Think About It

1. How could living in a foreign country help a person get ready for a trip in outer space?

2. How can studying in school help a person make his or her dreams come true?

Sundial

How can you use the sun to tell time?

Materials

- small ball of clay
- short pencil
- cardboard, about 15 cm x 20 cm

Procedure

1 Use the lump of clay to stand the short pencil in the center of the cardboard as shown.

2 Draw a circle around the pencil. The radius of the circle should be the length of the pencil.

3 Put your sundial on a windowsill that gets sun all day. Each hour, trace the shadow of the pencil on the cardboard. Mark the time at the end of each line. Do this for six hours.

4 On the next five sunny days, use your sundial to tell time.

Draw Conclusions

How does your sundial use Earth's movement to tell time? Why did you use it for five days rather than just one day?

Moving Constellations

How do the positions of the constellations change?

Materials

- ruler

Procedure

1 Observe the Big Dipper and the Little Dipper twice each night. One time should be in the early evening. The second time should be at least one hour later.

2 Find a reference point, such as the top of a tree. Hold the ruler at arm's length, and measure the distance from the reference point to the constellations. Draw your observations.

3 Repeat Steps 1 and 2 at the same time each night for four weeks. Remember to put the dates on your drawings.

Draw Conclusions

How did the constellations change their positions? What caused the changes?

Chapter ② Review and Test Preparation

Vocabulary Review

Use the terms below to complete the sentences. The page numbers in ( ) tell you where to look in the chapter if you need help.

solar system (B34)

orbit (B34)

planet (B34)

asteroid (B40)

comet (B40)

star (B44)

constellation (B45)

telescope (B48)

1. A large body of rock or gas that orbits the sun is a ____.

2. An ____ is a chunk of rock or metal that orbits the sun.

3. A ____ makes faraway things look clearer and bigger.

4. A ____ is a large ball of ice and dust that orbits the sun.

5. A ____ is a group of stars that forms a pattern.

6. The ____ is made up of the sun and all the objects that orbit around it.

7. An ____ is the path of an object as it moves around another object in space.

8. A ____ is a ball of hot, glowing gases.

Connect Concepts

List the planets, and classify them by their position in the solar system. Be sure to list them in the correct order from the sun.

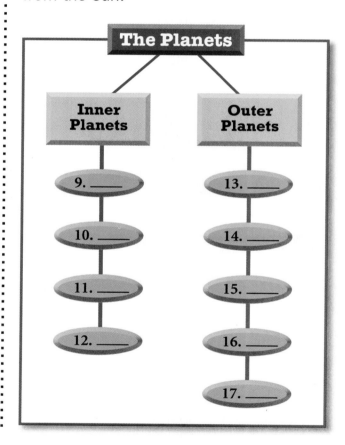

The Planets

Inner Planets

Outer Planets

9. ____

10. ____

11. ____

12. ____

13. ____

14. ____

15. ____

16. ____

17. ____

Check Understanding

Write the letter of the best choice.

18. The outer planets are —
    A like Earth
    B Mars and Jupiter
    C mostly larger than Earth
    D made of rock

19. A reflecting telescope in space is —
    F Keck   H Hubble
    G Arecibo   J Galileo

20. ＿＿ is the outer planet that is **NOT** a gas giant.
    A Saturn   C Uranus
    B Pluto   D Jupiter

21. Which of these planets has a ring?
    F Jupiter   H Earth
    G Pluto   J Venus

22. This type of telescope never has problems seeing through Earth's atmosphere. It uses lenses to enlarge an object.
    A Earth-based telescope
    B reflecting telescope
    C refracting telescope
    D space-based telescope

Critical Thinking

23. In what ways is Pluto like an inner planet?

24. Describe two ways constellations appear to move in the sky. Give a reason for each.

Process Skills Review

25. **Compare** reflecting and refracting telescopes.

26. **Use the numbers** in the table to **order** the planets from largest to smallest based on their mass.

Planet	Mass of Planet
Earth	17
Jupiter	5300
Mars	2
Mercury	1
Neptune	288
Pluto	$\frac{1}{5}$
Saturn	1587
Uranus	243
Venus	14

27. **Compare** asteroids, comets, and meteors. How are they alike? How are they different?

Performance Assessment

Model Solar System

Work with a partner to draw an imaginary solar system. Include one star, five planets, and two comets. Also include at least one more object that would be found in a solar system. Compare your model solar system with the one we live in.

Unit Project Wrap Up

Here are some ideas for other projects you can do.

Make a Chart

Use a computer software program to make a chart that explains the phases of the moon.

Write a Book

Do some research to find out how people have learned about space. Write and illustrate a book to share what you learn.

Investigate Further

How can you make your project better? What other questions do you have about Earth and space? Plan ways to find answers to your questions. Use the Science Handbook on pages R2–R9 for help.

Pedro   Kiesha   Tim

★Take It to the Top★

Investigating Matter and Energy

Investigating Matter and Energy

Unit Project Soap Tests

Analyze advertisements for soap, and record the manufacturer's claims. Choose at least three kinds of soap, and plan ways to test them to see if the claims are true. Organize your findings on graphs, tables, or charts. Compare the results of your tests to the advertisements.

Chapter 1

Properties of Matter

Vocabulary Preview

matter
physical property
solid
liquid
gas
atom
molecule
melting
evaporation
volume
mass

Every day we look at, listen to, feel, smell, and taste different kinds of matter. We even breathe it! Because matter comes in so many shapes and sizes, people have come up with many ways to measure it.

FAST FACT

People use lasers and satellites to measure really big objects. Mt. Everest in the Himalayas is the tallest mountain in the world. At 8848 meters (29,028 ft), it is as tall as a building with 2,950 stories!

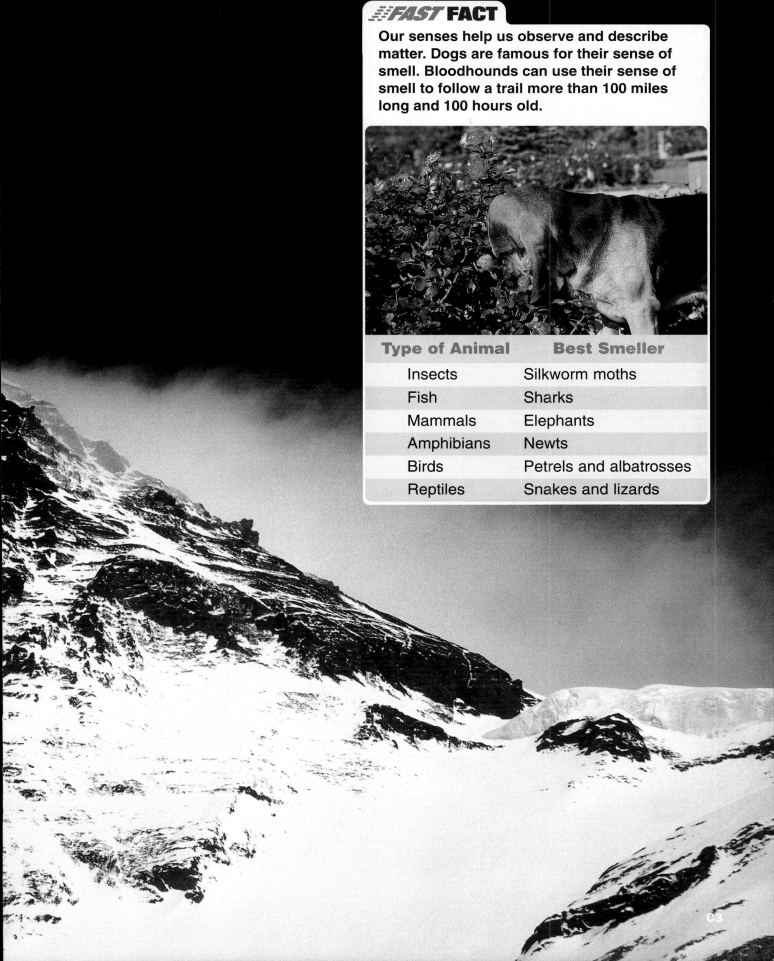

Our senses help us observe and describe matter. Dogs are famous for their sense of smell. Bloodhounds can use their sense of smell to follow a trail more than 100 miles long and 100 hours old.

Type of Animal	Best Smeller
Insects	Silkworm moths
Fish	Sharks
Mammals	Elephants
Amphibians	Newts
Birds	Petrels and albatrosses
Reptiles	Snakes and lizards

What Are Physical Properties of Matter?

In this lesson, you can . . .

INVESTIGATE kinds of matter.

LEARN ABOUT the properties of different objects.

LINK to math, writing, art, and technology.

INVESTIGATE

Physical Properties

Activity Purpose

Can you pour paper? Can you fold milk? Why not? Different objects have different properties. In this investigation you will **observe** different properties of matter.

Materials

- penny
- nickel
- marble
- key
- cotton balls
- piece of peppermint candy
- index card
- book
- uncooked macaroni
- twist tie
- peppercorns

Activity Procedure

1 Copy the charts shown.

2 Look at the objects you have been given. Notice whether they look shiny or dull. Notice how many colors each one has. **Record** your **observations.**

◀ This picnic basket is made of straw. The basket can hold many other things that are made of matter.

How It Looks				How It Feels			
Object	Shiny	Dull	Color	Hard	Soft	Rough	Smooth

How It Smells				How It Sounds			
Object	Sweet	Sharp	No Smell	Loud	Soft	Makes a Ping	No Sound

3 Touch the objects. Feel whether the objects are hard or soft. Feel whether they are rough or smooth. **Record** your **observations.** (Picture A)

4 Next, tap each object lightly with your fingernail. What kind of sound does it make? **Record** your **observations.**

5 Smell each object. **Record** your **observations.**

Picture A

Draw Conclusions

1. Which objects are hard and rough? Which objects are hard and smooth? Which objects are soft and rough? Which objects are soft and smooth?

2. **Compare** your chart with the chart of another group. Are any objects in different columns? Why?

3. **Scientists at Work** Scientists learn about the world by **observing** with their five senses. Which of the five senses did you *not* use in the investigation?

Process Skill Tip

Scientists study the world closely and **record** what they sense. This is called **observing.** Observing is one way scientists answer questions about matter.

C5

Physical Properties of Matter

FIND OUT

- **how to observe matter**
- **about three states of matter**

VOCABULARY

matter
physical property
solid
liquid
gas

Matter

Look around your classroom. You may see desks, books, other students, and the teacher. What else do you see? Everything you see takes up space. Your classroom must have enough space to hold you and all the other things that are in it. Everything in the classroom is matter. **Matter** is anything that takes up space.

Look at your desk. Can you pick it up with one arm? It is probably too heavy. Can you bend it? It is probably too stiff. You can use many different words to describe your desk. Each word you use to describe an object names a physical property of the object. A **physical property** (FIZ•ih•kuhl PRAHP•er•tee) is anything you can observe about an object by using your senses.

✔ **What is matter?**

◄ The girl, the raincoat, and the rain are matter. Even the air is matter. Everything in this picture is matter.

What Matter Looks Like

You can observe some physical properties of matter with your sense of sight. In the investigation you observed some things that are dull and some things that are shiny. You also looked at the colors of the objects.

There are some things, such as most glass windows, that you can see through. Some of these things don't have any color. Then you can see the colors of the things on the other side. But some things you can see through, such as tinted windows, do have color. Then you can't tell the colors of things on the other side.

Another physical property you can see is size. Have you ever seen a group of basketball players? They don't seem tall by themselves. But when a player is standing next to you, you can see that the player is tall. Size is easiest to see when you can compare one object to another.

A property you cannot see is temperature. But you can see the effects of temperature. You can

▲ The glass has no color, so when you look through it, you can see that the liquid in it is pink. You can tell the drink is cold because it has ice in it. The steam rising from the cup of tea lets you infer that it is hot.

infer that something is hot if you see steam coming from it. You can guess that something is cold if you see it with ice or snow.

✓ **What properties of matter can you learn about with your sense of sight?**

One of these horses is much larger than the other one. Size is a physical property of matter. ▶

C7

What Matter Feels Like

Many people wear shirts under wool sweaters because wool sweaters feel scratchy. You can learn about some physical properties of matter by using your sense of touch.

Sandpaper feels rough, but sand feels smooth. The bark on a tree and gravel against bare feet both feel rough. *Smooth* can describe objects as different as a mirror and a book cover.

You can feel some things that you can't see. You can feel the push of the wind. You can also feel whether something is hot or cold.

Different parts of the same object may feel different. A wool jacket feels rough, but the buttons may feel smooth. A cat's fur is soft, but its claws are sharp.

✔ **What are some words you can use to describe how matter feels?**

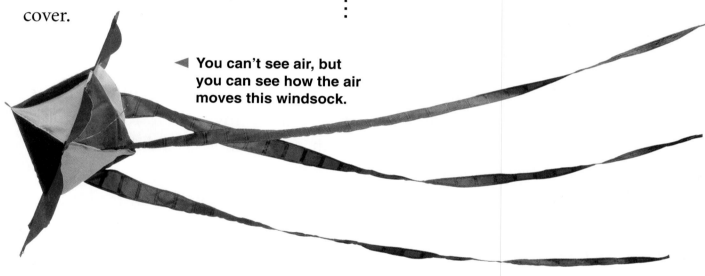

◄ **You can't see air, but you can see how the air moves this windsock.**

◄ **Snow feels cold and wet. Temperature and wetness are both physical properties of matter.**

Different parts of these slippers feel different. The fur is soft, but the soles feel hard and smooth. ▼

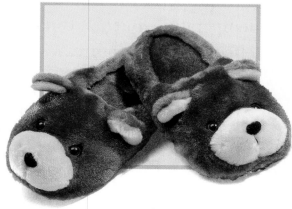

What Matter Tastes and Smells Like

People have to be careful about tasting things. Some things can make you ill, even if you taste just a small piece of them. But if you are careful, you can learn by tasting things. Your tongue can taste things that are sweet, sour, salty, and bitter.

You enjoy your favorite foods partly because of their smell. You may begin to feel hungry when good smells come from the kitchen.

Not all smells are pleasant. But people can get used to smells so they don't notice them anymore. Barnyards have strong smells. A visitor from the city might notice them right away. A farmer who works every day in a barn may not notice the strong smells at all. Smell is a physical property of matter.

✔ **What can we learn from our senses of taste and smell?**

▲ **The unpleasant odor of a skunk is a warning to stay away.**

◀ **Roses usually smell nice.**

Humans can taste many foods but don't always like what they eat. ►

Other Properties of Matter

Matter has many other properties that you can see, hear, and feel. Many objects break if you drop them. Others bounce. Rubber bands stretch. Kite string doesn't stretch at all. A paper clip can bend, but a twig will snap in two if you try to bend it. Magnets attract objects that contain iron. You can feel the force it takes to pull the object away from the magnet.

✔ **What are some of the other properties of matter?**

▲ Magnets attract objects that contain iron.

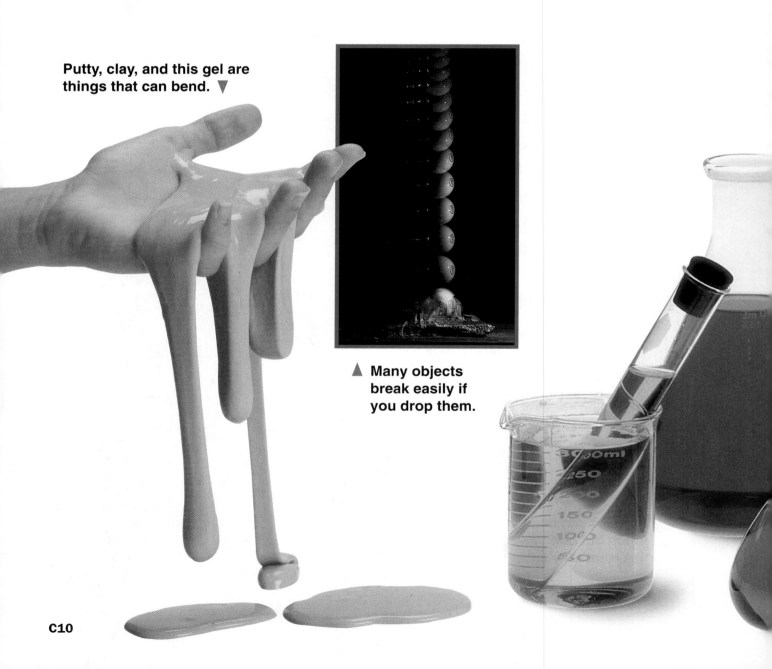

Putty, clay, and this gel are things that can bend. ▼

▲ Many objects break easily if you drop them.

Three States of Matter

Matter has different forms, called states. The three states of matter we can observe are solids, liquids, and gases.

Solids A **solid** takes up a specific amount of space and has a definite shape. A solid does not lose its shape. For example, a book keeps its shape when it is on a shelf or in your hands. A solid also has a volume that stays the same. That means a solid object takes up the same amount of space all the time.

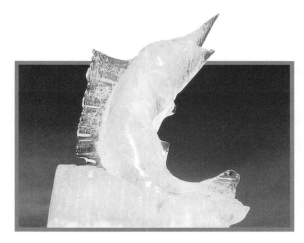

▲ This sculpture of a fish is made of ice. Ice is a solid. As long as the sculpture stays frozen, it will keep its shape. If the ice warms up, it will melt and become a liquid. Then the sculpture will lose its shape.

Liquid

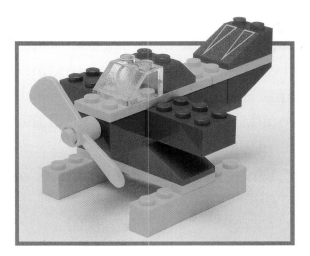

▲ Solid

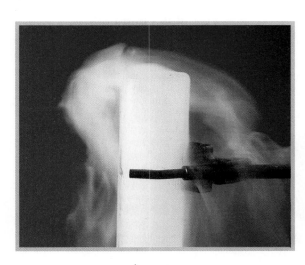

▲ Gas

Liquids A **liquid** has a volume that stays the same, but it can change its shape. A liquid takes the shape of any container it is put into. But one cup of water always takes up one cup of space, in any container.

One cup of water might not look like very much in a short, wide glass. But in a tall, skinny glass, one cup of water can look like a lot. No matter what it looks like, it is the same volume of water in both glasses.

Gases You may know that a gas takes the shape of the container it is in. A **gas** does not have a definite shape or a definite volume. It takes up all the space in its container. The air in your classroom is a gas. It takes the shape of your classroom. It also takes up all the space inside the classroom. If you put the same amount of air into a larger classroom, the air would spread out to take up all the space in that room.

✔ **What are the three states of matter we can observe?**

▲ The shape of the water changes as it falls. When it hits the stream, the banks help it hold a shape.

We breathe a gas. It is called air. ▼

Summary

Matter is anything that takes up space. Matter has many physical properties that you can observe using your five senses. You can feel matter, taste matter, see matter, hear matter, and smell matter. Matter has different states. The three states we can observe are solids, liquids, and gases.

Review

1. What is matter?
2. What is a physical property?
3. How can we learn about matter?
4. **Critical Thinking** Think of last night's dinner. What properties of matter did you observe?
5. **Test Prep** Which set of words all name physical properties of matter?
   A solids, liquids, diamonds
   B ice, water, steam
   C hard, soft, sticky
   D rocks, rubies, emeralds

LINKS

MATH LINK

Cups Per? How many cups of matter does it take to fill a liter container? A gallon container?

WRITING LINK

Narrative Writing—Story
Helium is a gas that is lighter than air. When you fill a balloon with helium, the balloon rises. Write a story for your classmates about the travels of a helium balloon that floats away.

ART LINK

Statues in Stone Sculptors choose their stone carefully. Different kinds of stone have different physical properties that can make it easier or harder to work with. Investigate the stone statues in your city or state. Find out what kind of stone they are made from.

TECHNOLOGY LINK

Visit the Harcourt Learning Site for related links, activities, and resources.
www.harcourtschool.com/ca

What Are Solids, Liquids, and Gases?

In this lesson, you can . . .

INVESTIGATE three states of matter.

LEARN ABOUT the differences between the three states of matter.

LINK to math, writing, language arts, and technology.

INVESTIGATE

One Way Matter Can Change

Activity Purpose Matter can change from one state to another. Think about what happens when you make ice cubes. You put water in a freezer, and it turns into ice. What might happen to an ice cube that is left out in a warm room? Investigate to see if your idea is correct.

Materials
- clear plastic cup
- paper towel
- 2 ice cubes
- marker

Activity Procedure

1. Place the plastic cup on the paper towel. Put the ice cubes in the cup. (Picture A)

◄ Three states of matter surround us everywhere. Liquid water is in the ocean and in fog. The lighthouse is a solid. We breathe air, which is a gas.

2 **Predict** what the ice cubes will look like after 45 minutes. Use your past observations of ice cubes to predict what will happen this time. **Record** your prediction.

3 **Observe** what's in the cup after 45 minutes. **Record** what you see. Was your prediction correct?

4 Mark the outside of the cup to show how high the water is. **Predict** what you will see inside the cup in the morning if you leave it out all night.

Picture A

5 **Observe** the cup the next morning. **Record** what you see. **Compare** your prediction to the actual result.

Draw Conclusions

1. What do you think caused the ice to change?

2. What do you think happened to the water when you left it out all night?

3. **Scientists at Work** Scientists make **predictions** based on things they have **observed** before. What had you observed before that helped you make your predictions?

Investigate Further Fill half an ice cube tray with water. Fill the other half with orange juice. **Predict** which will freeze first, the water or the orange juice. **Communicate** what you **observe.**

Solids, Liquids, and Gases

FIND OUT

- what matter is made of
- how matter changes

VOCABULARY

atom
molecule
melting
evaporation

Atoms

A puzzle has many pieces that fit together to form a picture. If you look closely, you can see each piece. If you look even more closely, you can see the tiny dots of color on each piece. All matter is like the puzzle. The more closely you look, the smaller the pieces you can see.

Some pieces of matter are so small that you can see them only by using special tools. Some pieces are so small that you cannot see them at all. These pieces are called atoms. **Atoms** are the basic building blocks of matter. Atoms are often found linked together rather than being separate. These linked atoms are called **molecules**.

✔ **What are atoms?**

◄ **From far away, you can see the carved figure of a woman sitting down.**

◄ **When you move closer, you can see the colors and roughness of the stone.**

◄ **If you use a microscope, you can see some of the tiny pieces that make up the stone.**

How Molecules Are Connected

The atoms and molecules in matter are arranged differently in each state of matter. But in all the ways they are arranged, the particles move.

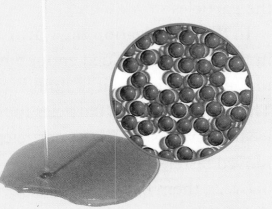

▲ In a gas, such as this iodine gas, the molecules are not connected to each other and are not close to each other. Each molecule moves in a straight line until something stops it. Then it bounces. It moves off in another straight line until something else stops it.

▲ In a liquid the molecules are more loosely arranged than in a solid. This allows the molecules to slide past each other.

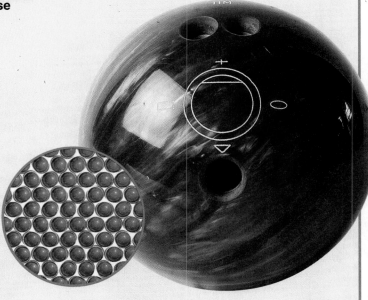

▲ A solid is hard because its molecules do not move very much.

How Matter Changes States

Adding heat or taking heat away causes matter to change states. This is because adding heat makes the particles in matter move faster. Taking away heat, or cooling, makes the particles slow down.

In the investigation the warm air in the classroom added enough heat to the ice to change it to liquid water. The heat caused the particles in the ice to move faster. As the particles moved faster, the connections between them became looser. In time, the connections got so loose that the particles could slide past each other. At that point, the solid ice became liquid water. The process by which a solid becomes a liquid is called **melting**.

With still more heat, the particles broke apart from each other completely. The liquid became a gas. The process by which a liquid becomes a gas is called **evaporation** (ee•vap•uh•RAY•shuhn).

If you take heat away from liquid water, the opposite happens. The particles slow down and solid ice forms.

✔ **What causes matter to change state?**

Hot lava, or liquid rock, comes from this volcano. When the lava hits water, the heat in the lava causes some of the water to turn to steam. Then the lava cools and changes into solid rock. ▼

Summary

Atoms are small particles that make up matter. Atoms are often linked together to form molecules. In solids atoms fit tightly together and do not move very much. In liquids, they slide past each other. The atoms in gases are far apart and are not connected. They keep moving until something stops them. Adding or taking away heat can cause matter to change states.

Review

1. What are the building blocks of matter?

2. In which state of matter are the atoms or molecules most tightly connected?

3. Why does gas **NOT** have a definite shape?

4. **Critical Thinking** When you boil water, what makes the liquid water turn into a gas?

5. **Test Prep** Which set of words names three states of matter?

   A solid, gas, water

   B solid, liquid, gas

   C hard, soft, smooth

   D salty, sweet, sour

LINKS

MATH LINK

Measuring Heat People often need to know the temperature of what they cook. Find out the names of two kinds of kitchen thermometers and what each kind is used for.

WRITING LINK

Informative Writing— Description Write a description of a lake or pond for a younger child. Tell what it is like in each season. Be sure to describe what happens to the water in each season.

LANGUAGE ARTS LINK

Parts of Speech Find out what parts of speech the words *solid, liquid,* and *gas* are. Use each word in a sentence.

TECHNOLOGY LINK

Learn more about how matter changes state by investigating *Solids, Liquids, and Gases* on **Harcourt Science Explorations CD-ROM.**

LESSON 3

How Can Matter Be Measured?

In this lesson, you can . . .

 INVESTIGATE the mass and volume of objects.

 LEARN ABOUT ways to measure mass and volume.

 LINK to math, writing, language arts, and technology.

Measuring Mass and Volume

Activity Purpose If you pick up a C-cell battery and a D-cell battery, which feels heavier? In this investigation you will find out the difference in mass between the two batteries. You will also **measure** the amount of space a liquid takes up.

Materials

- balance
- 3 C-cell batteries
- 3 D-cell batteries
- clear plastic cup
- water
- masking tape
- 3 clear containers of different sizes
- marker

Activity Procedure

Part A

1. Put a C-cell in the pan on the left side of the balance. Put a D-cell in the pan on the right side. **Record** which battery is heavier. (Picture A)

◀ Tools have been invented for measuring all sorts of things. Here an elephant is being weighed.

C20

2 Add C-cells to the left side and D-cells to the right side until the pans are balanced. You may need to use some of the small masses from the balance to make the batteries balance perfectly. **Record** the number of C-cells and D-cells you use.

Part B

3 Fill the cup half-full with water. Use a piece of tape to mark how high the water is in the cup. **Predict** how high the water will be in each container if you pour the water into it. Mark each prediction with a piece of tape. Write *P* (for *Predict*) on the tape. (Picture B)

4 Pour the water into the next container. Mark the height of the water with a piece of tape. Write *A* (for *Actual*) on the tape.

5 Repeat Step 4 for each of the other containers.

Picture A

Picture B

Draw Conclusions

1. **Compare** the numbers of C-cells and D-cells it took to balance the pans. **Draw a conclusion** from these numbers about the masses of the batteries.

2. Describe the height of the water in each container. Why did the same amount of water look different in the different containers?

3. **Scientists at Work** Scientists **measure** matter by using tools that are marked with standard amounts. What was the standard amount you used in this activity to measure the water?

Process Skill Tip

Using tools to **measure** allows scientists to study and **compare** different pieces of matter.

Measuring Matter

FIND OUT

- how to measure matter
- how to use tools to measure matter

VOCABULARY

volume

mass

Measuring Volume

Suppose you fill a glass all the way to the top with orange juice. Then you try to put ice cubes into it. The orange juice will spill out over the top of the glass. The orange juice takes up space, and the ice cubes take up space. If you want to add ice cubes to the drink, you have to leave enough space for them.

All matter takes up space. The amount of space matter takes up is called its **volume** (VAHL•yoom). Scientists measure volume by using tools. The volume of a liquid can be measured by using a measuring cup.

✔ **What is volume?**

The same volume of liquid looks different in different containers. A measuring cup will show the volume in a standard unit you can understand.

Like liquids, solids have volume. Since a solid holds its shape, you cannot measure its volume easily in a measuring cup. A rock or a marble will not take the shape of the cup. ▶

◀ You can measure the volume of a small rock. Pour some water into a measuring device. Record the level of the water. Gently place the rock in the water. Record the new water level. The difference in the water levels equals the volume of the rock.

Measuring Mass

All matter has mass. **Mass** is the amount of matter in an object. You can't tell how much mass an object has if you just look at it. A golf ball and a Ping Pong ball are about the same size. But a golf ball has much more mass than a Ping Pong ball. You have to measure to find out how much mass an object has.

In the investigation you used a pan balance to measure mass. You may have used another kind of balance in the grocery store to measure the

The balloon filled with air has more mass than the empty balloon. This shows that air has mass. ▶

An empty pan balance has the same amount of mass on both sides. ▼

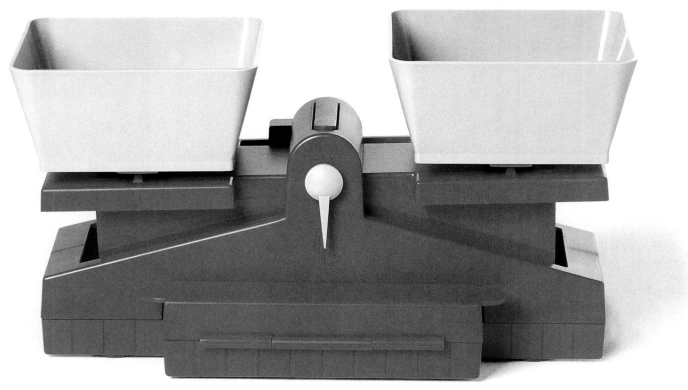

masses of fruits and vegetables. You may use a scale at home to measure your own mass.

You can't see air. In fact, you can't see most gases. But like all matter, gases have mass. Look at the balloons on the previous page. You can see that when you put air into a balloon you add to its mass. If you put too much air into a balloon, the balloon will pop. Then you can feel the mass of air rushing out of the balloon.

✔ **What is mass?**

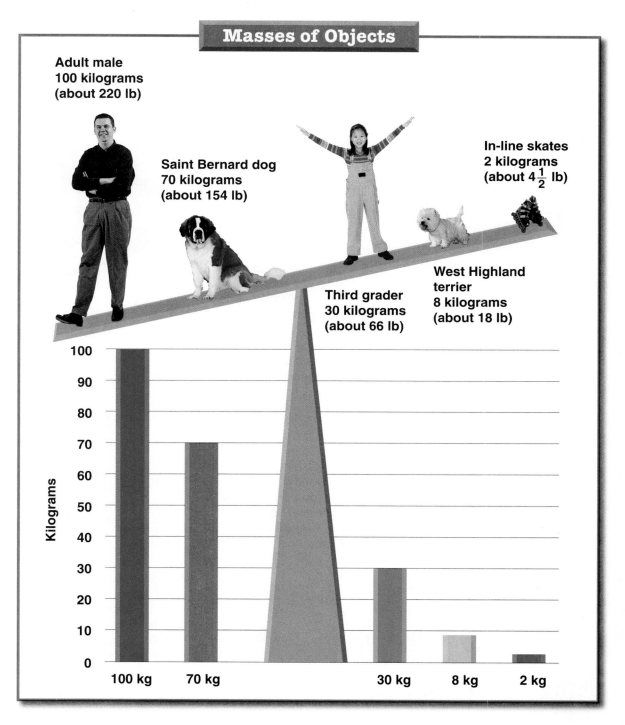

Masses of Objects

Adult male
100 kilograms
(about 220 lb)

Saint Bernard dog
70 kilograms
(about 154 lb)

In-line skates
2 kilograms
(about $4\frac{1}{2}$ lb)

Third grader
30 kilograms
(about 66 lb)

West Highland terrier
8 kilograms
(about 18 lb)

Kilograms

100 kg   70 kg   30 kg   8 kg   2 kg

Tools for Measuring Mass and Volume

Suppose you need 1 teaspoon of salt. You would use a measuring spoon, not a scale. Measuring tools are made for certain tasks. Using the right tool makes measuring easy.

This scale makes measuring fruits and vegetables easy. The large pan can hold big items like bags of apples or bunches of bananas. ▶

▲ When you need medicine, it is important to take the right amount. This spoon measures the correct volume of medicine.

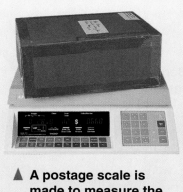

▲ A postage scale is made to measure the masses of letters and packages. A letter has a small mass. To measure its mass, you need a scale that can measure small masses.

◀ To find a person's mass, you need a scale a person can stand on. When the boy stands on this scale, he can read his mass.

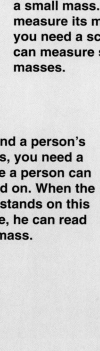

▲ Restaurants make food in large volumes. This measuring tool can hold large amounts of liquid.

◀ Scientists often measure liquids. This container, called a *graduate,* is marked along the side. By using it, a scientist can see exactly what the volume of a liquid is.

Adding Masses

Suppose you draw a picture on a large sheet of paper. Then you cut the paper into pieces to make it into a puzzle. When you put the puzzle back together, it's the same size as the whole sheet of paper. And it still has the same mass.

Suppose you measure the mass of an apple. Then you cut the apple in half and measure the mass of each piece. If you add the masses of the two pieces, you will find that the total is the same as the mass of the whole apple.

When you cut the apple in half, you still have the same amount of apple to eat. In any way matter is arranged, its mass stays the same.

✔ **What happens to the mass of an object when you cut the object into pieces?**

The balance is holding two identical boxes of crayons. Taking the crayons out of the box does not change their mass. The mass is the same when the crayons are in the box and when they are out of the box. ▼

Comparing Mass and Volume

Different kinds of matter can take up the same amount of space but have different masses. A Ping Pong ball takes up about the same amount of space as a golf ball. But the Ping Pong ball has much less mass. A lime has about the same volume as an egg. But the lime has more mass.

✔ **Which do you think has more mass, a cup of water or a cup of air?**

Mass and Volume

All the jars are filled. They all have the same volume of matter in them. But look closely at the matter in each jar. Each kind of matter has a different mass. For example, the jelly beans have more mass than the pasta.

Summary

Volume is the amount of space an object takes up. Mass is how much matter is in an object. The mass of an object stays the same in any way its matter is arranged. Different objects can have the same volume but different masses.

Review

1. Name one kind of tool for measuring the volume of a liquid.
2. Do objects that are the same size always have the same mass? Explain.
3. Name some tools you could use to measure mass.
4. **Critical Thinking** Name two kinds of fruit. Which do you think has more mass? Explain.
5. **Test Prep** Choose the best definition of *volume*.
   - **A** the amount of air an object holds
   - **B** how much something weighs
   - **C** the amount of matter in an object
   - **D** the amount of space something takes up

MATH LINK

Measuring Water Fill a film canister to the top with water, and put the lid on it. Measure the height of the canister. Then freeze it. In two hours, measure the height of the canister again. What happened to the water?

WRITING LINK

Informative Writing—Explanation Think about going shopping for milk. Tell what it would be like if there were no standard volumes of milk sold. Write a story for your teacher that explains what you would have to do.

LANGUAGE ARTS LINK

Many Word Meanings Look up the words *volume* and *mass* in a dictionary. Write two sentences for each word. But use meanings that are not from science.

TECHNOLOGY LINK

Learn more about measuring matter by visiting this Internet Site.
www.scilinks.org/harcourt

Classifying Matter

Many centuries ago, Greek thinkers tried to understand what matter was made of. They thought that everything—gold, silver, sulfur, trees, dogs, and horses—was made of different combinations of four different materials. These materials, called elements, were earth, air, fire, and water. Some other Greek thinkers thought matter was made up of small particles. They called these particles atoms. But the element theory was more popular. Nobody thought or wrote about atoms again until the early 1800s.

The Atomic Theory

In 1803 John Dalton published his studies of what he called ultimate particles. He had carried out many experiments with water. Using electricity, he split water into its two elements—hydrogen and oxygen. He found that the two elements had different weights. He found that he could predict the amount of oxygen formed if he knew how much hydrogen was formed. Dalton had read about the old Greek idea of atoms. He thought it explained many of the things he had observed. From

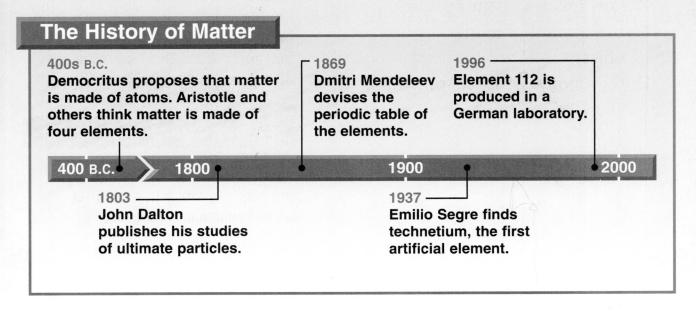

The History of Matter

400s B.C.
Democritus proposes that matter is made of atoms. Aristotle and others think matter is made of four elements.

1869
Dmitri Mendeleev devises the periodic table of the elements.

1996
Element 112 is produced in a German laboratory.

400 B.C. — 1800 — 1900 — 2000

1803
John Dalton publishes his studies of ultimate particles.

1937
Emilio Segre finds technetium, the first artificial element.

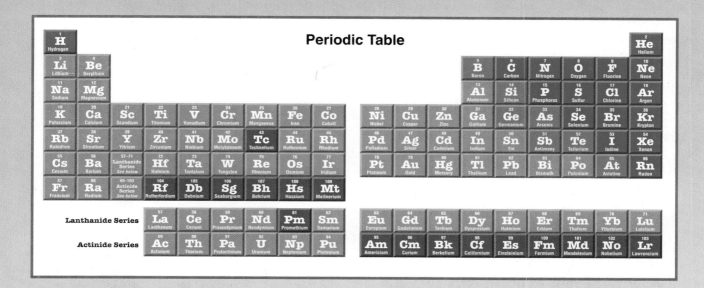

Periodic Table

his experiments, he inferred three things about atoms:

- Atoms of different elements have different weights.
- Two atoms of the same element are identical.
- An atom of one element can't be changed into an atom of a different element.

Making Sense of Elements

In the 1700s and 1800s, many scientists searched for new elements. As more and more elements were discovered, people began to look for an order. Could they predict the elements that hadn't been discovered yet?

In 1869 a Russian scientist named Dmitri Mendeleev studied each of the 63 known elements. He grouped the elements by their properties. He grouped all the metals together and all the nonmetals together. Then he ordered the elements in each group by how much their atoms weighed. He organized his ordered groups in a table, called the periodic table. The table is arranged in rows and columns. Mendeleev left gaps in his table where none of the known elements fit. He predicted that these gaps would be filled as new elements were discovered. Today, more than 100 elements are listed on the periodic table.

Think About It

- Why did Mendeleev's periodic table let him predict new elements that hadn't been discovered yet?

Dorothy Crowfoot Hodgkin

CHEMIST

"You're finding what's there and then trying to make sense of what you find."

Dorothy Crowfoot Hodgkin won the Nobel Prize in chemistry in 1964. She was only the third woman ever to win it. By the time she won the award, she had spent more than 30 years studying insulin. Insulin is a chemical made in the body that allows us to use sugar for energy. The results of her studies helped fight diseases and save lives.

Hodgkin did most of her research at Oxford University in England. While there, she attended meetings of the research club. At these meetings she was able to communicate her ideas and research findings with other students and scientists.

Hodgkin loved studying how things were put together. She became interested in crystals. She used X rays to find the shapes of the crystals. She did much of her work before computers had been invented, so her research took a very long time. She used the first IBM computers to help do her calculations. Later, she sent her data to a professor in Los Angeles who had a faster computer. They used mail and telegrams to send information back and forth.

Hodgkin traveled around the world to meet and talk with other chemists. She continued to do research, teach, and travel throughout her life.

Think About It

1. How did not having a computer slow down Hodgkin's research?
2. How can communicating with others help solve a problem?

Insulin

Properties of Metals

Which metals have magnetic properties?

Materials

- magnet
- penny
- piece of aluminum foil
- straight pin
- scissors
- dime
- paper clip

	Objects
Magnetic	
Non-Magnetic	Objects

Procedure

1. Copy the chart onto a sheet of paper. Predict which objects are magnetic.

2. Place the magnet close to the penny. Does the penny stick to the magnet? Write down the results on your chart.

3. Repeat Step 2 for each of the other objects. Compare the results with your predictions.

Draw Conclusions

Study your completed chart. Are all metals attracted by a magnet? Which kinds are?

Mass of Liquids

Which of three liquids has the greatest mass?

Materials

- clear measuring cup
- water
- oil
- red vinegar

Procedure

1. Will water float on oil? Or will oil float on water? Predict which liquid will float on the other.

2. Pour some water into the measuring cup.

3. Add some oil. Observe what happens to the oil. Write down your observations. Was your prediction correct?

4. Will the vinegar float on the water? Make a prediction.

5. Pour some red vinegar into the measuring cup. Let it stand still for five minutes. Write down your observations.

Draw Conclusions

The lightest liquid floats on the others. List the liquids from lightest to heaviest.

Floating Eggs

How can you change the density of a substance?

Materials

- plastic cup half-full of water
- 1 fresh egg in shell, uncooked
- table salt
- water
- spoon

Procedure

1. Carefully place the egg in the cup of water. Does it float?

2. Remove the egg, and stir several spoonfuls of salt into the water.

3. Carefully replace the egg in the water. Does it float now?

Draw Conclusions

Did the egg ever float? If so, when and why? What physical property of the water changed during the experiment?

Rust

How is a compound formed?

Materials

- pencil
- steel wool
- test tube
- plastic cup
- water
- masking tape
- metric ruler

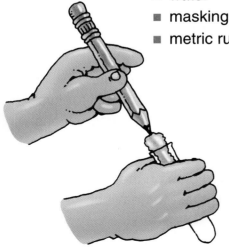

Procedure

1. Using the pointed end of the pencil, push a small wet ball of steel wool to the bottom of one test tube.

2. Fill the cup half-full with water. Place the test tube upside down in the cup. Tape the test tube to the side of the cup.

3. Measure and record the height of the water in the test tube once a day for 4 days.

Draw Conclusions

How did the steel wool change? What compound formed? What would prevent the compound from forming?

Signs of Chemical Change

How can you tell if a chemical change has taken place?

Materials

- 6 zip-top plastic bags
- wax pencil or permanent marker
- 3 packets of quick-acting yeast
- measuring cup
- warm water
- cold water
- sugar
- spoon

Procedure

1. Make a chart like the one below.

2. Use the wax pencil to number the bags.

3. Add one cup of cool water to Bag 1. Seal it shut. Add one cup of warm tap water to Bag 2. Seal it shut.

4. Add one cup of cool water and one spoonful of yeast to Bag 3. Seal it shut. Add one cup of warm water and one spoonful of yeast to Bag 4. Seal it shut. Mix the contents of each bag by kneading it.

5. Add one cup of cool water, one spoonful of yeast, and one spoonful of sugar to Bag 5. Seal it shut. Add one cup of warm water, one spoonful of yeast, and one spoonful of sugar to Bag 6. Seal it shut. Mix the contents of each bag by kneading it gently.

6. Let the bags sit for 10 minutes. Observe what has happened in each bag. Record your observations in the chart.

Draw Conclusions

In which bags did chemical changes occur? What clues did you see that helped you infer that chemical changes were taking place?

Bag Contents	Results
1. cool water	
2. warm water	
3. yeast and cool water	
4. yeast and warm water	
5. yeast, cool water, and sugar	
6. yeast, warm water, and sugar	

Vocabulary Review

Use the terms below to complete the sentences 1 through 11. The page numbers in ( ) tell you where to look in the chapter if you need help.

matter (C6)   **molecules** (C16)

physical   **melting** (C18)
 property (C6)   **evaporation** (C18)

solid (C11)   **volume** (C22)

liquid (C12)   **mass** (C24)

gas (C12)

atoms (C16)

1. A ____ is matter that has a definite shape.

2. All matter is made of ____.

3. Stickiness is a ____ of matter.

4. ____ is the amount of matter in an object.

5. Everything that takes up space is ____.

6. The amount of space that matter takes up is its ____.

7. A ____ has particles that are not tightly connected.

8. A ____ has no definite shape and no definite volume.

9. When a liquid changes into a gas, the process is called ____.

10. Atoms are sometimes linked to form ____.

11. When a solid changes to a liquid, the process is called ____.

Connect Concepts

Write the terms needed to complete the concept map.

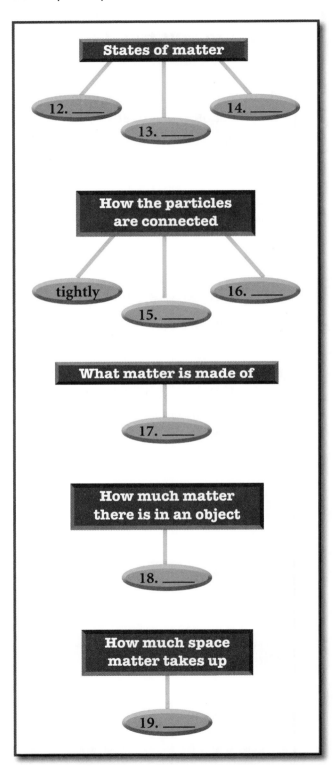

States of matter

12. ____   13. ____   14. ____

How the particles are connected

tightly   15. ____   16. ____

What matter is made of

17. ____

How much matter there is in an object

18. ____

How much space matter takes up

19. ____

Check Understanding

Write the letter of the best choice.

20. There are two jars that are the same size. One is filled with peanut butter, and the other is filled with jelly. They have the same volume, but they may not have the same —

    A heat   C evaporation

    B mass   D gas

21. One physical property that a football and a soccer ball share is that both —

    F bounce   H fold

    G stretch   J crackle

22. Syrup pours because its atoms are —

    A tightly connected

    B not connected

    C loosely connected

    D split

23. A shallow pond can dry up because of —

    F ice

    G cold weather

    H heat and evaporation

    J snow falling during the winter

Critical Thinking

24. Explain what happens to a liquid when heat is added to it.

25. A solid has a definite shape. Sand can take the shape of its container. Then why is sand a solid?

Process Skills Review

Write *True* or *False*. If a statement is false, change the underlined words to make it true.

26. **Predicting** means explaining what underlined{happened in the past}.

27. **Measuring** is underlined{using tools} to find the volume or mass of something.

28. **Observing** means underlined{watching something for a second}.

Performance Assessment

Make Models

Make clay models of the particles in a solid, a liquid, and a gas. Make the models small, but be sure each one looks different. Use an index card to make a label for each model. Place the labels in front of the models.

Changes in Matter

When you put the silverware away, it's easy to separate the spoons from the forks. But if you tried to unscramble an egg, you'd have a pretty hard time. What changes mixtures so you can't separate them? In this chapter, you'll find out.

Vocabulary Preview

physical change
mixture
solution
chemical change

FAST FACT

When you cut yourself, blood looks like a thick red liquid. But blood is really a mixture of liquids and cells of different sizes. Here are some other things that you might not think of as mixtures.

Different Kinds of Mixtures

Kinds of Matter Mixed	Result
Carbon and iron	Steel
Water and gelatin	Jelly
Air and rock	Pumice
Fat and water	Milk
Ash and air	Smoke
Water and air	Fog

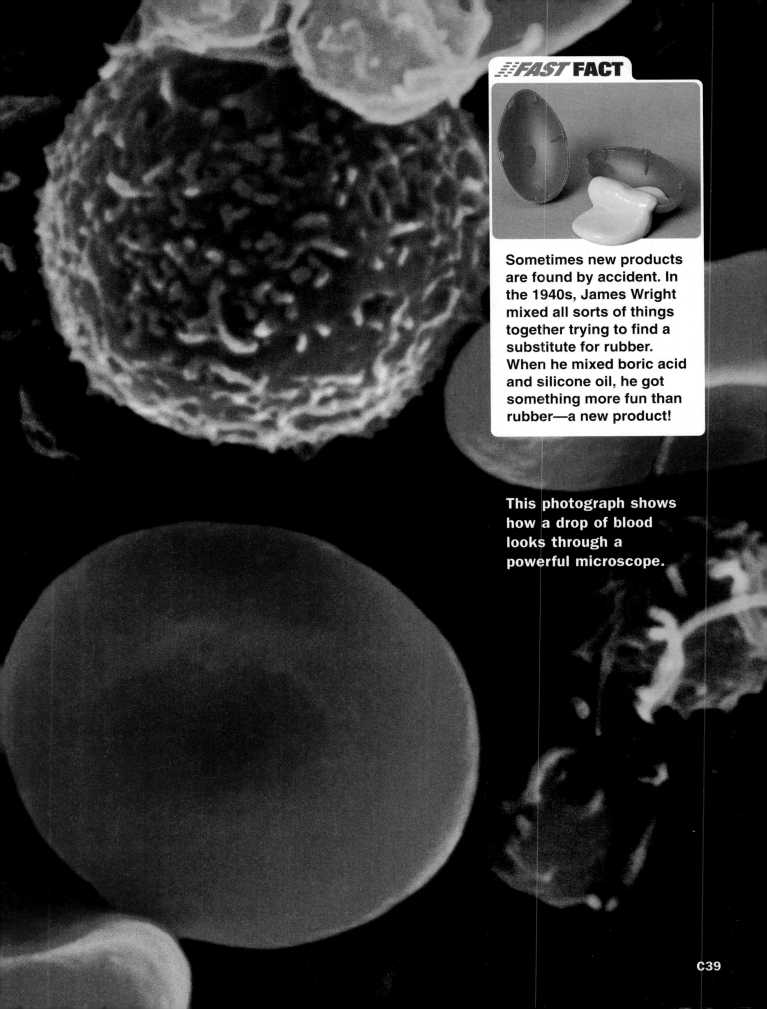

Sometimes new products are found by accident. In the 1940s, James Wright mixed all sorts of things together trying to find a substitute for rubber. When he mixed boric acid and silicone oil, he got something more fun than rubber—a new product!

This photograph shows how a drop of blood looks through a powerful microscope.

LESSON 1

What Are Physical Changes?

In this lesson, you can . . .

INVESTIGATE how to separate mixtures.

LEARN ABOUT physical changes in matter.

LINK to math, writing, social studies, and technology.

Separate a Mixture

Activity Purpose In a mixture of sand, shells, twigs, and seaweed, you might want to separate the shells. You could do it easily with your hands. To separate other mixtures, you might need to use different methods or tools. **Plan and conduct an investigation** to discover methods for separating mixtures.

Materials

- 4 clear plastic cups
- 6 marbles
- water
- steel paper clips
- rice
- magnet
- measuring cup
- paper towels
- funnel

Activity Procedure

1 In one cup, make a mixture of marbles and water. Plan a way to separate the marbles from the water. Try it. **Record** your method and your results.

◀ Heat causes a physical change in the ice pop. It melts.

2 In another cup, make a mixture of marbles, paper clips, and rice. Plan a way to separate the mixture. Try it. **Record** your method and your results.

3 If your method doesn't work, plan a different way to separate the mixture. Try different methods until you find one that works. Try using the magnet. **Record** each method you try.

4 In another cup, mix $\frac{1}{4}$ cup of rice with 1 cup of water. How could you separate the rice from the water? **Record** your ideas.

Picture A

5 Make a filter with the paper towels and the funnel. **Predict** how this tool could be used to separate the mixture. Then use the filter to separate the mixture. (Picture A)

Draw Conclusions

1. When would it be easy to use only your hands to separate a mixture?

2. When might you need a tool to separate a mixture?

3. **Scientists at Work** Scientists often use charts to **record** the results of an investigation. How would setting up charts help you **plan and conduct an investigation**?

Investigate Further Make a mixture of sand and water. **Plan and conduct an investigation** to separate the mixture. Would a tool be useful? Which tool would you use?

Process Skill Tip

Scientists ask questions about the world around them. To find the answers, they **plan and conduct investigations**. First, they think about the question they want to answer. Then, they plan a way to answer the question. As they conduct the investigation, they **record** their results.

C41

Physical Changes in Matter

FIND OUT

- how matter can change and still be the same
- about two kinds of mixtures

VOCABULARY

physical change
mixture
solution

Kinds of Physical Changes

When you wash your clothes, they get wet, soapy, and wrinkled. Even with all these changes, they are still your clothes. No new kinds of matter are formed. Changes to matter in which no new kinds of matter are formed are called **physical changes**.

Some physical changes make objects look very different. Paper can be cut, painted on, written on, torn, folded, and glued. Each time, the paper looks different, but it is still paper.

Changing the temperature can make matter change. Cooling makes liquid water change to ice. The ice has the same particles in it that the liquid water had. No new kinds of matter are formed.

✔ **What are some ways that matter can change and still be the same matter?**

People make paper so they can use it. ▼

One way people change paper is by giving it a different shape. ▶

◀ Another way people change paper is by cutting it into smaller pieces.

C42

Mixtures

A **mixture** is a substance that contains two or more different types of matter. The types of matter in a mixture can be separated. After a mixture is separated, the matter is the same as it was before it was mixed.

In the investigation you made a mixture of rice, paper clips, and marbles. Then you separated the pieces back into separate piles of rice, paper clips, and marbles. Making a mixture is a physical change.

Separating the parts of a mixture is another physical change.

Some mixtures can be separated by hand. You separated the rice from the marbles with your hands. Some mixtures can be separated by evaporation or by condensation. In *evaporation* a liquid part of a mixture turns into a gas. This leaves the other parts behind. In *condensation* a gas in a mixture turns into a liquid. The liquid can be separated from the rest of the mixture.

✔ **What is a mixture?**

This alphabet soup is a mixture of broth, peas, pasta, carrots, and other vegetables.

Solutions

Have you ever put sugar in iced tea? After you stir the tea, you can't see the sugar anymore. You know the sugar is still there because you can taste it. This mixture of sugar and tea is called a solution. In a **solution** the particles of the different kinds of matter mix together evenly.

The different kinds of matter in a solution can't be separated by hand. But evaporation can separate some solutions. If you heat the iced tea or leave the glass out for a while, the water in the tea will evaporate. Then the sugar will be left.

✔ **What is a solution?**

THE INSIDE STORY

Solutions

This bright-blue substance is called copper sulfate. Watch what happens when it is mixed with water.

Copper sulfate mixes with water to form a solution. Like the copper sulfate, the solution is a bright-blue color.

To separate the copper sulfate from the water quickly, you can heat the solution. The heat makes the water evaporate.

After the water is gone, only the copper sulfate is left.

Summary

Matter can change size, shape, and state. Matter can be mixed. Changes to matter that don't form any new kinds of matter are called physical changes. A mixture contains two or more types of matter. A solution is a kind of mixture. In a solution the particles of the different kinds of matter are mixed evenly.

Review

1. What is a physical change?
2. Name three ways to cause a physical change in matter.
3. What is the difference between a mixture and a solution?
4. **Critical Thinking** Suppose you have a mixture of water and salt. You use evaporation to separate the water from the salt. Where does the water go?
5. **Test Prep** Which one is a solution?
   A marbles mixed in water
   B sugar mixed in water
   C clay, rocks, and twigs
   D rice mixed in water

◀ **Mixture**

LINKS

 MATH LINK

Trail Mix Make a food mixture. Use a $\frac{1}{4}$-cup measuring cup and a 2-cup measuring cup. Measure $\frac{1}{4}$ cup each of raisins, dried banana chips, sunflower seeds, and pretzel circles. Put all these into the 2-cup measuring cup. How much trail mix do you have altogether?

 WRITING LINK

Expressive Writing—Song Lyrics Almost all soups are mixtures. Choose a familiar tune and write song lyrics for a younger child about your favorite soup.

 SOCIAL STUDIES LINK

Gold Rush Look up the California gold rush. Find out how people separated mixtures of water, sand, and rock to find gold.

 TECHNOLOGY LINK

Visit the Harcourt Learning Site for related links, activities, and resources.
www.harcourtschool.com/ca

WELCOME TO THE LEARNING SITE

LESSON 2

What Are Chemical Changes?

In this lesson, you can . . .

 INVESTIGATE a change in matter.

 LEARN ABOUT how new matter is formed.

 LINK to math, writing, language arts, and technology.

Chemical Changes

Activity Purpose You mix flour, eggs, milk, and oil. Then you pour some of the mixture into a hot pan. Pancakes! The pancakes are a different kind of matter than the flour and eggs. Many changes happen to cause the new kind of matter to form. You can **observe** a new kind of matter being formed in this investigation.

Materials
- safety goggles
- cookie sheet
- large glass bowl
- measuring cup
- baking soda
- vinegar

Activity Procedure

1 **CAUTION** Put on your safety goggles.

◄ The yellow liquid mixes with the clear liquid. Together they form a new kind of matter that is a pink solid.

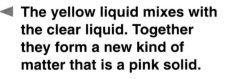

C46

2 Place the cookie sheet on the table. Place the bowl on the cookie sheet.

3 **Measure** $\frac{1}{4}$ cup of baking soda. Pour it into the bowl.

4 **Measure** $\frac{1}{4}$ cup of vinegar. Hold the cup with the vinegar in one hand. Use your other hand to fan some of the air from the cup toward your nose. Do not put your nose directly over the cup. (Picture A)

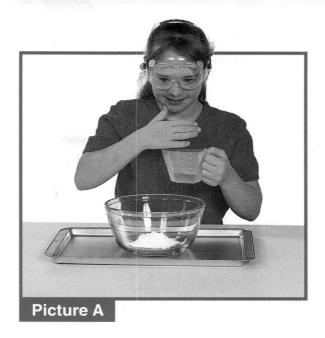
Picture A

5 Pour the vinegar into the bowl.

6 **Observe** the matter in the bowl. **Record** what it looks like. Use the procedure from Step 4 to smell the matter in the bowl. Record what it smells like.

Draw Conclusions

1. How is the material in the bowl like the baking soda and vinegar you started with? How is it different?

2. What can you **infer** about where the bubbles came from?

3. **Scientists at Work** Scientists do not rely on **conclusions** unless they are backed by **observations** that can be confirmed. How could you confirm your observations for this investigation?

Investigate Further Mix warm water and a fresh packet of dry yeast. **Observe** the mixture. **Record** what you see. What can you **infer** about the changes you see?

Scientists **observe** matter carefully. Sometimes they see things they don't understand right away. Sometimes they can use their experience to **infer** what those things mean. When you infer, you use your observations to form an opinion.

Chemical Changes in Matter

FIND OUT

- how new kinds of matter are formed
- some ways we use chemical changes every day

VOCABULARY

chemical change

Forming Different Kinds of Matter

Matter is always changing. Some changes are physical changes. In physical changes the kind of matter stays the same.

Some changes form new kinds of matter. Changes that form different kinds of matter are called **chemical changes**. In chemical changes the particles in the matter change. Cooking food makes new kinds of matter. Flour, eggs, milk, and oil turn into pancakes. The particles in the flour, eggs, milk, and oil change. The pancakes will never be just flour, eggs, milk, and oil again.

✔ **What is a chemical change?**

▲ This liquid looks like water. It is actually a solution with lead in it.

This is a solution with iodine in it. It also looks like water. ▶

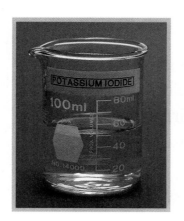

When the two liquids are mixed, they form a yellow solid. This is an example of a chemical change. ▶

Some Chemical Changes

Burning People burn things every day. Many people burn oil or gas to heat their homes. When things burn, different kinds of matter form. So burning is a chemical change. When wood burns, it combines with the oxygen in the air. The matter that forms includes smoke and ash. Another kind of matter forms that you can't see. It is a gas that mixes with the air.

Rusting Have you ever noticed orange-brown spots on the metal of a bike or a car? This orange-brown matter is rust. Rust forms when air and water mix with the iron in metal. The rust is a different kind of matter. It is flaky and soft. It is not strong like iron. When a metal gets rusty, it loses some of its strength. Often you can break the rusty part off. Rusting is a chemical change.

✔ **What are two common chemical changes?**

A chemical change is happening in this fire. The wood is combining with oxygen in the air to form new kinds of matter. ▼

The new bolt is shiny. The other bolts are old. The iron in the old bolts has rusted. It has combined with air and water to form a new kind of matter. ▼

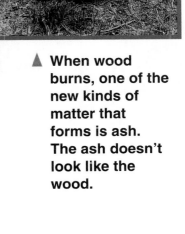

▲ When wood burns, one of the new kinds of matter that forms is ash. The ash doesn't look like the wood.

Using Chemical Changes

Chemical changes go on all around us. We burn fuel to heat our homes. The engines of cars and buses burn fuel to make them move. Chemical changes happen when we cook food. Many of the materials in our clothes are made by chemical changes. Plants use chemical changes to make their food. The film in a camera goes through chemical changes to make photographs.

✔ **Name three chemical changes.**

1 First you take a picture.

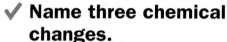

2 The film inside a camera has chemicals on it. These chemicals change when light hits them. The changes are the beginning of your photograph.

3 This first process makes a negative. On a negative, the colors are backward. The negative is used to make a print.

4 A machine shines light through the negative and onto a sheet of paper. This sheet of paper is coated with chemicals. The paper is put through a chemical bath.

Summary

Chemical changes cause new kinds of matter to form. Chemical changes can be very useful. We use chemical changes to cook. We use chemical changes to take pictures. Some chemical changes are harmful. Rust on metal makes the metal weak.

Review

1. What happens to particles of matter in a chemical change?
2. Name two common chemical changes.
3. Describe some ways we use chemical changes to help us.
4. **Critical Thinking** What is the difference between a chemical change and a physical change?
5. **Test Prep** Which of the following is a chemical change?
   A tearing
   B soaking
   C rusting
   D folding

4

LINKS

MATH LINK

A Fire Problem A log had a mass of 5 kilograms before it burned. After the fire was out, the ashes had a mass of 1 kilogram. What was the mass of the smoke and gas that were formed?

WRITING LINK

Narrative Writing—Story
Write the story of a forest fire for your teacher. Tell how the fire begins. Describe what is left of the forest when the fire is over.

LANGUAGE ARTS LINK

Many Uses of Fire Look up the word *fire* in a dictionary. Write two sentences that use the word. But use the word in ways that are different from the way *fire* is used in science. Explain what *fire* means in each sentence.

TECHNOLOGY LINK

To learn more about how matter that has undergone a chemical change can be used, watch *Recycled Roads* on the **Harcourt Science Newsroom Video** in your classroom video library.

Plastic Bridges

Physical changes can be useful. When you fold a sheet of paper, you want it to change shape. And you want a plastic bag to change its shape to hold the groceries you buy at the store. But if a bridge you were driving on changed shape as much as the paper or the plastic bag, you'd be in trouble.

Choosing Materials

When engineers design and make something, they choose their materials carefully. They use materials that change in ways that are useful and don't change in ways that cause problems. When they want to build a bridge, they use materials that are strong. They look for materials that won't bend or break when cars and trucks drive over them. They might use steel, or concrete—or plastic.

Why Build Plastic Bridges?

People don't usually think of plastic when they think of bridges.

▲ Building a plastic bridge

plastic building material

Plastic bags get holes in them. Plastic milk bottles bend and break. Even the hard plastic used in toys and computers breaks. But scientists have developed a new kind of plastic that is strong enough to hold the weight of cars and trucks. It is a kind of composite, or a material made of several different things put together.

Composite plastic is as strong as steel, but it is much lighter. Bridges built with plastic can be put together and used in about a day. Bridges made with steel and concrete take much longer to build.

Weathering wears out bridges made of steel and concrete. Heat, cold, rain, ice, and wind slowly break them apart. Water can erode cement and make steel rust. But water and salt don't affect composite plastic. The plastic doesn't break down or rust.

Using Plastic in Bridges

Today plastic bridges are being tested in different places around the country. These bridges aren't made completely of plastic. They still have steel rails on the sides and concrete on the road surface. They look just like the bridges you're used to. But scientists hope they will last longer.

Plastic is also being used to fix old bridges. Plastic can be wrapped around parts of these bridges to add support. The plastic coating also keeps the bridges from being damaged by heat, cold, wind, water, and salt.

Think About It

1. Why do we still need to use concrete and steel to make bridges?

2. Why might you want to wrap plastic around the supporting parts of a building?

WEB LINK:
For Science and Technology updates, visit the Harcourt Internet site.
www.harcourtschool.com/ca

Careers Civil Engineer

What They Do
Civil engineers design buildings, bridges, roads, airports, and tunnels and make sure these things are safe to use.

Education and Training Civil engineers have at least a bachelor's degree in engineering. They study physics, chemistry, and math so that they can test and design structures.

Enrico Fermi
PHYSICIST

"I'm hungry. Let's go to lunch!"

Enrico Fermi was a man who lived on a schedule. It was noon and he was hungry. So work on his great experiment could wait awhile. That afternoon, December 2, 1942, his experiment succeeded and made it possible to develop the atomic bomb. The work of many scientists over several years had been completed.

Fermi became interested in atoms after reading about the research done by other scientists. In 1938 he was awarded the Nobel Prize in physics.

After Fermi, his wife, and their two children went to Sweden to accept the prize, they did not return to Italy. Fermi's wife, Laura, was Jewish. She

was in danger because of the prejudice against Jews in Italy. So the Fermi family came to the United States. Fermi taught at Columbia University. A few years later, he went to the University of Chicago, where many of his experiments took place.

In 1943 Fermi went to Los Alamos, New Mexico, to help develop the first atomic bomb. All of the major countries involved in World War II were racing to make this bomb. After the war ended, Fermi returned to the University of Chicago.

Think About It

1. Why did all the major countries in the war want to make an atomic bomb?
2. Why is it important for scientists to write about their discoveries?

Changes in Cooking

What happens to muffins as they bake?

Materials

- 1 box of muffin mix
- other needed ingredients
- mixing bowl
- spoon
- muffin pan

Procedure

1. Read and follow the directions on the box of muffin mix.

2. Halfway through the cooking time, open the oven or turn on the oven light and observe the muffins. Record your observations.

Draw Conclusions

What is happening to the muffins?

Making a Solution

Which works better, hot water or cold water?

Materials

- 2 small, heat-proof glass containers
- cold water
- spoon
- sugar
- clock with second hand
- warm water (from the tap)

Procedure

1. Fill one container with cold water.

2. Mix a spoonful of the sugar into the water. Stir until the sugar dissolves.

3. Watch the clock to see how long it takes. Record the number of seconds it takes.

4. Repeat Steps 1–3 using warm water.

5. Do the activity again. Record your results.

Draw Conclusions

How were the results different for cold water and warm water? Why do you think they were different? Did the results change when you repeated the experiment? Why or why not?

Vocabulary Review

Choose a term below to match each definition. The page numbers in ( ) tell you where to look in the chapter if you need help.

physical change (C42)

mixture (C43)

solution (C44)

chemical change (C48)

1. Matter that contains two or more different things that can be separated

2. A change in which no new kinds of matter are formed

3. A change that makes new kinds of matter

4. A mixture in which the particles of the different kinds of matter mix together evenly

Connect Concepts

Complete the diagram below by listing three examples of physical change and two examples of chemical change.

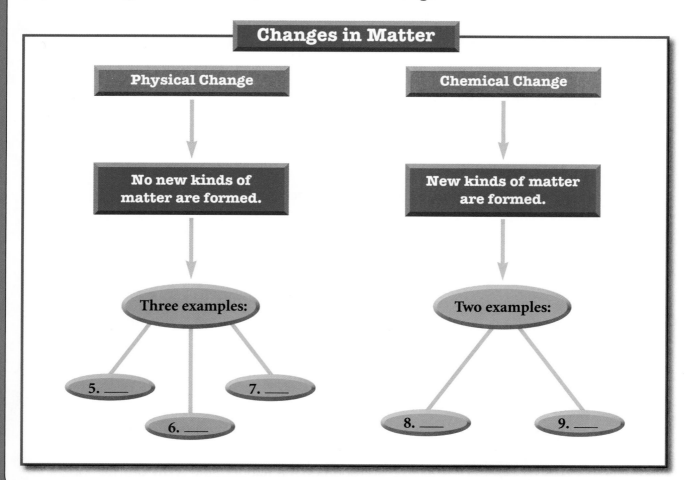

Changes in Matter

Physical Change	Chemical Change
No new kinds of matter are formed.	New kinds of matter are formed.
Three examples:	Two examples:

5. _____
6. _____
7. _____

8. _____
9. _____

Check Understanding

Write the letter of the best choice.

10. Which of the following involves a chemical change?

    A dissolving soap in water

    B cutting paper with scissors

    C burning paper

    D filling a balloon with air

11. Which of the following is a physical change?

    F mixing blueberries, strawberries, and raspberries

    G rusting of iron on a car

    H burning a log

    J cooking pancakes

12. When you add heat to ice to turn it into liquid water, you make a —

    A solution   C chemical change

    B mixture   D physical change

13. Which of the following is a solution?

    F twigs, leaves, and bugs

    G sugar and water

    H newspapers and magazines

    J milk and cereal

14. What new kind of matter forms when iron is mixed with air and water?

    A wood   C ice

    B rust   D ash

Critical Thinking

15. Think of the investigation you did with vinegar and baking soda. What happened that showed a gas was forming?

16. Suppose you leave a shovel out in the rain. Two weeks later there are orange-brown spots on it. Explain what has happened.

Process Skills Review

Write *True* or *False*. If the statement is false, change the underlined part to make it true.

17. A scientist who <u>wants to find an answer to a question</u> **plans and conducts an investigation.**

18. When you **observe** something, you <u>watch it carefully</u>.

19. When you **infer**, you <u>make a wild guess</u>.

Performance Assessment

Mixtures and Solutions

Work together with three or four other students. Your teacher will give you the following things: a pitcher of water, two cups, paper clips, safety pins, salt, a spoon, and unpopped popcorn. Make one mixture and one solution and correctly label each.

Chapter 3

Energy

Energy is all around you. It is in sunlight, moving water, gasoline, and batteries. It can move and change from one form to another. Without energy, plants could not grow, animals could not move, and machines could not operate.

Vocabulary Preview

energy
electricity
fossil fuel
vibrate
circuit
thermal energy
heat
waste heat

FAST FACT

The Earth is struck by lightning 100 times every second. Most lightning strikes do not cause any damage, but sometimes they start fires. About 75,000 forest fires are started every year by lightning.

It takes a ray of sunlight 8 minutes to travel from the sun to Earth. It would take a car going 60 miles per hour about 170 years to travel the same distance.

Animals get their energy from the food they eat. Racehorses can run as fast as 43 miles per hour. But ostriches can run even faster—up to 45 miles per hour.

Running Speeds	
Human	22 mph
African elephant	25 mph
Cat	30 mph
Alligator	35 mph
Pronghorn antelope	55 mph
Cheetah	62 mph

How Is Energy Stored?

In this lesson, you can . . .

INVESTIGATE how energy can be stored.

LEARN ABOUT the different ways stored energy can be used.

LINK to math, writing, health, and technology.

◀ **This hurricane lamp burns oil to produce light energy.**

INVESTIGATE

Twisting Up Energy

Activity Purpose You use energy to do lots of things every day. It takes energy to brush your teeth, walk to the bus stop, play kickball, or jump rope.

In this investigation, you will **hypothesize** what happens to the energy you use to twist two clothespins held together by a rubber band.

Materials
- safety goggles
- 1 rubber band
- 2 clothespins

Activity Procedure

CAUTION

1 **CAUTION** **Put on safety goggles to protect your eyes in case a clothespin pops loose.**

2 Attach the rubber band to each clothespin. Work with a partner to twist the rubber band between the clothespins. (Picture A)

3 When you have finished, the rubber band should be twisted and curled up. (Picture B)

4 Holding the clothespins tightly, lay them on the table and **hypothesize** what will happen to them when you let them go. **Communicate** your hypothesis to your partner.

5 **Observe** what happens to the clothespins when you let them go. Then do the investigation again, this time twisting the pins more tightly than you did before. **Compare** what the clothespins did the first time with what they did the second time.

Picture A

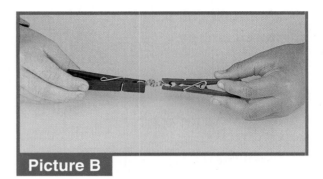
Picture B

Draw Conclusions

1. Describe what happened each time you put the clothespins on the table and let go of them. How did your hypothesis compare to the actual results?

2. Where did the energy to move the clothespins come from?

3. **Scientists at Work** Scientists **conduct simple investigations** to learn more about how things work. What did you learn about energy and twisted rubber bands from your investigation?

Investigate Further **Observe** what happens to a third clothespin that you twist around the other two with a second rubber band.

What Energy Is

FIND OUT

• **about different forms of energy**

• **how energy can be stored**

• **about uses of stored energy**

VOCABULARY

energy
electricity
fossil fuel

Energy to Live and Move

Think about what happens when you are riding your bike. How are you able to pump the pedals or stop? These actions use energy. **Energy** is the ability to cause change. Energy allows movement in the world. It lets athletes run, trees bend, water drip, and planes fly. Without it, nothing would move, including you.

All living things need energy. When people walk, talk, eat, laugh, or even sleep, they are using energy. Plants need energy to grow and reproduce. Tools like computers and flashlights need energy to operate.

People depend on energy to heat homes, cook food, run machines, and light streets. As the number of people on Earth grows, the need for energy grows also.

✔ **What is energy?**

Energy keeps this rubber ball bouncing.

Sources of Energy

Almost all energy on Earth comes from the sun. The food we eat, the gas we put in our cars, even the electricity that lights our homes can all be traced back to the sun's energy.

Light and heat are forms of energy that come directly from the sun. Plants need energy from light to make food. Heat from the sun warms everything on Earth.

What kinds of energy come indirectly from the sun? The food we eat is one example. Food contains the energy we use to power our bodies. Another example is fuels. Fuels, such as coal and oil, contain huge amounts of energy.

Fuels can release energy that can be changed into electricity. **Electricity** is a form of energy that people make by using other kinds of energy found in nature, such as wind, oil, or coal. Energy that comes into our homes as electricity can be used to light lamps, run computers, or cook popcorn.

Wind and moving water can also be used to produce energy. Wind can be used to keep a hang glider or a kite up in the air. Moving water can be used to carry logs downstream to a sawmill.

People can use other kinds of energy to open cans, print newspapers, or lift steel beams to build a skyscraper. Energy is needed for almost all the activities that make up our lives.

✔ **Where does almost all the energy on Earth come from?**

These children skate by using the energy from the food they have eaten. ▼

Stored Energy

At all times, the sun's rays are striking about half of Earth's surface. Plants use the energy in sunlight to make food, which they then use to grow and reproduce. Animals eat the plants to get the energy stored in the plant tissues. Then the animals use this energy to run, climb, hunt, and stay warm. So, organisms use a lot of the energy just by the things they do every day to stay alive. The energy that they don't use is stored in their bodies.

People can use the energy stored in plants and animals. You use stored energy when you eat a hamburger or ride the school bus. Fuel and food are both forms of stored energy that people use.

Fuel Have you ever seen a fire burning? What was used to make the fire? Chances are, it was wood. Wood comes from trees. Like other plants, trees store energy from the sun. When wood burns, this stored energy is released as heat. The heat warms you as you sit near the fire.

All living organisms store energy. When they die, their bodies are slowly buried by soil and rocks. Over millions of years, some of this material may be pressed together until it turns into fuel, like oil or coal. This kind of fuel is called **fossil fuel**. Gasoline, heating oil, and tar are made from fossil fuels.

To release the energy stored in fossil fuels, the fuels must be burned. Burning releases heat that can be changed into other types of energy.

◄ Gasoline, which is made from a fossil fuel, can be used as an energy source for a lawn mower engine.

Food Just before winter, when it begins to get colder outside, do you notice anything different about the squirrels in your neighborhood? Watch them closely. You will soon see that they are collecting nuts, berries, and other bits of food. They hide some of the food and eat it later in the winter when food is hard to find.

Food is one way energy from the sun can be stored. Leaves, stems, roots, and fruits are structures in which plants store energy.

When an animal eats a plant, it gets the energy stored inside the plant and uses it to keep warm and move around. Squirrels get the energy they need to keep warm during the long, cold winter months by eating the food they collected in the fall.

Squirrels will eat a lot of nuts over the winter. Any energy from the nuts that their bodies don't use will be stored as fat. Suppose that another animal, such as a fox, eats a squirrel.

The fox gets the energy stored in the squirrel's body. So while acorns are food for squirrels, squirrels are food for foxes.

✔ **Where does the energy in food and fuels come from?**

▲ Energy from the sun is stored in many of the fruits and vegetables we eat, including apples, broccoli, bananas, and lettuce.

This mountain goat is eating grass. The goat's body will break down the grass to release the energy stored inside. ▶

Batteries

In nature, energy is stored in the form of food and fuel. But people can store energy too. You can store energy in a battery.

Batteries come in many shapes and sizes. Some are so small that they have to be handled with tweezers. Others are bigger than a suitcase— and a whole lot heavier. You probably use batteries that look like cylinders, or tubes.

Companies that make batteries charge them. To do this, the batteries are filled with chemicals that contain energy. Batteries change the energy in the chemicals into the electricity needed to make many things work.

THE INSIDE STORY

How a Battery Works

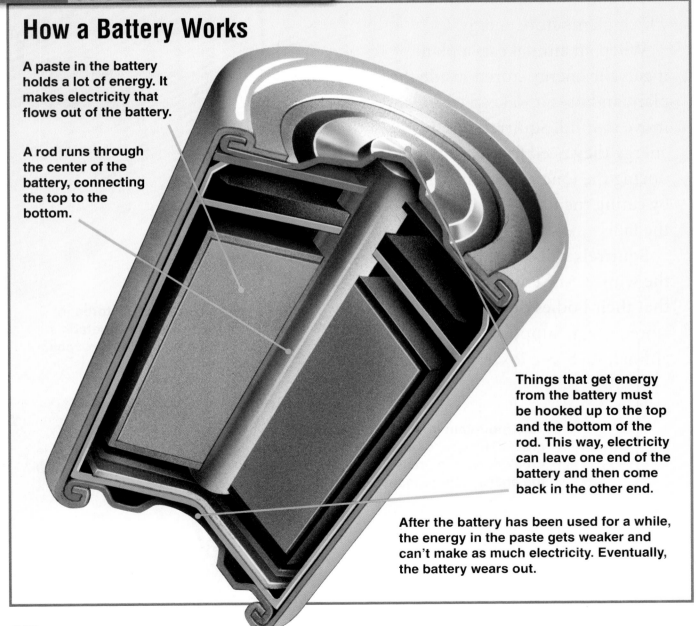

A paste in the battery holds a lot of energy. It makes electricity that flows out of the battery.

A rod runs through the center of the battery, connecting the top to the bottom.

Things that get energy from the battery must be hooked up to the top and the bottom of the rod. This way, electricity can leave one end of the battery and then come back in the other end.

After the battery has been used for a while, the energy in the paste gets weaker and can't make as much electricity. Eventually, the battery wears out.

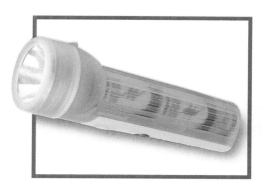

▲ Flashlights are also powered with batteries. They use the energy from batteries to make light.

▲ You can tell that the battery in your calculator is out of energy when you can't see numbers on the screen anymore.

▲ Batteries in this stereo supply the energy needed to play the radio or the cassette inside.

The stereo that you use to play music probably takes many big batteries. These batteries supply the stereo with the electricity it needs to play the music. Do you wear a wristwatch? Chances are, there is a small, flat battery inside. That battery provides the electricity needed for the hands to turn or the digital numbers to change on the face of the watch.

As batteries are used, the energy inside is used up. Some batteries can be recharged, or refilled with energy. Others cannot be recharged and must be recycled or thrown away.

✔ **How are batteries charged?**

The remote-control device for this toy gets its energy from batteries inside the control box. ▶

How Stored Energy Can Be Used

You have just learned that energy can be stored as food or fuel. You also saw that energy can be stored in batteries. People store energy so they can use it when they need it. During the day, you might feel warm and be able to see objects clearly. But on a dark, cold night, you need stored energy to supply heat and light to your home.

Think about what you and your family did last night after supper. Maybe you had the radio on as you all played a game. The energy to play the music came from energy that was stored earlier so that you could use it when you needed it.

If you've ever been to a farm and seen hay bales stacked in the barn, you know that food can be stored and used to feed the animals for many months. If you look in your cupboards at home, you will probably see cans and boxes of all kinds of food. Your family stores this food so that it is available when you need it for food energy.

Look at the picture of the women rowing in the boat below. Their muscles need energy to be able to pull the oars and move the boat forward. To get this energy, they eat foods such as sandwiches, spaghetti, and fruit. All this food originally got its energy from sunlight.

These athletes are using energy from food they have eaten to pull the oars on this boat, called a racing shell. ▼

▲ This model rocket uses the energy in fuel to lift it into the sky.

Fuel is a form of stored energy that people depend on a great deal. We either burn it to release the energy inside or use it to make electricity, which is another form of energy that can be used to make all sorts of things work. Fuel gives us energy to heat our homes, to cook our food, and to drive our cars. It even lets us launch model rockets.

Remember that the energy in fossil fuels came to Earth millions of years ago in the form of sunlight. First, it was stored in the tissues of living organisms. Then, it was stored underground as coal or oil until someone dug or pumped it up and used it. Millions of years have passed between the time living organisms stored energy and the time people burn the fossil fuel.

✔ **Why is stored energy useful?**

Electricity

Later in this chapter, you will learn how electricity can be used to make different forms of energy. Electricity is probably the most common form of energy because we use it to do so many things.

Look at the city lights shown in the picture on page C71. They are lit by electricity. Where did the electricity come from? A different form of energy—such as sunlight, fossil fuels, wind, or moving water—was used to make the electricity. The electricity was then stored until it was needed to light up the city at night.

But electricity isn't needed only at night. Think of all the things in your home that use electricity every day. The refrigerator and air conditioner use electricity to keep things cold. The furnace and oven use electricity to keep things warm or hot. Fans are powered by electricity, as are blenders, hair dryers, and washing machines. Almost all of this electricity comes from energy that was produced at an earlier time and stored as fuel until it was needed.

✔ **Why is electricity commonly used?**

This train is carrying a load of coal to the power station where it will be used to make electricity. ▼

▲ These city lights are powered by electricity, a kind of energy made from other forms of energy.

Summary

Energy is the ability to cause change. All living things need energy to survive. Tools and machines need energy to operate. Energy comes mainly from the sun and can be found in many different forms. It can be stored and used later when it is needed. Food and fuel are both forms of stored energy. Electricity is a form of energy that is made by using other forms of energy.

Review

1. What is the main source of energy on Earth?
2. What are fossil fuels?
3. Why are batteries useful?
4. **Critical Thinking** What would the world be like if the sun did not shine?
5. **Test Prep** Which of the following is not a source of energy?

   A wind   **C** engine

   B moving water   **D** coal

LINKS

MATH LINK

Solar Energy Scientists estimate that the sun produces about 4 million metric tons of energy every second. About how many metric tons does it produce each minute?

WRITING LINK

Persuasive Writing— Business Letter Fossil fuels are still commonly used in the United States. Scientists are trying to develop other kinds of fuels. Write a letter to the Department of Energy to find out more about other fuels being explored.

HEALTH LINK

Recycling Batteries People throw away millions of used batteries. Find out what recycling centers do with old batteries.

TECHNOLOGY LINK

To learn more about energy from the sun, watch Solar Float on the **Harcourt Science Newsroom Video** in your classroom video library.

LESSON 2

How Does Energy Move?

In this lesson, you can . . .

INVESTIGATE how energy moves as waves.

LEARN ABOUT how warm objects can become cold and how cold objects can become warm.

LINK to math, writing, social studies, and technology.

INVESTIGATE

Waves of Energy

Activity Purpose Energy can move through the air, through water, through wires—even through our bodies! One way energy moves is as waves.

In this investigation, you will **use models** to show two of the ways energy can move.

Materials
- rope about 6 feet long
- coiled spring toy

Activity Procedure

1 Do this investigation with a partner. Hold one end of the rope while your partner holds the other. Stand so that the rope hangs loosely between you.

2 While your partner holds his or her end of the rope still, move your end of the rope gently up and down. Now move the rope faster. **Compare** what the rope looked like before with what it looks like now. (Picture A)

◄ This coiled spring toy can be used to show one way energy can move.

3. Now take the coiled spring toy and place it on a table or on the floor. Hold one end, and have your partner hold the other. (Picture B)

4. Ask your partner to hold the end still as you quickly push your end of the toy in about 4 inches. Now push and pull the end backward and forward. **Observe** what happens to the coils.

5. Draw and label a diagram explaining what happened to the rope when you moved one end. Make another diagram showing what happened to the coiled spring toy when you pushed one end in.

Picture A

Picture B

Draw Conclusions

1. What happened to the rope when you moved one end up and down? How did it move? What happened when you moved it faster?

2. What happened when you pushed your end of the coiled spring toy toward your partner? What happened when you moved it back and forth?

3. **Scientists at Work** When things in nature can't be seen, scientists **use models** to see how they work. They then **communicate** what they learn. How did your diagram help you to communicate what you learned about how energy moves as waves?

Process Skill Tip

Using models is a good way to learn more about things that you can't see. Carefully drawn and labeled diagrams can then be used to **communicate** what you learned.

Energy Can Move as Waves

FIND OUT

• how energy can move as waves

• how energy can move as electricity

• how energy can move as heat

VOCABULARY

vibrate
circuit
thermal energy
heat

One kind of wave, like the one you made with the rope, moves up and down. ▼

Kinds of Waves

Have you ever seen a painting of the ocean? How did the artist draw the waves? Most of the waves we see every day look like curvy lines. If you were to draw a wave, it would probably start low, go up high, and then come back down low again. It would keep going like this over and over again.

Wind moving over water makes waves on the surface. Sometimes the waves are small, but at other times they are big enough to toss a boat about. You may even have made your own waves in the bathtub as you moved around. Waves in water are the easiest waves to see.

Look at the diagram below of a wave. If you wanted to measure the wave, what would you do? You might look at how high and how low each curve went. Or you might measure the distance from the top of one curve to the top of the next curve.

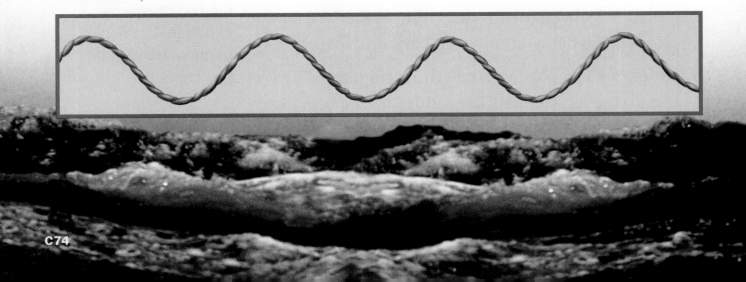

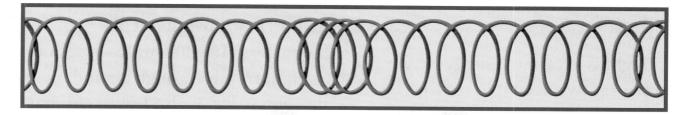

▲ The kind of wave you make with a coiled spring toy moves back and forth.

But what about the other kind of wave you made in the investigation? You don't see this kind of wave every day. It moves back and forth instead of up and down.

Look at the diagram above. It shows the kind of wave you made by using a coiled spring toy. If you look closely, you'll notice that some parts of the spring are very close together and others are spread out.

If you wanted to measure this wave, what would you do? You could look at the distance between one bunched-up part and the next.

Energy often moves. Light is one kind of energy that moves from the sun to Earth. Sound is another kind of energy that moves. It travels from our mouths to the ears of people when we speak.

Some forms of energy, including light and sound, move through the air as waves. Light moves as up-and-down waves, like the rope wave. Sound moves as back-and-forth waves, like the coiled spring toy waves.

✔ **How is a rope wave different from a coiled spring toy wave?**

This sailboat is being tossed about by ocean waves. ▼

Light Waves

Light is a form of energy we use every day. We need it to see the things around us. Light comes from many different sources. The sun is the most important. Other light sources, such as lamps and candles, provide light when the sun doesn't give us light.

Light has something in common with water waves. When you throw a pebble into a pond, ripples move away from the spot where the pebble hit. In the same way, light waves move away from a light source. Light, like water, moves in up-and-down waves. Light waves travel until they come to an object. When the waves strike the object, they bounce off it so that we can see the object.

You cannot see light waves. Light waves move too fast for you to see them. They move about 300,000 kilometers (186,000 mi) each second.

Light travels through air and through space. It also travels through clear materials such as glass and water. You know this because you can see fish in an aquarium. Light doesn't travel through most objects, though. A shadow is made whenever an object, like your body, stops the path of light waves. When you stand outside on a sunny day, light waves from the sun hit your body, but they can't move through you to the ground behind you. Your body blocks the light, and a shadow forms.

✔ How does light travel?

Lights placed all along this runway give off light waves, allowing pilots to see the runway and to land the plane safely—even at night. ▼

Sound Waves

Sound is another kind of energy that travels in waves. Sound travels as back-and-forth waves, like the coiled spring toy in the investigation.

Think of different sounds you hear every day—the voice of a friend, the jingle of a bell, the slamming of a door, the buzz of an insect, a song on the radio. Even though these sounds seem different, they all travel the same way.

Think about the sound from a bell. When you ring a bell, the clapper inside hits the sides of the bell. The sides then start to **vibrate**, or move back and forth very quickly. This makes the air around the bell vibrate too. Waves of vibrating air move away from the bell in all directions. When these waves reach your ears, your brain hears the bell ring.

◄ When this old-fashioned fire alarm rings, sound waves are sent out in all directions, warning people of the danger.

Have you ever been in a storm with lightning and thunder? As the storm was coming toward you, you probably saw the lightning before you heard the thunder. But the lightning and the thunder began at the same time. You saw the lightning first because light waves travel much faster than sound waves.

✔ **How does sound travel?**

Instruments made with wood, strings, and metal can be used to make beautiful sounds that we hear as music. ►

Energy Can Move as Electricity

Light and sound are both forms of energy, and both travel in waves. Another way energy can travel is as electricity.

In the last lesson you learned that batteries can store energy so that it can be used later. The kind of energy that batteries produce is called electricity. Electricity is also produced by energy companies and sent to your home. You can use this electricity by plugging something into a wall socket.

Electricity can be used to do many things. This is because electricity can easily be changed to other forms of energy. It can be used to start a car engine, to light a lamp, to turn the blades of a fan, or to make your favorite toy move.

▲ Energy, in the form of electricity, moves out of batteries and turns the blades of this fan.

Batteries, both big and small, can be used to supply electricity to objects. A car battery supplies the engine with electricity so that it can start. When the engine starts, the electric energy is changed to mechanical energy.

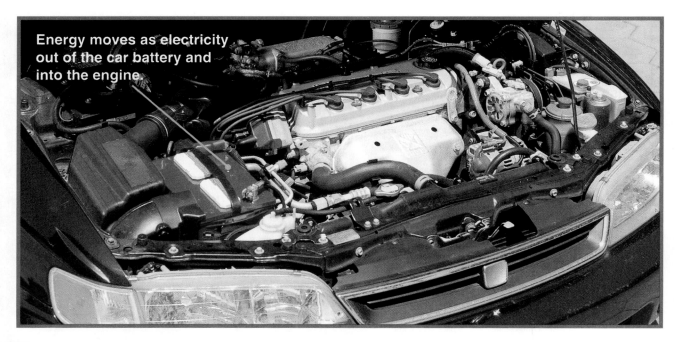

Energy moves as electricity out of the car battery and into the engine.

Have you ever made a bulb light by using a battery and some wires? The bulb lights because energy moves as electricity from the battery, through the wires, to the bulb, and back to the battery. When the bulb lights, electric energy is changed to light energy. The path the electricity follows from the battery, through the bulb, and back again is called a **circuit**.

If you took apart a flashlight, you would see a circuit that looked like the one shown. Instead of wires, though, you would see strips of metal on the inside of the case. The electricity from the battery travels along these strips to the bulb of the flashlight.

Electricity can change form to make things move or turn. A battery in a hand-held fan supplies electricity to a little motor in the fan that turns the blades of the fan.

Electricity can also move through the air. Lightning is electricity in the sky. When lightning hits the ground, energy moves from the sky into the ground.

✔ **What is a circuit?**

Energy stored in batteries supplies this bear with the energy needed to beat the drum. ▼

In a circuit, energy moves from the battery, through the wires, to the bulb, and then back to the battery. ▼

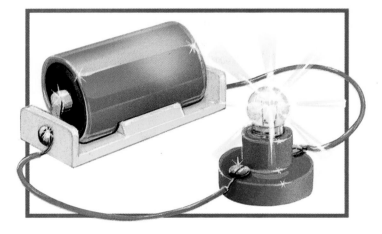

Energy Can Move as Heat

It's hot outside. My soup's cold. You know what hot and cold feel like, but do you know what causes them? It's heat.

The story of heat begins with energy. Every atom, or particle in matter, has energy. The atoms are always moving. The total energy of moving atoms in matter is called **thermal energy** .

A cup of something that is hot has more thermal energy than the same-sized cup of something that is cold. The particles in a bowl of hot soup are moving quickly. They have a lot of thermal energy. The particles in a bowl of cold soup are moving more slowly. They have less thermal energy.

The movement of thermal energy from one place to another is called **heat** . Suppose you warm some cocoa on the stove. Then you pour the cocoa into a cup. When you touch the cup, the outside of the cup feels hot. Thermal energy has moved from the cocoa to the cup. Then the thermal energy moved from the cup to your hand. You feel this movement of thermal energy as heat.

When you touch a warm cup, thermal energy moves from the cup to your hand. If you touch a cold glass of milk, thermal energy moves from your hand to the glass. Thermal energy moves from a hot place to a cold place. It never moves from a cold place to a hot place.

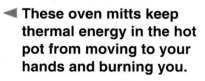

◀ **These oven mitts keep thermal energy in the hot pot from moving to your hands and burning you.**

Making Thermal Energy There are many ways to produce thermal energy. Burning fuel is one way. Remember that fuel is a form of stored energy. Suppose you light a gas stove. The energy stored in the gas is changed to thermal energy.

Another way to produce thermal energy is to rub two things together. For example, when you rub your hands together, the particles in your left hand rub against the particles in your right hand. This makes the particles in both hands move faster. Both of your hands now have more thermal energy, and they feel warm.

▲ This brick oven contains lots of thermal energy. It transfers that thermal energy to the pizza inside it. The thermal energy then cooks the pizza.

These students are blowing warm air from their lungs onto their hands. Doing this warms their hands on a chilly day. ▶

Heat from the Sun When you are holding a warm cup, thermal energy in the cup moves to your hands, and your hands warm up. But what if your hands and the cup aren't touching? Can thermal energy be transferred without touching?

If you've ever sweated under the heat of the sun, you know that you don't have to touch a hot object in order to get heat from it. Thermal energy that moves without touching anything is called *radiation*.

Energy from the sun warms the air and the Earth. Even though we cannot touch the sun, we can feel its heat. Remember that light waves travel from the sun to Earth. The sun radiates heat energy, which travels to Earth as another kind of wave.

These energy waves from the sun make the particles in our skin move around more, and we feel this thermal energy as heat. All plants and animals on Earth depend on energy from the sun to keep them warm.

✔ **How can thermal energy move without touching anything?**

When it is hot outside, a thermometer tells us how hot. The panting dog doesn't need a thermometer to know it's hot.

Summary

Energy can move in many ways. Light energy moves as up-and-down waves. Sound energy moves as back-and-forth waves. Electricity is a form of energy that can move from a battery to other objects. Heat is the movement of thermal energy. Thermal energy can be transferred when two things come into contact or by radiation.

Review

1. What do all sounds have in common?
2. How does electricity move to light the light bulbs in a room?
3. What does thermal energy do to particles of matter?
4. **Critical Thinking** If you want to carry two cups of hot cocoa to a friend's house, should you use metal cups or plastic cups? Explain your answer.
5. **Test Prep** When you pick up a snowball, thermal energy moves —
   A from the snowball to your hand
   B from your hand to the snowball
   C back and forth between your hand and the snowball
   D not at all

LINKS

MATH LINK

How Much Sun? About 30 parts of every 100 parts of the energy coming to Earth from the sun reflect back into space when it hits the Earth's atmosphere. What part reaches the Earth's surface?

WRITING LINK

Narrative Writing—On the oceans there are different kinds of waves. Some you can see. Others you can't. Write a description for your teacher about an ocean and all the different kinds of waves you might see or feel.

SOCIAL STUDIES LINK

Ringing the Bell Research the role of the bell tower in ancient times. Why was the bell located in the middle of town? Who was in charge of ringing it? How was it used to send out information?

TECHNOLOGY LINK

Learn more about sound waves and music by investigating *Waves of Music* on **Harcourt Science Explorations CD-ROM**.

How Can Energy Be Changed?

In this lesson, you can . . .

INVESTIGATE how energy flows from a battery to light a bulb.

LEARN ABOUT how some forms of energy can be changed into other forms.

LINK to math, writing, and technology.

INVESTIGATE

Lighting a Bulb

Activity Purpose Have you ever put batteries in a flashlight the wrong way? What happened? In order for the bulb to light up, the batteries need to be connected to the bulb in a certain way.

In this investigation you will **experiment** with a battery, a bulb, and wires.

Materials

- masking tape
- D-cell battery
- 2 pieces of insulated electrical wire
- miniature light bulb

Activity Procedure

1 Use a piece of masking tape to tape the battery to your desk. This way, it won't roll around. (Picture A)

2 As your partner holds the light bulb a few inches away from the battery, use the wires to connect the ends of the battery with the base of the bulb. (Picture B)

◀ the sun

3 Now switch the wires. Do you **observe** any changes?

4 Try to make the bulb light by touching the wires to the glass part of the bulb. Can you make it light?

5 Can you make the bulb light by touching the wires to the sides of the battery?

Picture A

Draw Conclusions

1. What happened when you connected the ends of the battery to the base of the light bulb by using the wires?

2. What happened when you switched the wires?

3. Could you make the bulb light by touching the wires to the glass part of the bulb? Did the bulb light when you touched the wires to the sides of the battery?

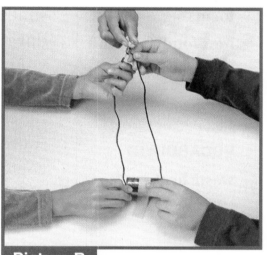
Picture B

4. **Scientists at Work** Scientists know that the results of experiments don't often turn out exactly the same every time. This can be caused by differences in materials or differences in procedure. How could you change the materials in this investigation to see if the results would change?

Investigate Further **Plan and conduct a simple investigation** to find out if you can make the bulb light by using something other than wires to connect the battery and the bulb. **Record** your observations.

> **Process Skill Tip**
>
> When you **experiment** with materials to see how they interact, you can figure out how to make them do something, like light a bulb. By experimenting, you can see the evidence that helps you **draw conclusions** about how things work.

Energy Can Change Forms

FIND OUT

- **how energy from sunlight can be changed into other forms**
- **how food, fuel, and electricity can produce motion and heat**

VOCABULARY

waste heat

Electricity is carried through wires to places where it is needed, like our homes. There, we change it into heat, light, motion, or other forms of energy. ▼

From Sunlight to Electricity

Sunlight brings us light and heat every day. We need light to see and heat to keep us warm. But sunlight cannot run our washing machines or play our radios. To do those things, we need electricity.

Electricity is a form of energy we use every day. You have probably already used electricity several times today. Electricity comes from many different sources, but almost all of them can be traced back to energy from the sun.

You may remember that plants can make their own food by using the energy from sunlight. When animals eat the plants, they convert, or change, the energy into energy they can use. When wood burns, the energy stored in the wood changes into thermal energy. These are just some of the ways that energy can be changed from one form to another.

✓ **Where did the energy in oil come from?**

The Formation of Fossil Fuels

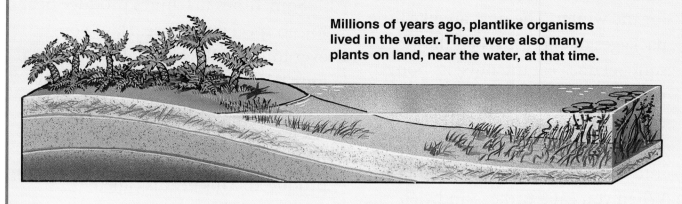

Millions of years ago, plantlike organisms lived in the water. There were also many plants on land, near the water, at that time.

When the plantlike organisms that lived in the water died, they were slowly covered with layers of soil and rock. Dead plants were buried in the same way.

Over millions of years, the energy in the plantlike organisms was pressed into a liquid fuel, called oil. Land plants that were buried and crushed became solid fuel, called coal.

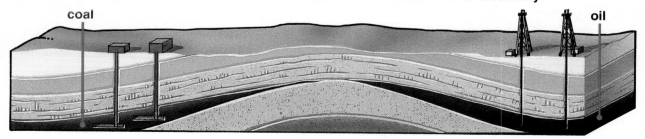

Today, people pump up oil and mine coal from beneath the ground. Then the oil and coal are converted to electricity.

Energy Into Motion and Heat

Recall that squirrels collect nuts for the winter. The nuts are like little packages of energy. When the squirrel does eat the nuts, its body will convert the food energy to the energy of motion and heat.

All animals convert food energy into the energy of motion and heat. When you eat a turkey sandwich, the energy contained in the meat and bread gives you the energy you need to walk to class, play kickball, and run across the schoolyard. Your body also uses the food energy to produce thermal energy to keep you warm.

Have you played outside on a cold day? Were you cold when you started and then warm once you had been playing for a while? This is because the energy of motion also produces heat. So it is better to move around on cold days than to stand still.

Machines also use energy to produce motion and heat. Fuel is the energy source. A car or boat engine uses fuel to produce motion. Furnaces use fuel to warm air or water.

Sometimes machines produce heat for no special purpose. Have you ever touched the hood of a car after a long trip? If you did, you would have noticed that the hood felt hot. As the engine worked to convert fuel energy into the energy of motion, heat was produced. This heat is called **waste heat** because it was not used for any purpose.

✔ **How are the energy of motion and heat energy related?**

This girl is using the energy contained in the food she ate to move this wagon. ▶

Summary

Energy can change forms. Sunlight can be changed into food, fuel, or electricity. Electricity can be changed into other kinds of energy, like light energy. Food and fuel can be changed into motion and heat by animals and by machines. The energy of motion often produces waste heat.

Lesson Review

1. How can sunlight be changed into electricity?
2. Where do you get the energy to climb stairs?
3. **Critical Thinking** If all coal disappeared tomorrow, could you still watch TV? Explain your answer.
4. **Test Prep** A car engine feels hot after a long ride because —
    A it contains a lot of electrical energy
    B the sun heats the engine
    C the energy of motion produces waste heat
    D the battery keeps it warm

LINKS

MATH LINK

Calculate Calories Scientists measure the energy we get from the food we eat in units called Calories. A gram of fat provides about 9 Calories. Bread, pasta, and meat provide about 4 Calories per gram. If you ate 112 grams (about 4 oz) of meat on 84 grams (about 3 oz) of bread with 56 grams (about 2 oz) of butter, about how many Calories would you consume?

WRITING LINK

Narrative Writing— Description Write a paragraph for a classmate describing how to make a bulb light up by using a battery, a bulb, and two pieces of wire. Then exchange paragraphs with a partner. Mark any places in the paragraph that you didn't understand. Rewrite your paragraph to make it clearer.

TECHNOLOGY LINK

Learn more about changing electricity to light by visiting the Smithsonian Institution Internet Site.
www.si.edu/harcourt/science

SOLAR POWER:
An Airplane That Soars on Sunlight

Most airplanes use fuel to run their engines. *Pathfinder* is not most airplanes; it is a solar-powered airplane. It runs on sunshine. *Pathfinder* is very lightweight and can fly higher than any other propeller-driven plane. The scientists who built *Pathfinder* think that solar-powered planes can do many of the same jobs that satellites do.

A Flimsy Flying Wing

Pathfinder is made of thin plastic film stretched over a skeleton of plastic and Styrofoam. It weighs only about 455 kilograms (1,000 lb)— about as much as five big men. *Pathfinder* doesn't look like an ordinary plane. It has one wing that's 40 meters (about 130 ft) long. The top surface of this long wing is covered with solar cells that turn sunlight into electricity. The electricity runs motors that turn *Pathfinder*'s eight propellers.

Pathfinder doesn't go very fast— only about 28 kilometers per hour (17 mph). Most kids can pedal a bike that fast! But it can go almost 42 kilometers (25 mi) high.

Pathfinder can't carry passengers. It doesn't even have a pilot. The plane is controlled by radio signals sent from the ground. So what good is a big, slow plastic airplane high in the sky? It can do some of the same jobs that satellites do. *Pathfinder* can take pictures while it is flying. The pictures can be used to keep track of

hurricanes and to help predict the weather, just like satellites do. It can carry instruments that help scientists learn about pollution, and it can relay signals for radios and cellular telephones.

What Happens When the Sun Goes Down?

Pathfinder can fly only when the sun is shining. It has to land at night. But engineers at AeroVironment are working on a new solar-powered plane with batteries that can store energy during the day. Energy from the batteries will keep the propellers spinning during the night. The new plane is called *Helios*, from the Greek word that means "sun." *Helios* could stay in the air for a long time. By using sunlight during the day and batteries at night, *Helios* could fly for six months without landing.

Where Else Could It Fly?

Pathfinder flies where the atmosphere is very thin. The atmosphere on other planets is thin, too. Scientists at NASA—the National Aeronautics and Space Administration—think a plane like *Pathfinder* could be used to explore other worlds. NASA hopes to have a small, lightweight solar-powered plane flying on Mars in 2003.

Think About It

1. Satellites use solar power in outer space. Have you seen any machines that use solar power on Earth?
2. What are some advantages and disadvantages of using sunlight for energy?

WEB LINK:
For Science and Technology updates, visit the Harcourt Internet site.
www.harcourtschool.com/ca

Careers   Energy Manager

What They Do Energy managers help people decide on the best way to use energy in homes, offices, and factories. They make  suggestions about what kinds of lights to use, when to turn air conditioning or heating on and off, and what kind of machines are the most efficient.

Education and Training An energy manager needs a college degree. He or she must know about different kinds of lighting, heating systems, and other machines that use energy. Energy managers also need to know about electricity and accounting.

Steven Chu

PHYSICIST

When Steven Chu was growing up in Garden City, New York, he wasn't crazy about school. "Learning seemed like work. I wanted it to be an adventure," he says. So he began asking questions that made learning fun—questions like "Why does that happen?"

Steven Chu was on his way to becoming a particle physicist—a scientist who studies atoms and the forces that hold them together or make them come apart.

In high school, Chu met a science teacher who encouraged him to keep learning about things by asking simple questions and then creating experiments that would give answers. Soon he was experimenting with chemistry sets and homemade rockets.

Chu's curiosity has led to some important questions and answers. In 1997 he received one of the most important awards in science—the Nobel Prize in physics. He won the award for thinking of a way to slow down tiny particles so other scientists can study them more carefully.

Steven Chu wants other people to know how much adventure there is in asking questions. He is a teacher at Stanford University in California. He loves working with students there. "They figure out that textbooks and professors don't know everything, and then they start to think on their own," he says. "Then I begin learning from them."

Think About It

1. What are you curious about? Pick a question, and try to think of some experiments that could help you find the answer.

2. Look for a story about science in a newspaper or magazine. What questions were the scientists asking?

Hot Ice

What environments make ice cubes melt fastest?

Materials
- 3 ice cubes of equal size
- 3 foam cups

Procedure
1. Place one ice cube in each cup.

2. Choose three different places to leave the cups. Predict which ice cube will melt most during the half-hour.

3. Place the cups in their locations. Thirty minutes later, get the cups and observe the ice cubes.

4. Which ice cube melted the most? Did your results support your hypothesis?

Draw Conclusions
How did heat affect your ice cubes?

Big Ears

How do big ears help animals hear?

Materials
- sheet of plain paper

Procedure
1. Work with a partner for this activity. Standing about 3 meters from your partner, have him or her whisper something to you. Can you hear what he or she said?

2. Now roll your sheet of paper into a cone, and hold the small end to your ear. Have your partner whisper at the same level as before. Were you able to hear your partner better this time?

Draw Conclusions
Explain how you think the cone helped you hear the whispering better. Use the term *sound waves* in your explanation.

Chapter ③ Review and Test Preparation

Vocabulary Review

Use the terms below to complete the sentences. The page numbers in ( ) tell you where to look in the chapter if you need help.

energy (C62)   **circuit** (C79)
electricity (C63) **thermal energy** (C80)
fossil fuel (C64) **heat** (C80)
vibrate (C77)   **waste heat** (C88)

1. We feel thermal energy as ____.

2. A ____ is made up of a battery, a bulb, and wires.

3. When objects ____, they make sounds.

4. ____ is energy that is given off and not used.

5. A source of stored energy called ____ was made over millions of years as the bodies of dead plants and animals were pressed together.

6. The ability to cause change is ____.

7. A hot cup of tea has more ____ than a cold cup of milk.

8. Other forms of energy can be used to make ____, which is the most common form of energy that we use.

Connect Concepts

Use the terms in the Word Bank to complete the concept map.

motion   **food**   **sunlight**   **batteries**
heat   **animals** **fuel**   **electricity**

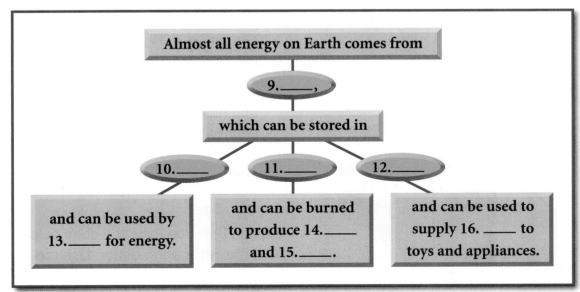

Almost all energy on Earth comes from

9.____,

which can be stored in

10.____   11.____   12.____

and can be used by 13.____ for energy.

and can be burned to produce 14.____ and 15.____.

and can be used to supply 16.____ to toys and appliances.

Check Understanding

17. Almost all energy on Earth comes from —
   A batteries   C the sun
   B electricity   D fuel

18. Sound waves move ____ light waves.
   F slower than
   G faster than
   H at the same speed as
   J in front of

19. Something that feels hot has more ____ than something that feels cold.
   A heat
   B fuel
   C thermal energy
   D electricity

20. Thermal energy always moves from ____ things to ____ things.
   F frozen, cool   H warm, hot
   G cool, warm   J hot, cold

21. Light waves can move through —
   A water   C walls
   B shadows   D the ground

Critical Thinking

22. What forms of energy can be found in your home? How does your family use each form?

23. Why do we need to store energy?

24. Draw a diagram that shows how a fossil fuel is formed. Use labels to show where the energy came from originally.

Process Skills Review

25. **Compare** food to fuel. How is each formed? What are they used for? Who are they used by? Present your ideas in a table or in a paragraph.

26. Based on your **observations** of the rubber bands and clothespins, what can you **infer** about what happened to the energy you used to twist up the rubber bands?

27. After you run around on a cold day, you notice sweat on your forehead. What **conclusions can you draw** about why you are sweating?

Performance Assessment

Diagram Energy

Working with a partner, draw a diagram showing everything you know about the energy in sunlight—who uses it directly, how it moves, how it can be stored, and into what other forms of energy it can be converted.

Vocabulary Preview

reflection
refraction
absorption
prism

Light

Flick! Bounce, reflect, bounce!
That's what happens to the light from
a flashlight if you turn it on and shine
it at your image in a mirror. The light
goes so fast it seems to hit the mirror
and you at the same instant you turn
the flashlight on!

FAST FACT

We see stars as they were when their light left them. This
table shows how long it takes the light from some space
objects to reach us.

The Speed of Light		
Object in Space	Distance from Earth	Light Reaches Us In
Moon	384,462 km	$1\frac{1}{3}$ seconds
Venus	41.2 million km	$2\frac{1}{3}$ minutes
Sun	149.7 million km	$8\frac{1}{2}$ minutes
Alpha Centauri	40.2 trillion km	$4\frac{1}{3}$ years
Sirius	81.7 trillion km	$8\frac{1}{2}$ years
Andromeda Galaxy	21.2 billion billion km	$2\frac{1}{4}$ million years

Andromeda Galaxy

Light travels at the speed
of 299,330 kilometers per
second (186,000 mi per sec).
If you could run that fast, you
would be able to circle the
Earth more than seven times
in just one second!

How Does Light Behave?

In this lesson, you can . . .

INVESTIGATE how light travels.

LEARN ABOUT things light can do.

LINK to math, writing, health, and technology.

INVESTIGATE

How Light Travels

Activity Purpose You can make shadows with your hands because of the way light travels. In this investigation you will **observe** how light travels.

Materials
- 3 index cards
- ruler
- pencil
- clay
- small, short lamp without a lampshade

Activity Procedure

1 Make a large X on each card. To draw each line, lay the ruler from one corner of the card to the opposite corner. (Picture A)

▲ Shadow puppets can be fun.

2 On each card, make a hole at the place where the lines of the X cross. Use the pencil to make the holes.

3 Use the clay to make a stand for each card. Make sure the holes in the cards are the same height. (Picture B)

4 Turn on the light. Look through the holes in the cards. Move the cards around on the table until you can see the light bulb through all three cards at once. Draw a picture showing where the light is and where the cards are.

5 Move the cards around to new places on the table. Each time you move the cards, draw a picture showing where the cards are. Do not move the light! **Observe** the light through the holes each time.

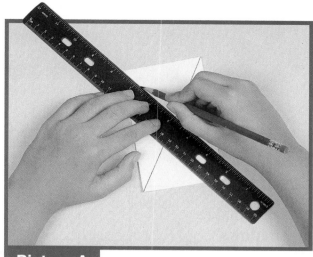
Picture A

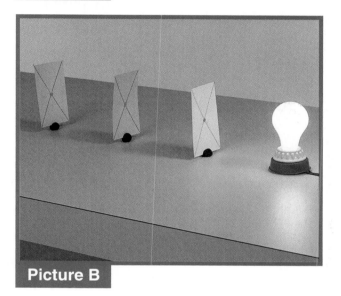
Picture B

Draw Conclusions

1. Where were the cards when you were able to see the light?

2. Were there times you couldn't see the light? Where were the cards then?

3. **Scientists at Work** Scientists **observe** carefully and then **record** what they observe. Often they draw pictures to **communicate** what they observe. Did drawing pictures help you describe what you saw? Explain.

Process Skill Tip

Scientists can learn many things about the world just by **observing**. Then they **record** what they see. After they observe the same thing many times, they **communicate** by telling other scientists what they have observed.

Light

Light Energy

You know that energy is the ability to cause things to change. The energy in a fire changes a sheet of paper into ashes. The heat from a fire can change your hands from cold to warm. Bacteria use energy to change a dead log into soil for plants.

Light is also a kind of energy. Light energy can make many changes. Without light energy, you could not see anything. Light energy gives things colors. The sun shines on the soil, and plants grow. Light energy can make cars move. In space, light energy powers satellites and space stations. Doctors use the light energy of lasers to perform some operations.

✔ **What are three changes light energy can cause?**

FIND OUT

- **what makes shadows**
- **how mirrors work**
- **why things look funny through water**

VOCABULARY

reflection
refraction
absorption

◄ **Plants can't live without light. Plants use the sun's light to make food.**

▲ **Scientists are finding new ways to use the sun's energy. Some new cars use light energy instead of gas.**

◀ **The sun provides energy to Earth.**

Shadows

When you put your hand in front of a lamp, you make a shadow on the wall. The shadows move and change shape as you move your hand. Shadows move and change because of the way light travels.

Light travels in straight lines. When you put your hand in front of a lamp, some of the straight lines of light hit your hand. The shadow on the wall shows where the light is blocked by your hand. When you move your hand, the shadow moves because your hand blocks different lines of light.

In the investigation you could see the light bulb only when the holes in the three cards were in a straight line. When one of the holes wasn't in line with the others, it blocked the line of light. How did this show that light travels in a straight line?

When you stand in the sun, you block some of the lines of sunlight. As the sun moves in the sky, you block different lines of light. When the sun is low in the sky, in the morning and in the afternoon, your shadow is long. When the sun is high overhead, your shadow is short.

✔ **How does light travel?**

▲ Shadows caused by sunlight are long in the morning. These shadows always point away from the sun.

▲ In the afternoon the sun is in a different place. Now the shadow points another way, but it still points away from the sun.

Bouncing Light

Look in a mirror. What do you see? You probably see yourself and some of the things around you. You are looking in front of you at the mirror. But the things you see in the mirror are next to you or even behind you. How is this possible?

Hold a lamp in front of a mirror, and you will see the lamp in the mirror. The light from the lamp moves in a straight line to the mirror. When it hits the mirror, it bounces off. It is still traveling in a straight line. But now it's going in a new direction. It is coming straight back to you. The bouncing of light off an object is called **reflection** (rih•FLEK•shuhn). You see objects in a mirror because their light is reflected straight back into your eyes. (See the diagram of the eye on page R32.)

◀ When light bounces off a mirror, the light changes direction. The letters on the sign are backward. This is because a mirror reverses an image from left to right.

Light travels in straight lines. Even if it bounces off many mirrors, you can still see the object. If the mirrors are lined up exactly right, you can see many reflections of the object. ▼

Light bouncing off a smooth surface gives an image you can see. A mirror is very smooth. So are shiny metal and still water. You can see yourself in these things. But most things aren't as smooth as mirrors.

Most things are bumpy. When light hits a bumpy surface, each straight line of light goes off in a different direction. Then you don't see any image.

✔ **What is reflection?**

◀ If the water is rippling, each wave reflects light in a different direction. Since the light is traveling in so many directions, it is hard to see a clear picture on the surface of the water.

The water on the lake is so still that it acts like a mirror. ▼

Bending Light

Light doesn't bounce off every surface. There are some things light goes through. That's why you can see through air, water, and glass.

Light travels at different speeds in air, water, and glass. So when light goes from one thing to another, such as from air to glass, it changes speed. Any time light goes from one kind of matter to another, it changes speed. If light hits the new matter straight on, it keeps going straight. But if light hits the new matter at a slant, the light bends. The bending of light when it moves from one kind of matter to another is called **refraction** (rih•FRAK•shuhn).

Light moving from air to glass is like a skater moving from a sidewalk to the grass. If the skater is going straight into the grass, both front wheels hit the grass at the same time. The skater slows down because grass is softer than concrete. But he or she continues to go straight. If the skater does not go straight into the grass, one wheel hits the grass first. The other is still on the sidewalk. The wheel that hits the grass first slows down first. This makes the skater change direction.

✔ **What is refraction?**

Half of this toy diver is in the water. You see the bottom half through the water. The light bends when it hits the water. You see the top half through air. This light isn't bending. So the toy diver looks as if it is broken in two. ▼

Light travels through air and glass. This light hits the glass straight on and keeps going straight. ▶

Here the light hits the glass at an angle. This time the light bends and changes direction. ▼

Here the light is refracted three times. So the pencil looks as if it is broken into four pieces. ▼

Stopping Light

You have learned that you can see through air, water, and glass. Light travels through these forms of matter. But most matter doesn't let light pass. When light hits a wall, the wall stops, or absorbs, the light. Stopping light is called **absorption** (ab•SAWRP•shuhn). Have you ever watched rain falling on grass? The soil absorbs the water. Most matter absorbs light in the same way.

When light hits most objects, some of the light bounces off and the rest is absorbed. Smooth, shiny objects reflect almost all the light that hits them. Other objects absorb most of the light that hits them and reflect the rest. If an object doesn't produce its own light, what you see when you look at it is the light that bounces off it.

✔ **What is absorption?**

▲ Light travels through this glass window because it is *transparent*. You can see a clear image of the girl through the window. Light also travels through the thin curtain. Matter that lets only some light through is called *translucent*. Light can't travel through the dark curtains. A material that doesn't let light through is *opaque*.

Summary

Light energy can cause things to change. Light travels in a straight line unless it bumps into something. An object that stops light can cause a shadow. Some objects let light pass through them. When light hits an object, it can be reflected, refracted, or absorbed.

Review

1. What does a mirror do?
2. At about what time of day is your shadow shortest?
3. What word describes stopping light so that it is not reflected or refracted?
4. **Critical Thinking** You stick your hand into an aquarium to get something out. Why does your hand look as if it is cut off from your arm?
5. **Test Prep** Which is an example of light energy being used?
   A water boiling
   B a seed sprouting
   C a ball bouncing
   D a girl lifting a chair

LINKS

MATH LINK

Elapsed Time Suppose the sun rises at 6:15 A.M. and sets at 7:15 P.M. How many hours of daylight are there?

WRITING LINK

Informative Writing— Description Write a short story for your classmates that describes a building reflected in a puddle. Include one description for when the water is smooth and one for when the water is rippling.

HEALTH LINK

The Eye Look at page R32 to see a drawing of the human eye. Copy the drawing onto your own paper. Use references to find out how light enters the eye and where light rays strike the inside of the eye. Draw a light ray onto your drawing of the eye.

TECHNOLOGY LINK

Learn more about how light can be used by watching *Using Natural Light* on the **Harcourt Science Newsroom Video** in your classroom video library.

How Are Light and Color Related?

In this lesson, you can . . .

INVESTIGATE rainbows.

LEARN ABOUT light and color.

LINK to math, writing, art, and technology.

INVESTIGATE

Making a Rainbow

Activity Purpose   The world is a colorful place. You know that you can see colors only when the light is shining. In the dark you can't see color. So is color in the objects or in the light? In this investigation you can **observe** where colors come from.

Materials
- small mirror
- clear glass
- water
- flashlight

Activity Procedure

1 Gently place the mirror into the glass. Slant it up against the side.

2 Fill the glass with water. (Picture A)

3 Set the glass on a table. Turn out the lights. Make the room as dark as possible.

◀ **You can get all the colors of the rainbow in a box of colored pencils.**

Picture A

Picture B

4 Shine the flashlight into the glass of water. Aim for the mirror. Adjust your aim until the light hits the mirror. If necessary, adjust the mirror in the water. Make sure the mirror is slanted.

5 **Observe** what happens to the light in the glass. Look at the light where it hits the ceiling or the wall. **Record** what you observe. (Picture B)

Draw Conclusions

1. What did the light look like as it went into the glass?

2. What did the light look like after it came out of the glass?

3. **Scientists at Work** Scientists **draw conclusions** based on what they **observe.** What conclusions can you draw about where color comes from?

Investigate Further Change the angles of the mirror and the flashlight. Which setup gives the best result? Draw a picture of the best arrangement.

Process Skill Tip

You **draw conclusions** when you have gathered data by observing, measuring, and using numbers. Conclusions tell what you have learned.

Light and Color

FIND OUT ——

• how many colors are in light

• what makes a rainbow

VOCABULARY

prism

Prisms

Have you ever drawn a picture of the sun? Did you color it yellow? People often do. But sunlight is really made of many different colors. Yellow is only one of them. The sunlight you see is really white light. White is the color of all the sun's colors mixed together.

Different colors of light travel at different speeds in water and in glass. So when white light moves from air to glass or from air to water, the different colors of light bend at different angles. They separate into each individual color.

In the investigation you used water and a mirror to break white light into different colors. Scientists use glass triangle prisms to experiment with light. A **prism** (PRIZ•uhm) is a solid object that bends light. When white light hits the prism, each color of light bends at a different angle. Light that passes through a prism separates into a rainbow.

✔ **What is a prism?**

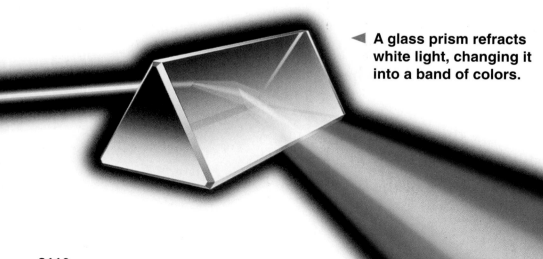

◀ A glass prism refracts white light, changing it into a band of colors.

C110

How Rainbows Form

You can sometimes see a rainbow in the sky during a summer rain when the sun is out. ▷

Each drop of falling water is like a tiny prism. So sunlight passes through all the raindrops, and the light rays bend. This bending separates the light into its colors, and you see a rainbow.

When white light separates, its colors always appear in the same order. The order is red, orange, yellow, green, blue, and violet.

Adding Colors

A prism breaks white light into colors. You can also add colors together. When you add different colored lights together, they form other colors. Shining a red light and a green light onto the same spot will make a yellow light. Shining a blue light and a red light onto the same spot will make a purple light. You can add red light, blue light, and green light in different ways to make all other colors.

✔ **What is one method for making colors?**

Seeing Colors

All the colors of light, called white light, hit every object you see. Most objects absorb most of the light, but not all of it. The light that is not absorbed is reflected and is the color you see. For example, green grass absorbs all of the white light except the green part. The green part reflects back to your eyes, and you see green grass.

✔ **Why do you see color?**

Three basic light colors are red, blue, and green. They will form all other colors. Adding all three of these colors will give white light.

 The red rose absorbs all parts of white light except red. Red light is reflected, and we see a red flower.

Summary

White light is made up of many colors mixed together. A prism separates the colors. Raindrops act like prisms to form rainbows. You can make colors by adding different colored lights. The colors of objects you see are the colors of light that the objects reflect.

Review

1. Describe how a prism works.
2. Name the colors that make up white light.
3. What happens if you add different colors of light?
4. **Critical Thinking** Why don't you see a rainbow during most rainstorms?
5. **Test Prep** Which light colors are absorbed by a yellow tulip?

   A red, orange, and yellow

   B red, orange, green, blue, and violet

   C violet, orange, green, and yellow

   D yellow, red, blue, and green

LINKS

MATH LINK

Solid Figures The bases of a triangular prism are triangles. What are the bases of a rectangular prism?

WRITING LINK

Informative Writing— Narration Find five different words that describe colors of red. Write a paragraph for your teacher describing a scene that includes each of these colors.

ART LINK

Color Wheel Find out what a color wheel is and how an artist might use one. Draw one, and explain it to a classmate.

TECHNOLOGY LINK

Visit the Harcourt Learning Site for related links, activities, and resources.

www.harcourtschool.com/ca

DISCOVERING LIGHT AND OPTICS

We use our eyes to see. A curved lens inside the eye bends light, focusing an image on the retina. This image is sent to the brain, which interprets the image.

Using Lenses

Lenses in tools such as microscopes, telescopes, and even eyeglasses work the same way. All lenses have at least one curved surface. The curve of the lens bends and focuses the light. The image formed by the lens might be smaller than, larger than, or the same size as the original object.

People have worn eyeglasses for hundreds of years. The Italian explorer Marco Polo saw people in China wearing glasses around 1275. After books became common in the late 1400s, glasses became common for reading. During the 1600s, people discovered that using lenses would correct nearsightedness. Nearsighted people have difficulty seeing objects far away. More than 125 million people in the United States now wear glasses or contact lenses.

The History of Optics

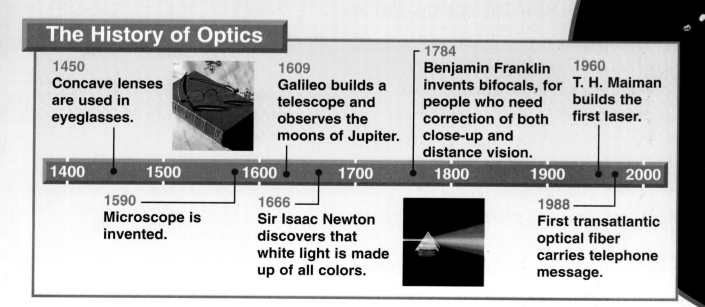

1450
Concave lenses are used in eyeglasses.

1609
Galileo builds a telescope and observes the moons of Jupiter.

1784
Benjamin Franklin invents bifocals, for people who need correction of both close-up and distance vision.

1960
T. H. Maiman builds the first laser.

1400 1500 1600 1700 1800 1900 2000

1590
Microscope is invented.

1666
Sir Isaac Newton discovers that white light is made up of all colors.

1988
First transatlantic optical fiber carries telephone message.

Lasers—Light in a Straight Line

If you've ever shone a flashlight into a dark room, you've seen a property of most light beams. The beams spread apart as they leave their source. Lasers turn a regular beam of light into a narrow, straight beam of bright light. Laser light is very focused and has only one color.

Laser light is used in many ways. Lasers are used to scan bar codes on products. Laser light has been bounced off the moon to accurately measure its distance from Earth.

◄ **Fiber Optics**

Physicians use lasers to do surgery. The most common use of lasers is in compact disc (CD) players. A laser beam cuts information onto the discs. The narrow beam allows a disc to hold more information than a tape. Lasers are then used to read and play back the recorded information. Besides music, entire encyclopedias have been put on CDs.

Telephones have long used electric current and copper wire to carry messages. Flashes of light can be used to send messages, too. Laser beams can carry many different messages along very thin glass fibers called optical fibers. Many fibers, each carrying a different message, can be squeezed into a single cable. Fiber-optic telephone lines are now used between many cities. Lines were laid across the Atlantic and Pacific Oceans in the late 1980s.

Fiber optics are also used in medicine to make surgery easier. Doctors can use the fibers to see inside the body while making only small cuts—or no cuts at all.

Think About It

1. How can lenses change an image?
2. What are two uses of optical fibers?

Lewis Howard Latimer

INVENTOR, ENGINEER

Every time you turn on an electric light, you can thank Lewis Latimer. His many inventions helped improve the first light bulb, which had been made by Thomas Edison. And if you've ever screwed a light bulb into a socket, you have used one of Latimer's inventions. He designed the threads of the socket. His model was made of wood, but we still use his idea.

Latimer was the youngest son of escaped slaves. He had to leave school when he was ten to earn money for the family. He never stopped learning, though. He taught himself mechanical drawing by watching the men in the office where he worked. They made detailed drawings of inventions for patent applications. (Having a patent means the inventor "owns" the idea and the invention.) Latimer's office was near the office of Alexander Graham Bell, who invented the telephone. When Bell applied for a patent, he asked Latimer to make the drawing.

Later Latimer worked with the Edison Pioneers, a group of 80 inventors. He was the only African American in the group. He helped install lighting systems in New York, Philadelphia, Montreal, and even London.

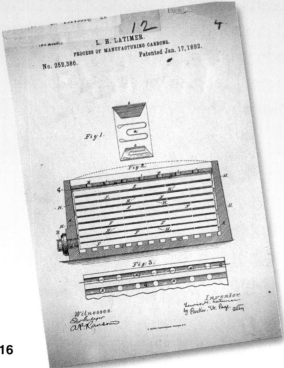

Think About It

1. What do inventing and writing poetry have in common?
2. How is teaching yourself something, perhaps by watching others, different from learning in a classroom?

Colors

What colors are reflected off different colors of paper?

Materials

- glue
- strips of colored construction paper
- prism

Procedure

1. Glue strips of construction paper together in the order of the colors of the rainbow: red, orange, yellow, green, blue, and violet.

2. Use a prism to separate the colors in sunlight. Aim the colors from the prism at the different colors of construction paper.

3. Observe how the light from the prism is reflected by the different colors of construction paper.

Draw Conclusions

What colors from the prism are reflected from the green piece of construction paper? Explain.

Make a Periscope

How can you see around a corner?

Materials

- glue
- aluminum foil
- 2 index cards
- shoe box
- black construction paper

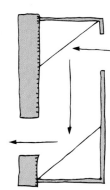

Procedure

1. Glue aluminum foil, shiny side out, to the index cards to make mirrors. Make the foil as smooth as possible.

2. Line the inside of the box with black paper. Cut out a hole in the bottom of the box, about 3 cm from one end. Cut a hole in the lid about 3 cm from one end.

3. Fold the ends of the aluminum foil mirrors to make tabs. Then glue the aluminum-foil mirrors to the inside of the box as shown.

4. Put the lid back on the box, and look through your periscope.

Draw Conclusions

How could you use a periscope to see around a corner?

Vocabulary Review

Use the terms below to complete the sentences 1 through 4. The page numbers in ( ) tell you where to look in the chapter if you need help.

reflection (C102)   **absorption** (C106)
refraction (C104)   **prism** (C110)

1. The bending of light is called ____.

2. A ____ breaks white light into colors.

3. The bouncing of light off objects is called ____.

4. Stopping light and holding it in is ____.

Connect Concepts

Follow the path of light as it travels. Use the terms in the Vocabulary Review to complete the concept map.

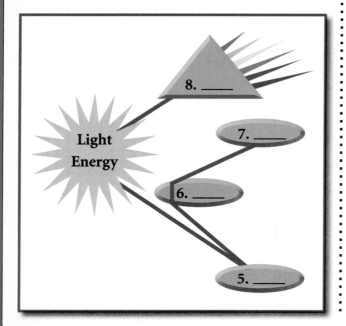

Check Understanding

Write the letter of the best choice.

9. Suppose you drop a penny into a shallow pool of water. You try to grab it but cannot seem to get your fingers in the right place. This happens because of —
   A reflection
   B absorption
   C refraction
   D light energy

10. Suppose you are standing at a pond. Your friend tries to sneak up on you, but you see him coming. You see him in the pond because of —
   F refraction
   G reflection
   H noise in the grass
   J absorption

11. White light is really —
   A all colors of light mixed
   B a mixture of yellow and white light
   C bright in the morning
   D a mixture of red and green light

12. Light travels —

   F through walls

   G around objects

   H in straight lines

   J in a curvy pattern

Critical Thinking

13. A skylight has water drops on it from a rainstorm. The sun comes out, and you see a rainbow on the wall. What is happening?

14. Describe how you could use a mirror to signal your friend in the house across the street.

15. You go to see a play. The light on the stage is yellow. You look up at the lights. They are red and green. Explain.

16. For art class, your teacher has you draw a bowl of fruit. The bowl contains a red apple, an orange, and a banana. After you have finished, your teacher puts a green spotlight on the fruit and asks you to draw it again. Why do you need to draw a new picture?

Process Skills Review

Write *True* or *False*. If the statement is false, correct it to make it true.

17. When you **observe** what is happening in an experiment, you use only your eyes.

18. Scientists sometimes draw pictures to explain their experiments.

Performance Assessment

Make a Model Prism

   With a partner, use construction paper to make a large model of a prism breaking a ray of white light into its colors. Be sure to show the colors in the right order. Label each color. Make a hole in the model and add some string so it can be hung up in the classroom. You will need construction paper, glue, scissors, string, and a pencil.

Unit Project Wrap Up

Here are some ideas for ways to wrap up your unit project.

Display at a Science Fair

Display the results of your project in a school science fair. Be prepared to explain how you identified and controlled variables in your experiments. Let volunteers conduct their own tests with materials you provide.

Draw a Billboard

Design a billboard advertisement for the best soap you tested. What claims could you make that you have evidence for?

Make an Ad Scrapbook

Collect advertisements that make claims that could be tested. Analyze the ads for proof for the claims.

Investigate Further

How could you make your project better? What other questions do you have? Plan ways to find answers to your questions. Use the Science Handbook on pages R2-R9 for help.

Extension Chapters

California Science Standards

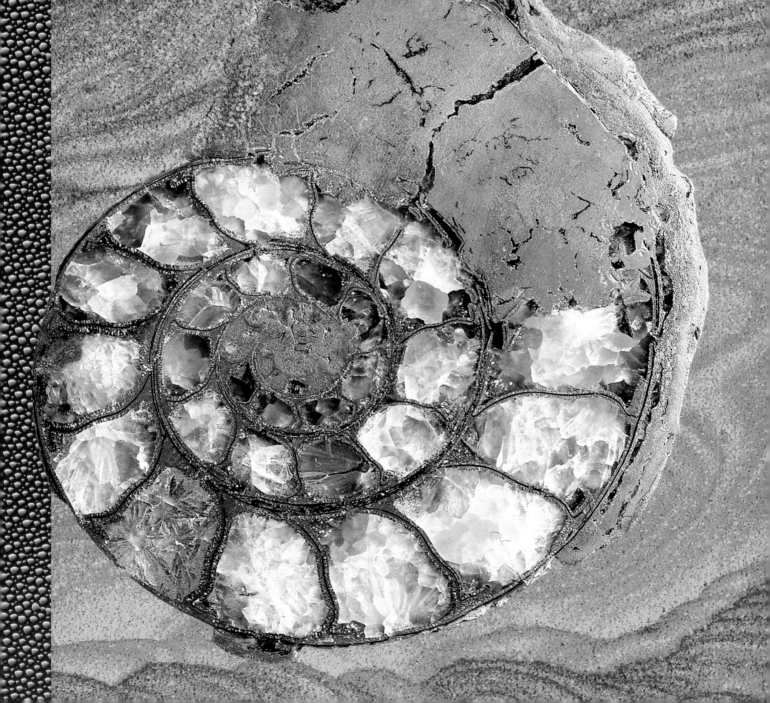

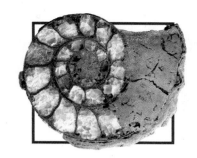

Extension Chapters

CALIFORNIA SCIENCE STANDARDS

Chapter 1

Vocabulary Preview

- interact
- producer
- consumer
- decomposer
- food chain
- energy pyramid
- food web
- predator
- prey

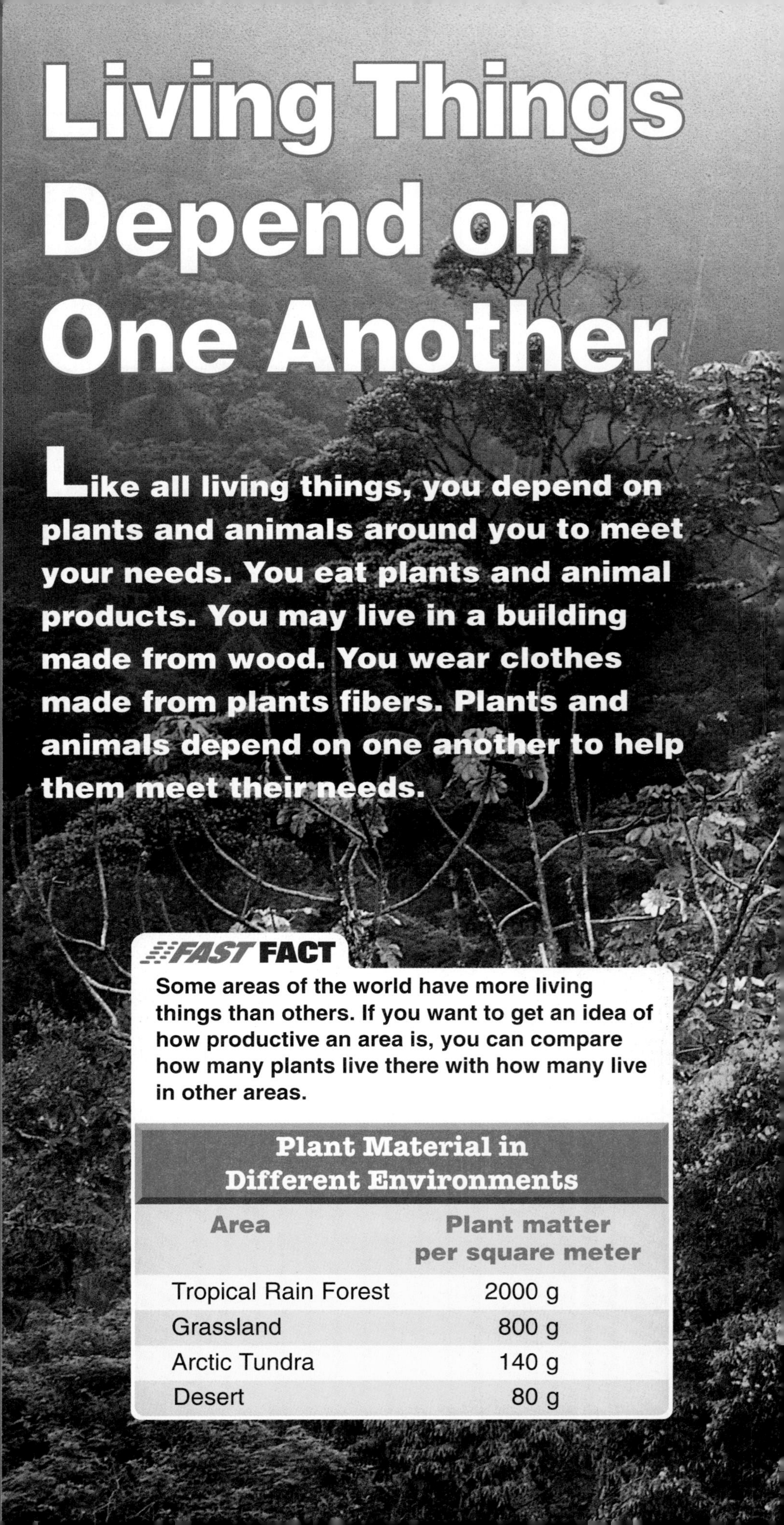

Living Things Depend on One Another

Like all living things, you depend on plants and animals around you to meet your needs. You eat plants and animal products. You may live in a building made from wood. You wear clothes made from plants fibers. Plants and animals depend on one another to help them meet their needs.

FAST FACT

Some areas of the world have more living things than others. If you want to get an idea of how productive an area is, you can compare how many plants live there with how many live in other areas.

Plant Material in Different Environments

Area	Plant matter per square meter
Tropical Rain Forest	2000 g
Grassland	800 g
Arctic Tundra	140 g
Desert	80 g

Tropical rain forest

FAST FACT

Hippopotamuses live in the rivers of central Africa. They eat grasses and other plants that grow in the water. The wastes they produce are rich in nutrients, and they help the plants to grow.

How Do Animals Get Food?

In this lesson, you can . . .

INVESTIGATE how animals use their teeth to help them get food.

LEARN ABOUT how living things get food.

LINK to math, writing, health, and technology.

Animal Teeth

Activity Purpose
Bite into an apple. Which teeth do you use? Which teeth do you use to chew the apple? In this investigation you will **observe** the shapes of teeth of different animals.

Materials
- blank index cards
- books about animals

Activity Procedure

1 **Observe** the pictures of the animals. Look closely at the shape of each animal's teeth.

2 Use one index card for each animal. **Record** the animal's name, and draw the shape of its teeth.

◀ Animals that are pets get their food from people. But animals that are wild must find their own food.

Shark ▼

Bobcat ▼

3 With a partner, make a list of words that describe the teeth. **Record** these words next to the drawings on the index cards. (Picture A)

4 Think about the things each animal eats. Use books about animals if you need help. On the back of each index card, make a list of the things the animal eats.

Picture A

Draw Conclusions

1. Which animals might use their teeth to catch other animals? Which animals might use their teeth to eat plants? Explain.

2. Some animals use their teeth to help them do other things, too. **Observe** the beaver's teeth. How do its teeth help it cut down trees?

3. **Scientists at Work** Scientists learn by **observing**. Scientists can learn how animals use their teeth by watching how and what the animals eat. From what you observed in this investigation, what can you **infer** about the shapes of animals' teeth?

Process Skill Tip

Observing and inferring are not the same. When you **observe**, you use your senses. When you **infer**, you form an opinion using your observations.

Wolf ▼

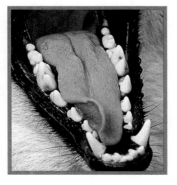

Horse ▼

Beaver ▼

E5

Living Things and Food

Making and Getting Food

FIND OUT

- how plants and animals interact with the environment
- how living things get food

VOCABULARY

interact
producer
consumer
decomposer

All living things need food. In the investigation you saw that an animal's teeth match the food it eats. But not all living things have teeth. Some living things get their food in other ways. For example, a bird uses its beak to get food. Plants make their own food.

Plants and animals work together, or **interact** (in•ter•AKT), with the environment to get what they need. Plants interact with sunlight, air, and water to make food. Animals interact with plants or other animals to get their food. Animals also interact with nonliving things in their environment, such as water, sunlight, soil, and rocks. For example, a snake lies in the sun for warmth and drinks water. The same snake may make its home in the soil or under a rock.

✔ **Why do plants and animals interact with the environment?**

This strawberry plant uses energy from the sun to make its own food. ▼

This strawberry provides a chipmunk with some of the energy it needs to live. ▼

The chipmunk provides energy for a snake that catches and eats it. ▼

E6

Producers

Plants are producers. A **producer** (proh•DOOS•er) is a living thing that makes its own food. Producers use the food they make to live and to grow.

Plants make more food than they need. This extra food is stored in roots, leaves, seeds, and fruit. People and other animals then eat this stored food as their own food.

✔ **What is a producer?**

▲ These foods come from plants. Plants are producers that make their own food. Animals then eat plants as food.

Consumers

Animals cannot make their own food. They must eat plants or other animals. An animal is a **consumer** (kuhn•SOOM•er). A consumer is a living thing that eats other living things as food.

Consumers can be grouped by the kinds of food they eat. Some consumers eat only plants. Sheep, like this bighorn sheep, eat the leaves, twigs, fruits, and nuts of many plants.

A few consumers eat only one kind of plant. Giant pandas eat only bamboo. To survive, they must live where bamboo grows.

Animals that eat only plants may have body parts that help them eat. For example, the giant panda has an extra bone in its hand that helps it hold bamboo as it eats.

The bighorn sheep is a consumer that eats grass. ▼

E7

Some animals get food by eating other animals. Often they must hunt and kill their food. Animals that get food in this way have body parts that help them catch and eat their food. For example, an owl has strong claws that it uses to catch animals. Its sharp beak helps it tear meat.

Some animals eat both plants and other animals. A box turtle eats both berries and insects. The meats you eat come from animals and the vegetables you eat come from plants.

✔ **What is a consumer?**

Decomposers

A **decomposer** (dee•kuhm•POHZ•er) is a living thing that breaks down dead things for food. Decomposers also break down the wastes of living things. As decomposers feed, they help clean the environment. Two decomposers you may know of are fungi, such as mushrooms, and earthworms.

✔ **What is a decomposer?**

This owl catches small animals for its food. ▼

▲ **Many bacteria are decomposers.**

The fungi growing on this log are decomposers. The fungi are using the dead log as food. ▼

Summary

Plants and animals interact. They depend on their environments and on one another to get the food they need. Plants are producers. Animals are consumers. Decomposers get food by breaking down wastes or dead things.

Review

1. How do producers get their food?
2. How do consumers get their food?
3. What are the three groups of consumers?
4. **Critical Thinking** How do decomposers help keep the environment clean?
5. **Test Prep** Which of the following is **NOT** a consumer?

   A bird   **C** squirrel

   B tree   **D** human

LINKS

MATH LINK

Consumers on an Island
Scientists studied 60 moose on an island. They found that during the summer, each moose eats the fruit of 25 blackberry bushes. What is the minimum number of blackberry bushes on the island?

WRITING LINK

Informative Writing—Explanation Suppose that the bushes on the island in the Math Link all die. Write a paragraph for your teacher explaining what you think might happen to the moose population.

HEALTH LINK

Teeth Think about how you use your teeth to eat. Which teeth do the cutting? The chewing? How are the teeth different?

TECHNOLOGY LINK

Learn how scientists help injured animals get food by visiting the Smithsonian Institution Internet Site.
www.si.edu/harcourt/science

LESSON 2

What Are Food Chains?

In this lesson, you can . . .

INVESTIGATE a food-chain model.

LEARN ABOUT food chains and energy pyramids.

LINK to math, writing, literature, and technology.

INVESTIGATE

Make a Food-Chain Model

Activity Purpose You get energy from the food you eat. All living things get energy from the food they eat. In this investigation you will **make a model** to show how living things interact to get their energy from food.

Materials

- index cards
- marker
- 4 pieces of yarn or string
- tape

Activity Procedure

1 In the bottom right-hand corners, number the index cards 1 through 5.

2 On Card 1, draw and label grass. On Card 2, draw and label a cricket. On Card 3, draw and label a frog. On Card 4, draw and label a snake. On Card 5, draw and label a hawk. (Picture A)

◄ A puffin eats different kinds of sea animals. It can catch as many as ten small fish at one time in its beak.

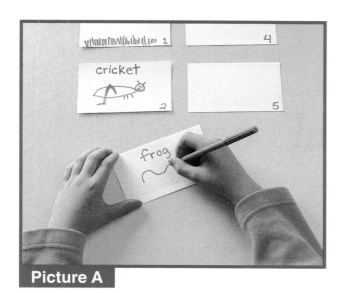

Picture A

Picture B

3. Order the cards in a line with Card 1 first and Card 5 last. Use yarn and tape to connect the cards. (Picture B)

4. Stretch the connected cards out on a table. The cards form a model called a food chain.

5. Discuss with a classmate how each living thing in the food chain gets its food. Tell which things in your model show producers. Tell which things show consumers.

Draw Conclusions

1. In your model, which living thing is last in the food chain? Why do you think it is in this place?

2. In which part of the food chain is the producer found? Why do you think it is there?

3. **Scientists at Work** Scientists **use models** to help them study things in nature. How does using a model of a food chain help you understand living things and the food they eat?

Process Skill Tip

It is hard to **observe** a real-life food chain. **Using a model** of a food chain helps you learn about the real thing.

Food and Energy

Food Chains

FIND OUT
- **how living things get energy**
- **how energy moves through a food chain**

VOCABULARY

food chain
energy pyramid

All living things need energy to live. Producers get energy from sunlight. They store the energy in the food they make. Consumers can't make their own food. They get their food by eating other living things. In this way, the consumers get the energy they need.

In the investigation you saw that the path of food from one living thing to another forms a **food chain**. A food chain also shows how energy moves through the environment. For example, grass uses the energy in sunlight to make its food. A cricket that eats the grass gets the energy stored in the grass. If a frog eats the cricket, it gets energy that is stored in the cricket. In this way, the energy that started with the sun is passed from the grass to the cricket to the frog.

✔ **What is a food chain?**

This turtle eats slugs that eat leaves. ▶

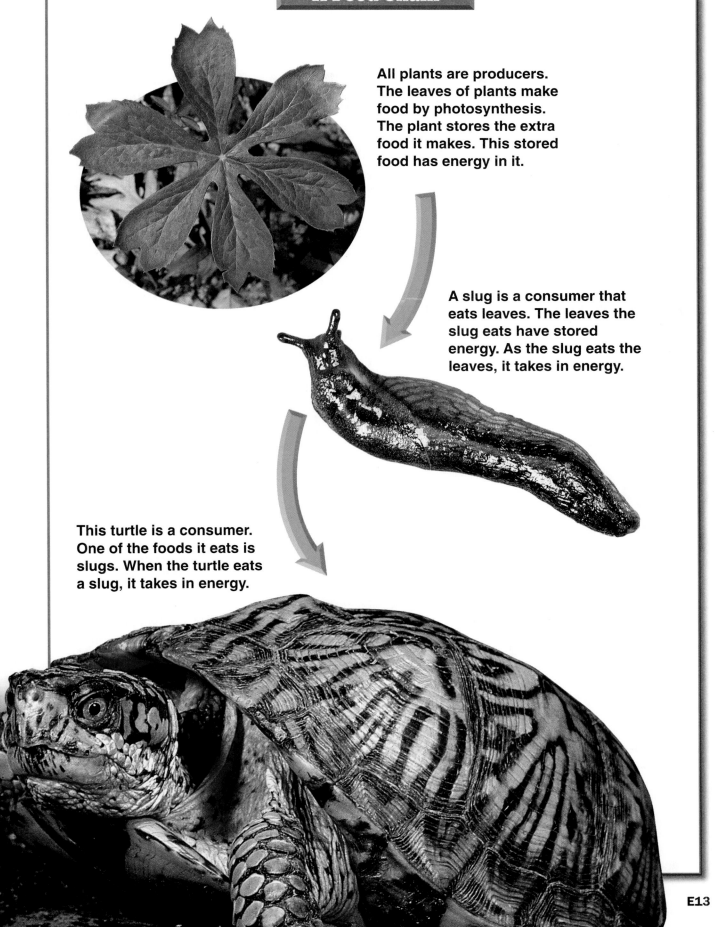

All plants are producers. The leaves of plants make food by photosynthesis. The plant stores the extra food it makes. This stored food has energy in it.

A slug is a consumer that eats leaves. The leaves the slug eats have stored energy. As the slug eats the leaves, it takes in energy.

This turtle is a consumer. One of the foods it eats is slugs. When the turtle eats a slug, it takes in energy.

Energy from Food

Every living thing uses energy to live and to grow. The energy that a living thing uses cannot be passed along through the food chain. Because of this, the higher on the food chain a living thing is, the less energy there is.

An **energy pyramid** shows that the amount of useable energy in an ecosystem is less for each higher animal in the food chain.

In an energy pyramid, there are more producers than any other kind of living thing. Most of the energy in an ecosystem is found in plants. Animals that eat plants make up the next level. The upper parts of the pyramid are made up of animals that eat other animals. The higher in the pyramid an animal is, the fewer of that animal there are. This is because there is less energy available to them.

✔ **What is an energy pyramid?**

1 Energy from the sun is taken in by plants and other producers. This energy is used by plants for growth and to make fruits and seeds. Energy that is not used by the plant is stored.

2 Animals that eat plants are called first-level consumers. These animals must eat many plants to get the energy they need. Energy not used by the animal is stored in its body.

3 Animals that eat other animals are called second-level consumers. There are fewer of these animals. Some of the energy that is stored in first-level consumers can be passed on to these animals.

4 There are very few animals at the top of the pyramid. The energy these top-level consumers get has been passed through all the other parts of the food chain.

THE INSIDE STORY

An Energy Pyramid

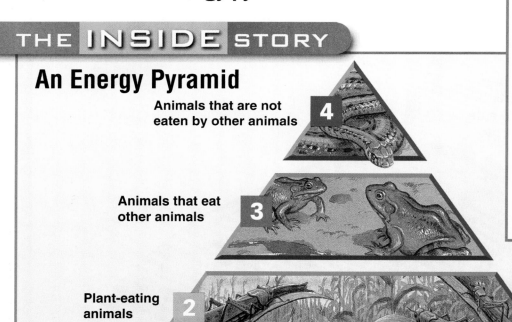

Animals that are not eaten by other animals **4**

Animals that eat other animals **3**

Plant-eating animals **2**

Plants **1**

▲ A hyena is a *scavenger,* an animal that feeds on dead animals.

Summary

Living things get their energy from food. Animals cannot make their own food, so they eat other living things to get energy. A food chain is the flow of food in an ecosystem from one living thing to another. An energy pyramid shows that the amount of useable energy in an ecosystem is less for each higher animal in the food chain.

Review

1. How does energy get from a producer to a meat-eating consumer?
2. What kind of living thing is at the top of a food chain?
3. Where is the most food energy in an energy pyramid found?
4. **Critical Thinking** What is the source of all the energy on Earth?
5. **Test Prep** Which is passed in a food chain from one living thing to another?

   A producers   C sunlight

   B animals   D energy

LINKS

MATH LINK

Animals in the Food Chain
One food chain is made up of a producer, a consumer that eats plants, a consumer that eats both plants and animals, and a consumer that eats only animals. What fraction of living things in this food chain eats plants?

WRITING LINK

Expressive Writing—Poem
You are part of many food chains. Pick your favorite dinner. Write a poem for your family about how the different foods fit into food chains.

LITERATURE LINK

Underwater Food Chains
Plants and animals that live in water are parts of food chains, too. In the book *Mangrove Wilderness,* Bianca Lavies tells about food chains in an estuary.

TECHNOLOGY LINK

To learn more about food chains, watch the video *Poisoned Eagles* on the **Harcourt Science Newsroom Video** in your classroom video library.

LESSON 3

What Are Food Webs?

In this lesson, you can . . .

INVESTIGATE
food webs.

LEARN ABOUT
how food chains overlap to form food webs.

LINK to math, writing, literature, and technology.

Make a Food Web

Activity Purpose Most animals eat more than one kind of food. Because of this, one living thing can be a part of more than one food chain. Food chains in an ecosystem overlap to form *food webs.* In this investigation you will **make a model** of a food web.

Materials
- index cards, cut into fourths
- poster board
- tape or glue
- crayons

Activity Procedure

1 Write the name of each living thing from the chart on its own card.

2 Glue the cards onto a sheet of poster board so they form a circle. Leave room for writing. (Picture A)

◀ A sea otter is part of an ocean food web. It feeds on abalone and other shellfish. As the otter floats on its back, it cracks open the shellfish by banging it against a rock it carries on its chest.

Living Thing	What It Eats
clover	uses the sun to make its own food
grasshopper	clover
frog	grasshopper
snake	frog, mouse
owl	snake, mouse
mouse	clover

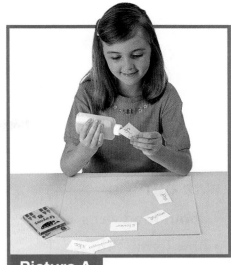

Picture A

3 Look at the chart again. List two different food chains you could make.

4 Draw arrows between the parts of each food chain. Use a different color for each food chain. You have now made a food web. (Picture B)

5 **Observe** your model to see how the food chains overlap. What other living things could you add to your food web?

Picture B

Draw Conclusions

1. What is the producer in this food web?

2. What does your food web tell you about producers and consumers?

3. **Scientists at Work** Scientists sometimes **make models** to help them learn about things. How did drawing a food web help you learn about animals in a real ecosystem?

Investigate Further Cut out magazine pictures of different plants and animals. Work with a partner to make a food web that includes these plants and animals.

Process Skill Tip

It is hard to observe a real-life food web. **Using a model** of a food web helps you learn about the real thing.

Food Webs

FIND OUT

- about food webs
- how living things interact in food webs

VOCABULARY

food web
predator
prey

This marsh ecosystem has many kinds of animals. These animals may be predators, prey, or both. ▼

Predator and Prey

There are many food chains in an ecosystem. Sometimes these food chains overlap. A model that shows how food chains overlap is called a **food web**. A food web contains producers and consumers that are used as food by more than one living thing.

Food webs contain animals that eat other animals. An animal that hunts another animal for food is called a **predator** (PRED•uh•ter). The animal that is hunted is called **prey** (PRAY). Some animals can be both predator and prey. For example, when a snake eats a mole, the snake is the predator. The mole is the prey. If the snake is eaten by a hawk, the snake becomes the prey. The hawk is the predator.

✔ **What is a food web?**

Marsh Ecosystem

Many overlapping food chains make up the food web for this marsh ecosystem.

1 The plants in the marsh use the energy of the sun to make food.

2 Insects eat the plants that grow in the marsh.

3 Fish eat the insects. Some fish also eat the plants. Smaller fish are eaten by larger fish.

4 Birds eat the fish in the marsh. Some birds also eat the insects and the plants that grow in the marsh.

5 Alligators eat both fish and birds. Alligators are top-level consumers. They are not eaten by other animals in the marsh.

What other food chains can you identify in this food web?

An Ocean Food Web

The living things in the ocean also interact to form food webs. Plants and other producers that grow in ocean waters are food for some ocean animals.

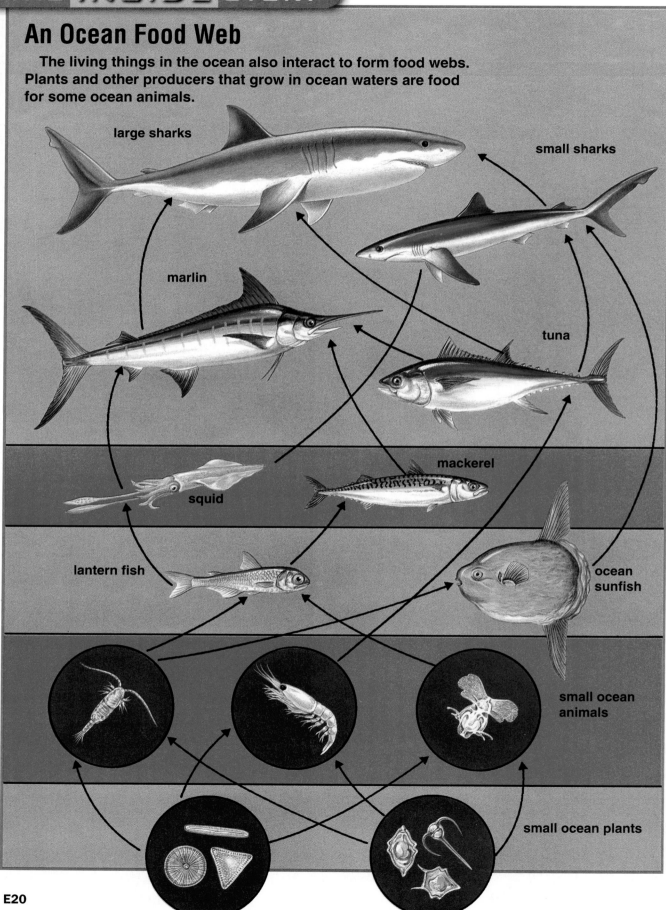

large sharks

small sharks

marlin

tuna

squid

mackerel

lantern fish

ocean sunfish

small ocean animals

small ocean plants

Summary

Most ecosystems have many food chains. These food chains overlap and link together to make food webs. An animal in a food web may be a predator, prey, or both.

Review

1. How are food webs and food chains alike? How are they different?
2. How can an animal be both predator and prey?
3. How does an alligator get energy?
4. **Critical Thinking** In the following food chain, name the predators and the prey.

   insect → frog → snake
5. **Test Prep** Which of the following is a producer in an ocean ecosystem?

   A shark   C starfish

   B seaweed   D fish

Other animals prey on these shrimp. Just like animals that live on land, many ocean predators have body parts that help them catch and eat their prey. ▼

LINKS

MATH LINK

Recording Food Web Data Choose a food web from this lesson. Count the different food chains in that web. How many animals in the web are predators, and how many are prey? Record your findings in a table.

WRITING LINK

Informative Writing— Explanation Study the ocean food web on page E20. Pick one of the animals and write a paragraph for your classmates that explains how the animal fits into a food chain and a food web.

LITERATURE LINK

Read About Predators Learn about some amazing predators, such as a fishing spider or a vampire bat. Read *Extremely Weird Hunters* by Sarah Lovett.

TECHNOLOGY LINK

Visit the Harcourt Learning Site for related links, activities, and resources.

www.harcourtschool.com/ca

People and Animals —A Long Relationship

Animals and humans have had a long relationship. People learned many thousands of years ago to domesticate, or tame, animals. Animals have also been hunted for food and clothing for thousands of years.

Uses of Animals

Animals are part of the web of life. They are consumers, living off plants and smaller animals. But people use animals and animal products as food. Some people choose not to eat animals. Many of those people do eat products that come from animals, such as milk, eggs, or honey. All of us depend on animals to pollinate the flowers of many fruits and vegetables.

Animal fur or skins may be used for clothing. Perhaps some of the clothing you are wearing today came

The History of People and Animals

15,000 B.C.
Horses are drawn in cave paintings in France.

15,000 B.C.   7500 B.C.   B.C./A.D.   1500   1600   1700

8000 B.C.
People begin to tame animals.

1400 B.C.
Hittites who live in Turkey train horses.

1519
Spanish explorers bring horses to North America.

from an animal. We get wool from sheep. Silkworms make silk.

Over the centuries, people have used animals to work. Large animals like oxen can be used to plow fields. Horses, camels, and elephants are good for carrying people and goods. Some dogs can guard, rescue, hunt, herd, or guide. Cats catch mice.

For some of us, domestic animals are best friends. You may have a cat or a dog as a family pet. Some people have more unusual pets, such as small reptiles or birds from foreign countries.

The Camel—A Very Useful Animal

The camel is one animal that is very useful to humans. Most camels now live in the deserts of Asia and Africa. But scientists have evidence that camels lived in North America before the Ice Age. They died out before Europeans came to the continent. But the U.S. Army brought camels back to North America to carry cargo from Texas to California during the mid-1800s. The railroad was faster than camels, though. After the railroad across the country was finished, most camels went to live in zoos and circuses.

People in Asia still use camels to carry heavy loads, especially in desert areas. One camel can carry more than 136 kilograms (300 lb). A working camel travels about 40 kilometers (25 mi) a day at about 5 kilometers per hour (3 mph). Also, camels can go for a long time without water.

Camels provide meat and milk. People make cheese and butter from their milk. Camel hair makes warm blankets, clothes, and tents.

As you can see, the relationship of animals and humans is complicated. Think of all the types of animals you have studied—fish, reptiles, birds, amphibians, and mammals. Then look around at home and at school. What should you thank an animal for today?

1850
Camels arrive in the United States.

| 1800 | 1900 | 2000 |

1973
The United States passes the Endangered Species Act to protect animals.

Think About It

- Why do you think people train animals to do specific jobs?

Akira Akubo

OCEANOGRAPHER

Growing up in Japan, a country surrounded by water, Akira Akubo became interested in the ocean. His interest led him to study oceanography.

Questions Akubo has studied include why and how fish live in schools. Fish gather in schools for protection. A school may break up at night to feed, but the fish gather again the next morning. A school may have as few as two dozen fish or as many as several million. All the fish in a school are about the same size. Adult fish and young fish are never in the same school. Some fish form schools when they are young and stay together all their lives. Other species of fish form schools for only a few weeks after hatching.

Akubo has also studied plankton—tiny animal-like and plantlike living things that float near the water's

surface. Most plankton are so small that they can be seen only with a microscope. Plankton is food for many other living things in the sea. Animal-like plankton eat the plantlike plankton. A lot of plankton is eaten by fish. Some whales eat nothing but tons of plankton!

Akubo is interested in land animals, too. He believes that studying land animals can help him learn more about animals in the water. He hopes that comparing ocean animals with land animals will help him predict animal behavior.

Think About It

1. Why is plankton important?
2. What is the advantage for fish of traveling in schools?

Food Chains

How do animals get their food?

Materials
- name tags
- colored game markers
- small plastic bags

Procedure
Play this game with ten or more people.

1 Have each player wear a tag that names him or her as a grasshopper, a snake, or a hawk. Scatter the game markers over a large area. The game markers are food.

2 Each round of the game is 30 seconds. In the first round, only grasshoppers play. They collect as many markers as they can and put them in their bags.

3 In the next round, only snakes play.

4 In the final round, only hawks play.

Draw Conclusions
Which animals have the most food after the three rounds? Talk about your answer.

Energy Flow

How does energy flow through a food chain?

Materials
- index cards
- crayons
- pushpins
- yarn

Procedure
1 Divide the class into five groups: producers, plant eaters, plant and animal eaters, animal eaters, and decomposers.

2 Have each person in your group draw on an index card and label a kind of plant or animal that is from your group.

3 Form teams made up of one member from each group. Each team should make a food chain with the pictures. Use yarn to connect the parts on a bulletin board.

Draw Conclusions
How does energy flow through the food chain?

Vocabulary Review

Use the terms below to complete the sentences 1 through 9. The page numbers in ( ) tell you where to look in the chapter if you need help.

interact (E6)
producer (E7)
consumer (E7)
decomposer (E8)
food chain (E12)

energy
pyramid (E14)
food web (E18)
predator (E18)
prey (E18)

1. A ____ feeds on the wastes of other living things.

2. A fish that is hunted and eaten by another consumer is called ____.

3. The path of food in an ecosystem from one living thing to another can be shown as a ____.

4. A ____ makes its own food.

5. A living thing that eats other living things is called a ____.

6. The living things in a community ____ with each other and with nonliving things.

7. Several linked food chains make up a ____.

8. A shark is a ____ because it hunts its food.

9. A model of how energy moves through a food web is called an ____.

Connect Concepts

Use the words listed below to complete the concept map.

consumer   horse
decomposer   mushroom
grass   producer

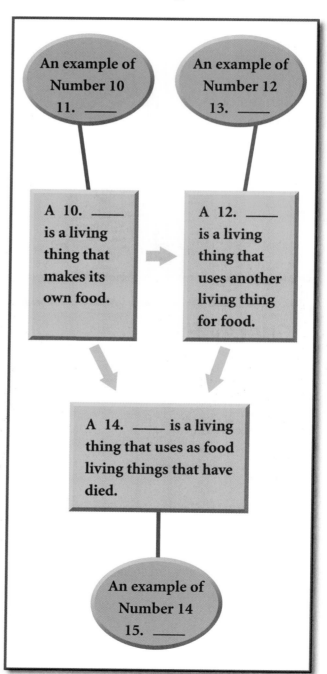

An example of Number 10
11. ____

An example of Number 12
13. ____

A 10. ____ is a living thing that makes its own food.

A 12. ____ is a living thing that uses another living thing for food.

A 14. ____ is a living thing that uses as food living things that have died.

An example of Number 14
15. ____

Check Understanding

Write the letter of the best choice.

16. Which is **NOT** a producer?
    - A tree
    - C grass
    - B flower
    - D bird

17. A model that shows how energy moves through a food chain is —
    - F a decomposer
    - G an ecosystem
    - H an energy pyramid
    - J a food web

18. A spider hunts and kills other animals for food. It is —
    - A prey
    - B a decomposer
    - C a predator
    - D a producer

19. Producers get their energy from —
    - F other living things
    - G the soil
    - H an energy pyramid
    - J the sun

Critical Thinking

20. A bear lives in the woods near a river. How might the bear interact with its environment to get food?

21. Where do you fit into a food chain? Draw a food chain that includes a plant or animal you ate for lunch.

Process Skills Review

22. How can you use **observation** to find out what a goat eats? How might you **infer** what the goat eats?

23. Use what you know about **models** to draw a food web that includes a bear, a water plant, berries, a big fish, a small fish, and a mouse.

Performance Assessment

Diagram a Food Web

Work with a partner. Choose an animal with which you are familiar. Draw a food web that includes the animal. Identify the producers and the consumers in each food chain. Identify predators and prey in as many food chains as you can.

Chapter 2

Rocks, Minerals, and Fossils

Take a look around at rocks. Some may be on the ground. Others may have been used to build homes and office buildings. Some rocks are shiny. Others may have different-colored pieces in them. You may even be able to see traces of once-living animals or plants in some rocks.

Vocabulary Preview

mineral
rock
crust
mantle
core
igneous rock
sedimentary rock
metamorphic rock
rock cycle
fossil

FAST FACT

If lightning strikes the beach, a new kind of rock may form. The heat from the lightning melts sand to make a glassy rock called fulgurite (FUHL·gyuh·ryt).

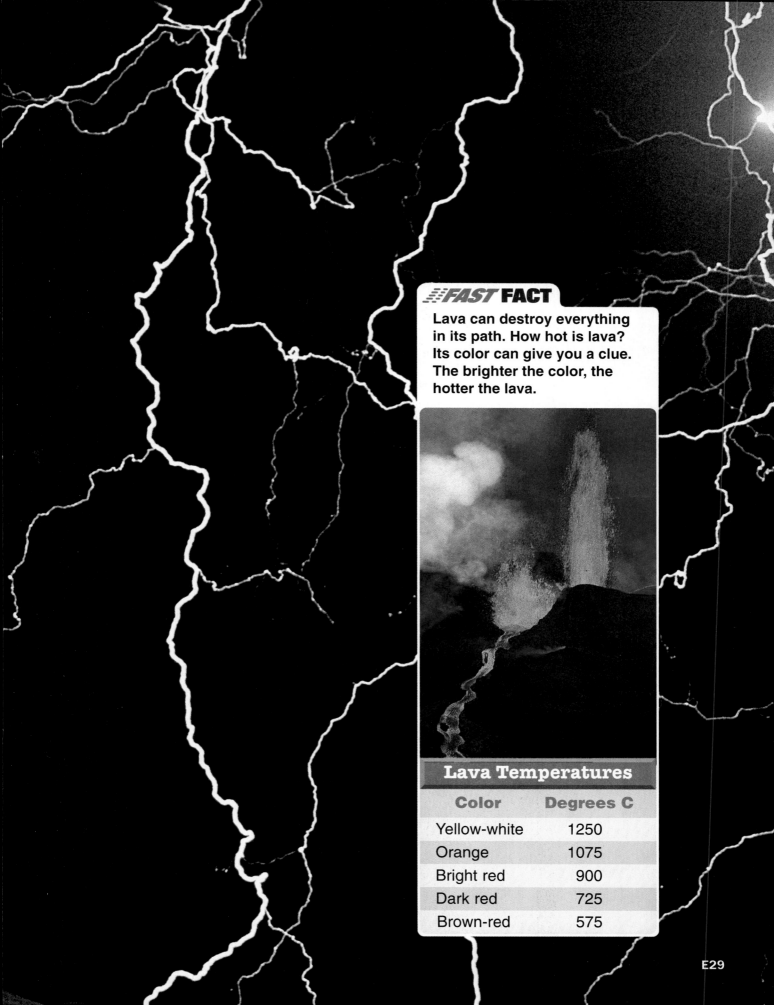

Lava can destroy everything in its path. How hot is lava? Its color can give you a clue. The brighter the color, the hotter the lava.

Lava Temperatures

Color	Degrees C
Yellow-white	1250
Orange	1075
Bright red	900
Dark red	725
Brown-red	575

What Are Minerals and Rocks?

In this lesson, you can . . .

INVESTIGATE the hardness of minerals.

LEARN ABOUT how people identify and use minerals and rocks.

LINK to math, writing, literature, and technology.

A geode is a hollow rounded rock with mineral crystals inside.

INVESTIGATE

Testing Minerals

Activity Purpose

How do scientists tell minerals apart? They test them for specific properties. A property is a feature that identifies something. In this investigation you will test seven minerals for the property of hardness. Then you will **order** the minerals from softest to hardest.

Materials

■ minerals labeled *A* through *G*

Activity Procedure

1 Make a chart like the one shown.

2 A harder mineral scratches a softer mineral. Try to scratch each of the other minerals with Sample A. **Record** which minerals Sample A scratches. (Picture A)

3 A softer mineral is scratched by a harder mineral. Try to scratch Sample A with each of the other minerals. **Record** which minerals scratch Sample A.

Mineral to Test	Minerals It Scratches	Minerals That Scratch It
Sample A		
Sample B		
Sample C		
Sample D		
Sample E		
Sample F		
Sample G		

4 Repeat Steps 2 and 3 for each mineral.

5 Using the information in your chart, **order** the minerals from softest to hardest. Give each mineral a number, starting with 1 for the softest mineral.

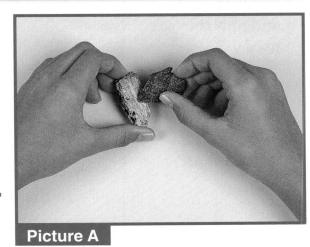

Picture A

Draw Conclusions

1. Which mineral was the hardest? Which was the softest? How do you know?

2. How did you decide the **order** of the minerals?

3. **Scientists at Work** Scientists often put objects in **order.** By doing this, they can show that different objects have different properties. How can putting objects in order of hardness help you identify them?

Investigate Further To test for hardness, scientists sometimes scratch an unknown mineral with common objects. That's because they don't always have other minerals with them. But to use common objects, scientists need to know how hard the objects are. Using the minerals from this investigation, find out the hardness of glass, a copper penny, and your fingernail.

Process Skill Tip

In a scratch test, you **observe** the results and **record** them on a chart. You use the chart to put the objects in **order.**

Minerals and Rocks

FIND OUT

• what minerals are and how they are used

• what is under the surface of the Earth

VOCABULARY

mineral
rock
crust
mantle
core

What Minerals Are

If an object is a solid, was formed in nature, and has never been alive, it's likely to be a **mineral** (MIN•er•uhl). There are many kinds of minerals. No two are exactly alike. For example, gold is bright and shiny. Graphite is dark and dull. Diamonds are hard enough to cut steel. Chalk is so soft that you can write with it.

In the investigation you saw that hardness is one property of minerals. Other properties of minerals are color and shape. Every mineral can be identified by its properties.

✔ **Name three properties of minerals.**

▲ Diamond is the hardest mineral.

▲ This sapphire has a beautiful deep blue color.

▲ Corundum, the second hardest mineral, may be many colors. The ruby shown here is a red corundum.

▲ Quartz is a common mineral. It is almost as hard as diamond.

▲ An emerald is among the most valuable minerals. It is very rare and very hard.

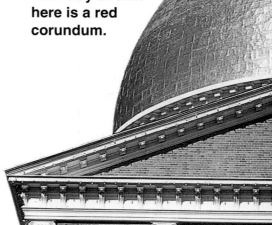

How Minerals Are Used

You use a mineral whenever you pick up a glass or put salt on your food. You use a mineral when you write with a pencil. The "lead" in the pencil is the mineral graphite.

Your body needs small amounts of minerals such as iron and zinc to stay healthy. You get these minerals from the foods you eat.

Minerals are in many of the things around you. For example, iron comes from the mineral hematite. Iron is used to make steel for airplanes, buildings, and washing machines.

Minerals such as gold and diamond are used to make jewelry. The pennies in your pocket contain copper. That's a mineral, too.

✔ **Name three ways that minerals are used.**

▲ **Aluminum comes from the mineral bauxite. Aluminum is molded into many products, such as baseball bats, cooking pots, and airplanes.**

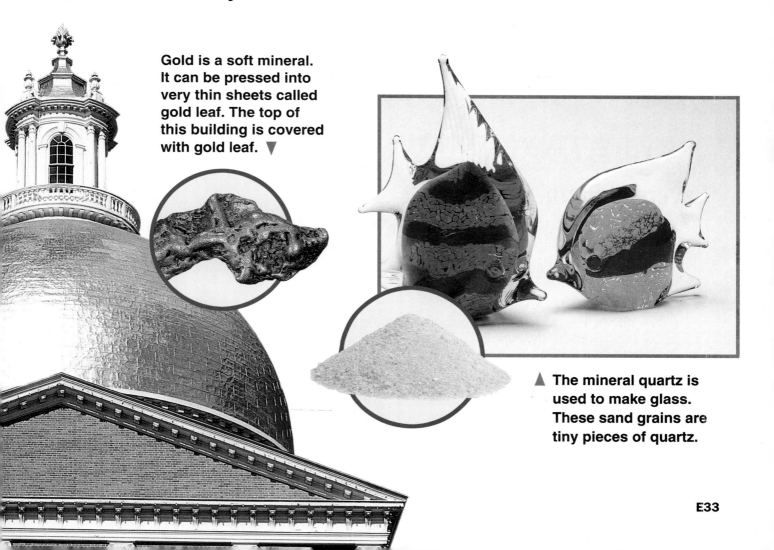

Gold is a soft mineral. It can be pressed into very thin sheets called gold leaf. The top of this building is covered with gold leaf. ▼

▲ **The mineral quartz is used to make glass. These sand grains are tiny pieces of quartz.**

What Rocks Are

The Earth is made mostly of rocks. A **rock** is made of minerals. Some rocks are made of just one. Other rocks are made of many minerals.

If you could cut the Earth open, you would see three different layers of rocks. At the surface of the Earth is the solid outside layer, called the **crust**. The crust is probably the only part of the Earth you have seen.

The crust sits on the **mantle**, the middle layer. The mantle is so hot that some of the rocks have nearly melted. They are soft like taffy.

Below the mantle, at the center of the Earth, is the **core**. It is even hotter than the mantle. The rocks in the outer part of the core are so hot that they are liquid. The liquid rock is called *magma*. The inner part of the core is much hotter than the mantle, but it is solid. Because the weight of the whole planet presses in on the core, the inner part stays solid.

✔ **Name the three layers of the Earth.**

Biotite

Feldspar

Quartz

Muscovite

THE INSIDE STORY

Layers of Earth

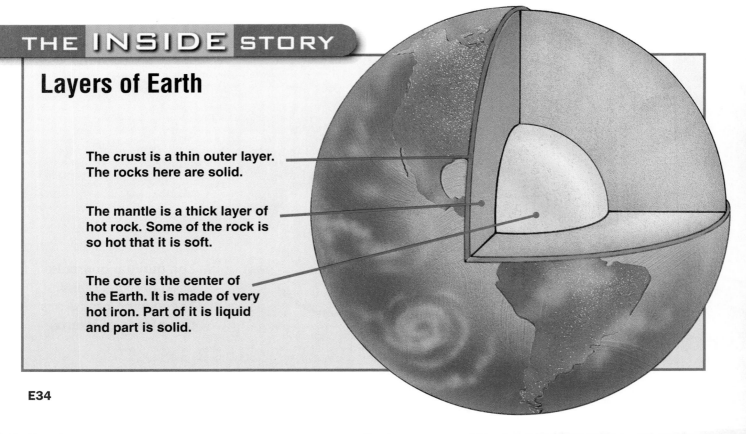

The crust is a thin outer layer. The rocks here are solid.

The mantle is a thick layer of hot rock. Some of the rock is so hot that it is soft.

The core is the center of the Earth. It is made of very hot iron. Part of it is liquid and part is solid.

◀ Granite is a rock that is made of the minerals shown here.

Summary

A mineral is a solid natural material that has never been alive. Rocks are made of minerals. The Earth is a ball of rock with three layers.

Review

1. What is a mineral? List three uses of minerals.
2. What is a rock?
3. Describe the layers of the Earth.
4. **Critical Thinking** How is the mantle of the Earth different from the crust? How are the mantle and crust alike?
5. **Test Prep** Which of these minerals is the hardest?
   A quartz
   B diamond
   C hematite
   D corundum

LINKS

MATH LINK

Crystal Shapes The particles in minerals form patterns called crystals. There are seven types of crystal shapes. Gather information on crystal shapes. How are they alike, and how are they different?

WRITING LINK

Informative Writing— Description Look for rocks where you live. Choose one that looks interesting. For a family member, make a list of words that describe it.

LITERATURE LINK

Magic School Bus Take a ride on the Magic School Bus to explore the center of the Earth. Read *Inside the Earth* by Joanna Cole. List three new things you learn about the Earth's layers.

TECHNOLOGY LINK

Learn more about rocks by visiting the Smithsonian Institution Internet Site.
www.si.edu/harcourt/science

How Do Rocks Form?

In this lesson, you can . . .

INVESTIGATE
different types
of rock.

LEARN ABOUT
how rocks form.

LINK to math,
writing, literature, and
technology.

INVESTIGATE

Types of Rocks

Activity Purpose In this investigation you will **observe** six different rocks and **compare** their properties. Then you will use your observations to group the rocks.

Materials

- 3 rocks labeled *I*, *S*, and *M*
- hand lens
- 3 unknown rocks labeled *1*, *2*, and *3*

Activity Procedure

1. Make a chart like the one shown.

2. Rocks *I*, *S*, and *M* are three different types of rocks. Look at them with and without the hand lens. **Record** your observations in the chart.

◀ **The Anasazi (ah•nuh•SAH•zee) people built homes in the rocky cliffs of Colorado hundreds of years ago.**

Rock	Observations
I	
S	
M	
1	
2	
3	

Picture A

3 Look at each of the numbered rocks with and without the hand lens. **Record** your observations in the chart. (Picture A)

4 **Compare** the properties of the lettered rocks with the properties of the numbered rocks. Think about how the rocks are alike and how they are different.

Draw Conclusions

1. What properties did you use to **compare** the rocks?

2. Which numbered rock is most like Rock *I*? Which numbered rock is most like Rock *S*? Which numbered rock is most like Rock *M*? Explain your answers.

3. **Scientists at Work** Scientists learn about new objects when they **compare** them with objects they have already studied. What did you learn about the rocks when you compared them?

Investigate Further Look near your school or home for small rocks. **Compare** them with Rocks *I*, *S*, and *M*. Try to **classify** the rocks as *I*, *S*, or *M*.

Process Skill Tip

When you **compare** objects, you **observe** their properties to find out how the objects are alike and how they are different. Comparing can help you put things into groups.

How Rocks Form

FIND OUT

- how rocks form
- ways people use rocks to make things

VOCABULARY

igneous rock
sedimentary rock
metamorphic rock
rock cycle

Three Types of Rocks

Exploding volcanoes, flowing water, and heat and pressure inside the Earth all form rocks. Rocks are grouped by how they form. There are three groups of rocks.

Igneous rock (IG•nee•uhs RAHK) is rock that was once melted but has cooled and hardened.

Sedimentary rock (sed•uh•MEN•ter•ee RAHK) forms from material that has settled into layers. The layers are squeezed together until they harden into rock.

Metamorphic rock (met•uh•MAWR•fik RAHK) is igneous or sedimentary rock that has been changed by heat and pressure.

✔ **What did the *I*, *S*, and *M* stand for in the investigation?**

◄ Rivers carry *sediment*, or pieces of rocks and soil. When a river slows down, it drops the sediment. Sediment builds up in layers at the bottom of rivers, lakes, seas, and oceans. These layers are pressed and stuck together to form sedimentary rocks.

Igneous rocks form from melted rock that has cooled and hardened. Some igneous rocks come from volcanoes. ▼

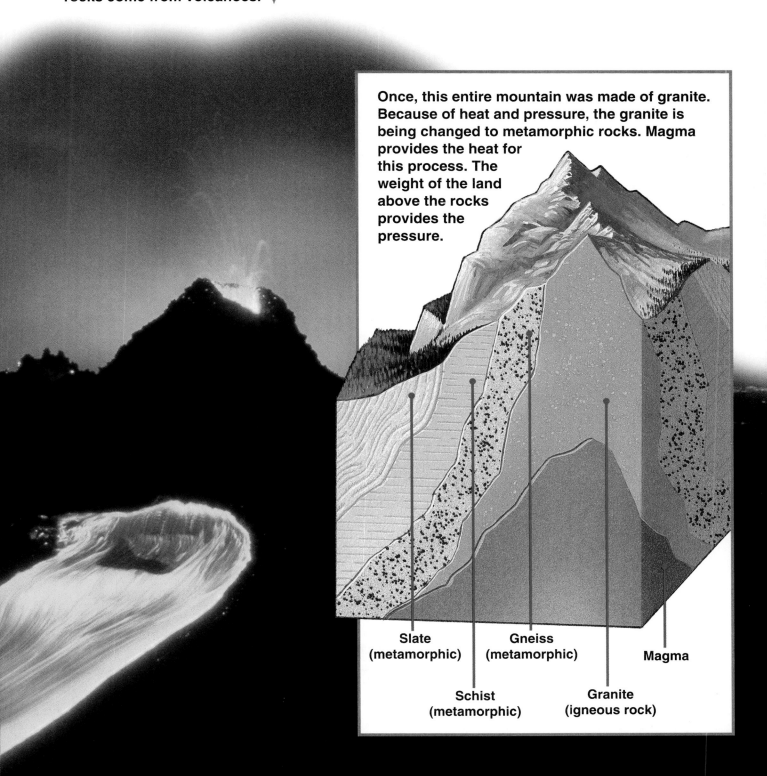

Once, this entire mountain was made of granite. Because of heat and pressure, the granite is being changed to metamorphic rocks. Magma provides the heat for this process. The weight of the land above the rocks provides the pressure.

Slate
(metamorphic)

Schist
(metamorphic)

Gneiss
(metamorphic)

Granite
(igneous rock)

Magma

How Rocks Form and Change

You know that there are three types of rocks—igneous, metamorphic, and sedimentary. But did you know that each type can be changed into the other types? This process of changing is called the **rock cycle** (RAHK SY•kuhl).

The diagram shows how rocks can change. The arrows show what is happening to make the rocks change. They tell about heat and pressure being applied to rocks. They also show how rocks break apart to form sediments. Use your finger to trace the changes that can happen to each type of rock.

✔ **What is the rock cycle?**

Metamorphic

Quartzite

Marble

Slate

Heat and pressure can change metamorphic rocks into other metamorphic rocks.

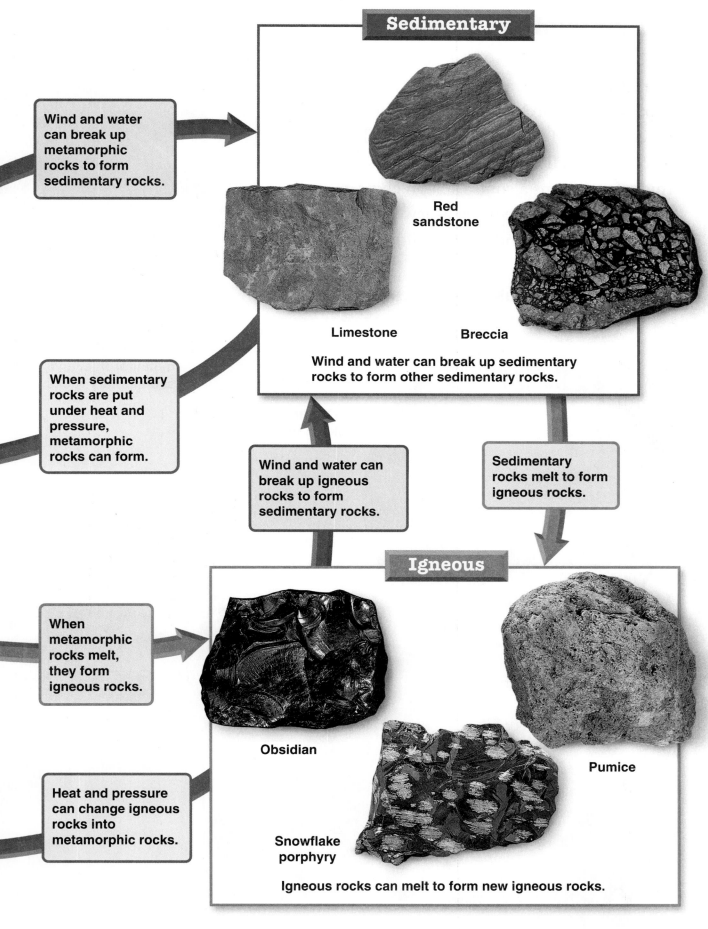

Sedimentary

Red sandstone

Limestone

Breccia

Wind and water can break up metamorphic rocks to form sedimentary rocks.

When sedimentary rocks are put under heat and pressure, metamorphic rocks can form.

Wind and water can break up sedimentary rocks to form other sedimentary rocks.

Wind and water can break up igneous rocks to form sedimentary rocks.

Sedimentary rocks melt to form igneous rocks.

Igneous

When metamorphic rocks melt, they form igneous rocks.

Heat and pressure can change igneous rocks into metamorphic rocks.

Obsidian

Snowflake porphyry

Pumice

Igneous rocks can melt to form new igneous rocks.

How People Use Rocks

Rocks are all around you. You see them all the time. But rocks are also in places you might not think of. Did you know that rocks help you play video games? The games use silicon chips, and silicon comes from rocks. Computers, satellites, and microwave ovens also use silicon chips.

Colorful rocks are worn as jewelry. Roads are paved with rocks, and many buildings and statues are made of rocks.

✔ **What are two uses of rocks?**

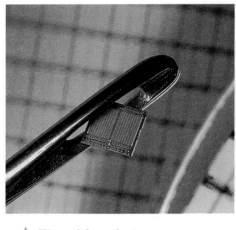

▲ The chips that run computers are made of silicon. Silicon comes from quartz, a very common mineral. Quartz is found in igneous, metamorphic, and sedimentary rocks.

◀ Metamorphic rocks such as marble are used to make statues.

Summary

There are three types of rocks. Igneous rocks form from melted rock that has cooled and hardened. Sedimentary rocks form from layers of sediment. Metamorphic rocks have been changed by heat and pressure. The rock cycle shows how one type of rock can be changed into another type of rock.

Review

1. Where do igneous rocks come from?
2. How can igneous rocks become sedimentary rocks?
3. How can metamorphic rocks become igneous rocks?
4. **Critical Thinking** Choose a rock, and tell about some things that are made from it.
5. **Test Prep** Which type of rock forms in layers?

   A igneous
   B metamorphic
   C sedimentary
   D All rocks form in layers.

◀ The Jefferson Memorial in Washington, D.C., is made of marble, a metamorphic rock.

LINKS

MATH LINK

Rock Model Suppose you were asked to make a model of the rock cycle. You were told to include 3 types of each kind of rock in your model. How many rocks are in the model?

WRITING LINK

Informative Writing—Report Interview someone who works with minerals and rocks. Find out how he or she uses them at work. Write a report for your teacher about what you learn. Share it with your class.

LITERATURE LINK

Rock On Want to find out more about rocks? Read *The Rock* by Peter Parnall. Tell how the rock changed over time.

TECHNOLOGY LINK

Learn more about the rock cycle by observing rocks as they change. Try *Rock Processor* on **Harcourt Science Explorations CD-ROM**.

What Are Fossils?

In this lesson, you can . . .

INVESTIGATE how fossils form.

LEARN ABOUT different types of fossils.

LINK to math, writing, literature, and technology.

INVESTIGATE

Fossil Layers

Activity Purpose You have never seen a live dinosaur. But you may know a lot about dinosaurs because of fossils (FAHS•uhlz). A *fossil* is what's left of a plant or animal that lived long ago. In this investigation you will **make a model** of rock layers and fossils.

Materials
- 5 colors of modeling clay
- 5 sheets of wax paper
- 5 different seashells labeled *A* through *E*

Activity Procedure

1 Make a chart like the one shown.

2 Use clay of one color to make a layer about the size and shape of a hamburger. Put the layer of clay on a sheet of wax paper.

3 Press a shell into the clay to make a print. Remove the shell. **Record** the clay color and the shell letter in your chart. (Picture A)

◀ **Fossil bones show how dinosaurs looked. This fossil is of a Tyrannosaurus rex.**

Rock Layer	Clay Color	Shell Letter
1 (bottom layer)		
2		
3		
4		
5 (top layer)		

4 Place a sheet of wax paper over the clay layer.

5 Repeat Steps 2, 3, and 4 until you have made new layers with each color of clay and each shell.

6 Trade your group's clay layers and shells with another group's. Make a second chart. Remove each layer of clay, and **observe** it. Do not change the order of the layers. Match each shell to its print. Fill in the second chart. Check your answers with the group that made the model.

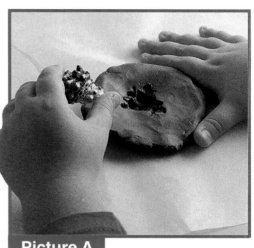

Picture A

Draw Conclusions

1. How did you know the correct layer for each shell?

2. Pretend the shell prints are fossils and the clay is sedimentary rock. List the shell letters from the oldest to the newest. Do this by using what you know about sedimentary rock layers.

3. **Scientists at Work** Scientists **use models** to understand how things happen. How did **using a model** help you understand how fossils are left in layers in time order?

Process Skill Tip

In class you can't see how real rock layers and fossils form. So **using a model** is helpful. It shows what the layers can tell you about the order in which the fossils were formed.

What Fossils Are

FIND OUT

• how fossils form

• how fossils show that life on Earth has changed

VOCABULARY

fossil

How Fossils Form

Some places are better for fossil hunting than others. Sedimentary rocks usually have more fossils than other kinds of rocks. That's because what's left of a plant or animal is sometimes trapped in the sediments that form the layers of the rock. The heat and pressure that form metamorphic and igneous rocks often destroy fossils.

Every **fossil** is something that has lasted from a living thing that died long ago. But there are different types of fossils. Some are body parts, such as bones or teeth, that have turned into stone. Other fossils are only marks, such as animal tracks.

The fossils of the shells in the picture on E47 show two ways fossils can form. The fossil shell on the top is a mold. You made a mold in the investigation.

Fossils often form in sedimentary rocks, such as limestone and shale.

1 The soft parts of an animal rot away.

2 Bones are slowly buried under layers of sediment.

A *mold* is the shape of a plant or animal left in sediments when the rock formed. The shell that made the mold in the picture dissolved.

The other fossil shell is a cast. A *cast* forms when mud or minerals fill a mold. The cast has the exact shape of the animal that made the mold.

Look at the fossil fern leaf. Fossil *imprints* are molds of leaves or other thin objects. Some imprints are of animal parts such as wings or feathers. The leaves or animal parts rotted away long ago.

✔ **What are fossils?**

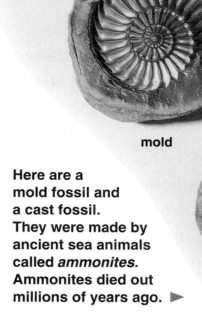

mold

Here are a mold fossil and a cast fossil. They were made by ancient sea animals called *ammonites.* Ammonites died out millions of years ago. ▶

cast

▲ **This is a fossil imprint of a dragonfly.**

Plant fossils are much less common than animal fossils. This is because plant parts are more easily destroyed as rocks form. ▶

3 Over a long time, the sediment turns into rock.

4 Movement of the Earth's crust brings the rock and fossils closer to the surface. Wind and rain wear away the rock on top of the fossils.

How Fossils Help Us Learn About Dinosaurs

Dinosaurs died out long before there were any scientists to study them. But scientists today can use fossils to learn how dinosaurs looked and how they lived.

Using fossil bones, scientists can put together skeletons of dinosaurs. The skeletons show how large the dinosaur was and whether it walked on two legs or four.

Fossil dinosaur teeth show the kinds of foods dinosaurs ate. The shapes of the teeth are suited to eating plants or other animals. Some dinosaurs ate other dinosaurs. How do we know that?

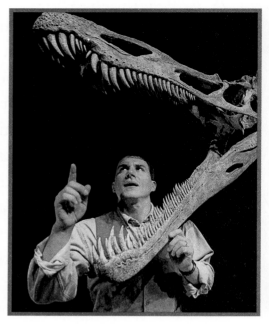

▲ This dinosaur fossil was recently discovered. Look at its teeth and you will see that it ate other animals.

This paleontologist (a scientist who studies fossils) is digging up fossil dinosaur bones. ▼

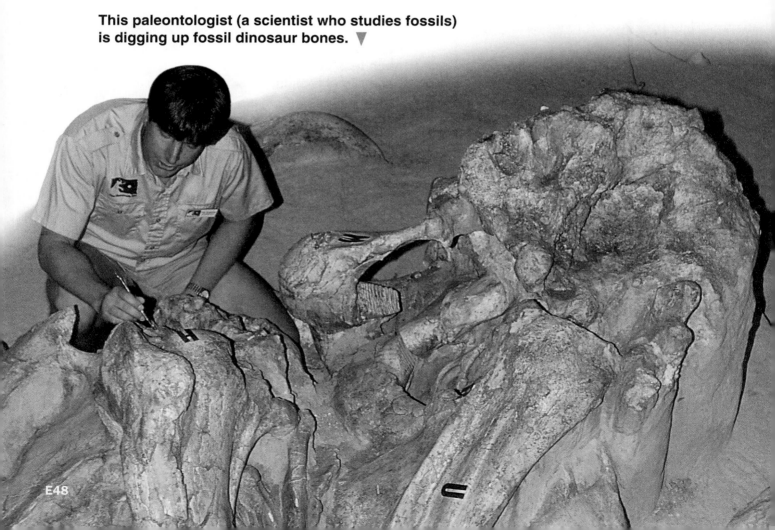

Scientists have found fossil dinosaur bones with the teeth of other dinosaurs broken off in them!

New dinosaur fossils are being discovered all the time. Each new discovery increases what we know about dinosaurs.

✔ **How do scientists learn about dinosaurs?**

Summary

A fossil is something that has lasted from a living thing that died long ago. Fossils are found mostly in sedimentary rocks. Scientists can use fossils to understand how dinosaurs looked and lived.

Review

1. Why are most fossils found in sedimentary rocks?
2. Name two types of fossils, and tell how they formed.
3. What dinosaur fossils have scientists used to learn how dinosaurs looked?
4. **Critical Thinking** Would you find fossils in igneous rock? Why?
5. **Test Prep** Which of the following rocks would be most likely to have a fossil in it?
   A granite
   B limestone
   C marble
   D quartz

LINKS

MATH LINK

How Big? Find the sizes of the largest and smallest dinosaurs. Make a model to show the difference in their sizes. Subtract to find the difference in their sizes.

WRITING LINK

Write to Describe Choose a type of dinosaur, and make a card that describes it. At the top of the card, draw the dinosaur. Then write information about it under your drawing. Share your card with your classmates.

LITERATURE LINK

Would you like to know more about fossils? Read *Dinosaurs Walked Here* by Patricia Lauber. Choose a fossil described in the book. Then make a model showing how the fossil formed.

TECHNOLOGY LINK

Learn more about finding dinosaur fossils by watching *Dinosaur Discovery* on the **Harcourt Science Newsroom Video.**

DISCOVERING Dinosaurs

As early as the third century, people in China wrote about dragon teeth and dragon bones. But what those people described weren't dragons. They were dinosaurs.

Dinosaur Discoveries

No one knew what dinosaur fossils were before the 1800s. One early scientist thought the giant thighbone he had found was from a giant human. In 1824 William Buckland gave the name Megalosaurus ("great lizard") to the animal whose jaw and teeth he had been studying. The next year, Mary Ann Mantell found a large tooth partly buried in a rock in England. She didn't know what it was. Her husband, Gideon Mantell, was a doctor who collected fossils. He thought the tooth came from a large reptile like an iguana. So he called it Iguanodon, which means "iguana tooth."

During the next few years, many remains were found. In 1842 Richard Owen, an English scientist, gave the name Dinosauria to the whole group of fossil remains. Dinosaur means "terrible lizard."

The first dinosaur craze was in the 1850s in England. There was an exhibit at the Crystal Palace in

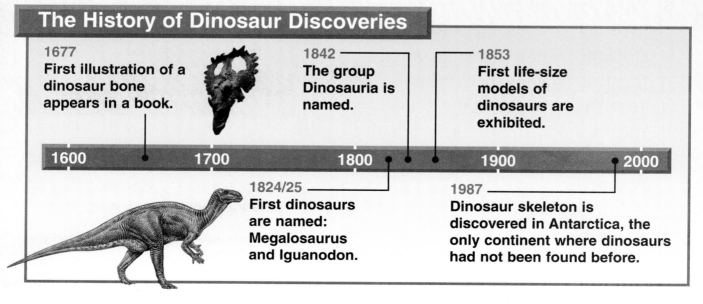

The History of Dinosaur Discoveries

1677 First illustration of a dinosaur bone appears in a book.

1842 The group Dinosauria is named.

1853 First life-size models of dinosaurs are exhibited.

1600   1700   1800   1900   2000

1824/25 First dinosaurs are named: Megalosaurus and Iguanodon.

1987 Dinosaur skeleton is discovered in Antarctica, the only continent where dinosaurs had not been found before.

London in 1853. Sir Richard Owen and Waterhouse Hawkins, an artist, made some life-size dinosaur models. The models have errors, but they are still on view at the Crystal Palace Park.

Studying Dinosaur Fossils

Dinosaur fossils have been found on every continent. The largest numbers of sites are in the United States and Europe. At a fossil site, or dig, scientists use chisels to carefully free the fossils from the surrounding rock. Each fossil is cleaned and carefully packed in a plaster or foam jacket. Detailed notes are taken about where the bones were found.

The bones are then taken to a laboratory to be analyzed. Scientists try to determine how the bones may have fit together. This job is easier if the muscles have left marks, called muscle scars, where they were attached to the bones. A scientific artist sketches the bones and muscles, and adds skin. Drawing the skin is mostly guesswork. No one knows for sure whether dinosaurs had stripes or spots, or what color their skin was.

Interesting Dinosaurs

Dinosaurs began to appear in books during the mid 1800s. Today, some museums feature exhibits of dinosaurs. Dinosaur robots that move and make noises are made of steel and latex. They are shown throughout the world at theme parks and museums.

Think About It

- Why do you think people in China thought dinosaur bones were from dragons?

Dinosaur Model

Charles Langmuir

PETROLOGIST, GEOCHEMIST

"I had no idea of the excitement of sea-going science."

Charles Langmuir says that when he was a boy, his father played at science with him. They made musical instruments together and changed the tone of a flute by blowing carbon dioxide through it instead of air. They made a model of a diver in a bottle. They watched dry ice evaporate and grew crystals. All this play taught Langmuir that science was a combination of fun, amazement, and careful observation. Although his mother didn't play at science with him, Langmuir says she taught him other things. She taught him that exploration never stops, that limits don't matter, and that a sense of humor is important.

These lessons led Langmuir to the study of geology and petrology, the study of rocks. Langmuir began studying ocean rocks while in graduate school. Most of the rocks he studies are basalts, a type of igneous rock. Studying the ocean leads to greater knowledge about Earth's land. Learning about Earth's land gives more information about the ocean.

Langmuir thinks of the ocean floor as a wonderful frontier. He finds it exciting to be working with the two-thirds of Earth's surface that is underwater.

Think About It

1. What kinds of things would you expect to find on the ocean floor?
2. What school subjects do you "play at" outside school?

Atlantic Coast   **Mid-Atlantic Ridge**

Growing Crystals

How do salt crystals grow?

Materials

- salt
- hand lens
- hot tap water
- small jar
- plastic spoon
- small nail
- cotton string
- pencil

Procedure

1. Observe the salt with the hand lens. Record what you see.

2. **CAUTION** **Be careful with hot water.** Fill your jar with hot water. Add salt one spoonful at a time. Stir. Keep adding salt until no more will dissolve.

3. Set up the jar as shown. The nail should not touch the jar.

4. Leave the jar for five days. Then describe what you see on the nail and string.

Draw Conclusions

Observe this material with the hand lens. Compare it with the salt crystals you examined in Step 1.

Minerals in Sand

What minerals are found in sand?

Materials

- sand
- sheet of paper
- hand lens
- toothpick
- mineral descriptions

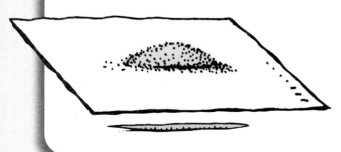

Procedure

1. Spread the sand on a sheet of paper.

2. Observe the colors and shapes of the sand grains with the hand lens. Each type of mineral grain has a different color and shape.

3. Use the toothpick to move the grains of each mineral into a separate pile.

Draw Conclusions

Identify the minerals. Use the descriptions your teacher gives you. Which mineral is the most common?

Chapter ② Review and Test Preparation

Vocabulary Review

Use the terms below to complete the sentences 1 through 10. The page numbers in ( ) tell you where to look in the chapter if you need help.

mineral (E32)   **sedimentary**
rock (E34)   **rock** (E38)
crust (E34)   **metamorphic**
mantle (E34)   **rock** (E38)
core (E34)   **rock cycle** (E40)
igneous rock (E38)   **fossil** (E46)

1. A ____ is something that has lasted from a living thing that died long ago.

2. Rock that has been changed by heat and pressure in the Earth is ____.

3. The ____ is the rock layer at the center of the Earth.

4. A solid material made of minerals is a ____.

5. A ____ is a solid natural material found in the Earth.

6. Rock that forms from layers of sediment is ____.

7. The ____ is Earth's middle layer of soft rock.

8. One type of rock turns into another type as rocks move through the ____.

9. The ____ is Earth's outer layer.

10. Melted rock that has cooled is ____.

Connect Concepts

Write the terms where they belong in the concept map.

minerals   sedimentary
igneous   metamorphic

melted rock that cools and hardens

layers of sediment and plant and animal remains

rock that has been changed by heat and pressure inside the Earth

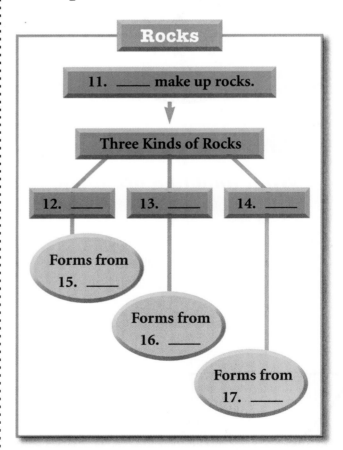

Rocks

11. ____ make up rocks.

Three Kinds of Rocks

12. ____   13. ____   14. ____

Forms from
15. ____

Forms from
16. ____

Forms from
17. ____

Check Understanding

Write the letter of the best choice.

18. A rock is made of —
    A only living things
    B one or more minerals
    C only two minerals
    D minerals that are hard

19. Heat helps form —
    F igneous and metamorphic rocks
    G sedimentary and metamorphic rocks
    H only igneous rocks
    J only metamorphic rocks

20. Fossils often last in sedimentary rocks because the rocks —
    A are very hot
    B are often near animals
    C have layers that save animal and plant shapes
    D don't ever change

21. A ___ mineral will scratch a ___ mineral.
    F rare, common H hard, soft
    G soft, hard   J small, big

22. As you go deeper into Earth, —
    A the pressure increases and it gets hotter
    B the rocks get smaller
    C it gets cold
    D the pressure decreases and the rocks get smaller

Critical Thinking

23. Why are fossils not often found in igneous rocks?

24. You find a mineral sample. You think it may be calcite or quartz. How could you decide which mineral your sample is?

Process Skills Review

25. What tools are useful in putting minerals in **order** by hardness?

26. You want to **compare** three unknown rocks with three known rocks. What properties would you use?

27. How can you **make a model** of the way sedimentary rocks form?

Performance Assessment

Changing Rocks

Choose a type of rock. Tell how it could move through the rock cycle by changing into different types of rocks. Draw a picture showing the stages your rock could go through.

References

Planning an Investigation

When scientists observe something they want to study, they use scientific inquiry to plan and conduct their study. They use science process skills as tools to help them gather, organize, analyze, and present their information. This plan will help you work like a scientist.

Step 1—Observe and ask questions.

Which food does my hamster eat the most of?

- Use your senses to make observations.
- Record a question you would like to answer.

Step 2—Make a hypothesis.

My hypothesis: My hamster will eat more sunflower seeds than any other food.

- Choose one possible answer, or hypothesis, to your question.
- Write your hypothesis in a complete sentence.
- Think about what investigation you can do to test your hypothesis.

Step 3—Plan your test.

I'll give my hamster equal amounts of three kinds of foods, then observe what she eats.

- Write down the steps you will follow to do your test. Decide how to conduct a fair test by controlling variables.
- Decide what equipment you will need.
- Decide how you will gather and record your data.

Step 4 — Conduct your test.

I'll repeat this experiment for four days. I'll measure how much food is left each time.

- Follow the steps you wrote.
- Observe and measure carefully.
- Record everything that happens.
- Organize your data so that you can study it carefully.

Step 5 — Draw conclusions and share results.

My hypothesis was correct. She ate more sunflower seeds than the other kinds of foods.

- Analyze the data you gathered.
- Make charts, graphs, or tables to show your data.
- Write a conclusion. Describe the evidence you used to determine whether your test supported your hypothesis.
- Decide whether your hypothesis was correct.

Investigate Further

I wonder if there are other foods she will eat . . .

Using Science Tools

Using a Hand Lens

1. Hold the hand lens about 12 centimeters (5 in.) from your eye.

2. Bring the object toward you until it comes into focus.

Using a Thermometer

1. Place the thermometer in the liquid. Never stir the liquid with the thermometer. Don't touch the thermometer any more than you need to. If you are measuring the temperature of the air, make sure that the thermometer is not in line with a direct light source.

2. Move so that your eyes are even with the liquid in the thermometer.

3. If you are measuring a material that is not being heated or cooled, wait about two minutes for the reading to become stable, or stay the same. Find the scale line that meets the top of the liquid in the thermometer, and read the temperature.

4. If the material you are measuring is being heated or cooled, you will not be able to wait before taking your measurements. Measure as quickly as you can.

Caring for and Using a Microscope

Caring for a Microscope

- Carry a microscope with two hands.
- Never touch any of the lenses of a microscope with your fingers.

Using a Microscope

1. Raise the eyepiece as far as you can using the coarse-adjustment knob. Place your slide on the stage.

2. Start by using the lowest power. The lowest-power lens is usually the shortest. Place the lens in the lowest position it can go to without touching the slide.

3. Look through the eyepiece, and begin adjusting it upward with the coarse-adjustment knob. When the slide is close to being in focus, use the fine-adjustment knob.

4. When you want to use a higher-power lens, first focus the slide under low power. Then, watching carefully to make sure that the lens will not hit the slide, turn the higher-power lens into place. Use only the fine-adjustment knob when looking through the higher-power lens.

You may use a Brock microscope. This sturdy microscope has only one lens.

1. Place the object to be viewed on the stage.

2. Look through the eyepiece, and raise the tube until the object comes into focus.

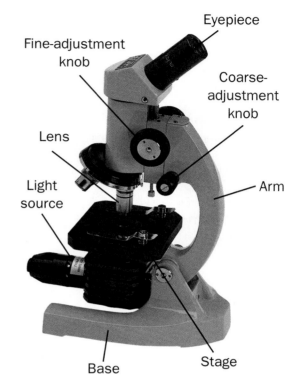

A Light Microscope

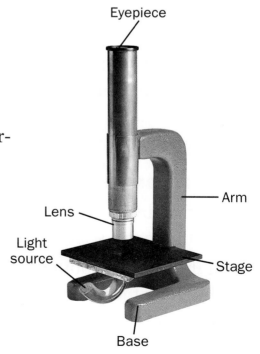

A Brock Microscope

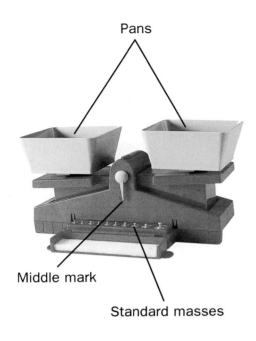

Pans

Middle mark

Standard masses

Using a Balance

1. Look at the pointer on the base to make sure the empty pans are balanced. Place the object you wish to measure in the left-hand pan.

2. Add the standard masses to the other pan. As you add masses, you should see the pointer move. When the pointer is at the middle mark, the pans are balanced.

3. Add the numbers on the masses you used. The total is the mass in grams of the object you measured.

Using a Spring Scale

Measuring an Object at Rest

1. Hook the spring scale to the object.

2. Lift the scale and object with a smooth motion. Do not jerk them upward.

3. Wait until any motion of the spring comes to a stop. Then read the number of newtons from the scale.

Measuring an Object in Motion

1. With the object resting on a table, hook the spring scale to it.

2. Pull the object smoothly across the table. Do not jerk the object.

3. As you pull, read the number of newtons you are using to pull the object.

Measuring Liquids

1. Pour the liquid you want to measure into a measuring container. Put your measuring container on a flat surface, with the measuring scale facing you.

2. Look at the liquid through the container. Move so that your eyes are even with the surface of the liquid in the container.

3. To read the volume of the liquid, find the scale line that is even with the surface of the liquid.

4. If the surface of the liquid is not exactly even with a line, estimate the volume of the liquid. Decide which line the liquid is closer to, and use that number.

Beaker   **Graduate**

Using a Ruler or Meterstick

1. Place the zero mark or end of the ruler or meterstick next to one end of the distance or object you want to measure.

2. On the ruler or meterstick, find the place next to the other end of the distance or object.

3. Look at the scale on the ruler or meterstick. This will show the distance or the length of the object.

Using a Timing Device

1. Reset the stopwatch to zero.

2. When you are ready to begin timing, press *Start*.

3. As soon as you are ready to stop timing, press *Stop*.

4. The numbers on the dial or display show how many minutes, seconds, and parts of seconds have passed.

Using a Computer

Writing Reports

To write a report with a computer, use a word processing software program. After you are in the program, type your report. By using certain keys and the mouse, you can control how the words look, move words, delete or add words and copy them, check your spelling, and print your report.

Save your work to the desktop or hard drive of the computer, or to a floppy disk. You can go back to your saved work later if you want to revise it.

There are many reasons for revising your work. You may find new information to add or mistakes you want to correct. You may want to change the way you report your information because of who will read it.

Computers make revising easy. You delete what you don't want, add the new parts, and then save. You can also save different versions of your work.

For a science lab report, it is important to show the same kinds of information each time. With a computer, you can make a general format for a lab report, save the format, and then use it again and again.

Making Graphs and Charts

You can make a graph or chart with most word processing software programs. You can also use special software programs such as Data ToolKit or Graph Links. With Graph Links you can make pictographs and circle, bar, line, and double-line graphs.

First, decide what kind of graph or chart will best communicate your data. Sometimes it's easiest to do this by sketching your ideas on paper. Then you can decide what format and categories you need for your graph or chart. Choose that format for the program. Then type your information. Most software programs include a tutor that gives you step-by-step directions for making a graph or chart.

Doing Research

Computers can help you find current information from all over the world through the Internet. The Internet connects thousands of computer sites that have been set up by schools, libraries, museums, and many other organizations.

Get permission from an adult before you log on to the Internet. Find out the rules for Internet use at school or at home. Then log on and go to a search engine, which will help you find what you need. Type in keywords, words that tell the subject of your search. If you get too much information that isn't exactly about the topic, make your keywords more specific. When you find the information you need, save it or print it.

Harcourt Science tells you about many Internet sites related to what you are studying. To find out about these sites, called Web sites, look for Technology Links in the lessons in this book.

If you need to contact other people to help in your research, you can use e-mail. Log into your e-mail program, type the address of the person you want to reach, type your message, and send it. Be sure to have adult permission before sending or receiving e-mail.

Another way to use a computer for research is to access CD-ROMs. These are discs that look like music CDs. CD-ROMs can hold huge amounts of data, including words, still pictures, audio, and video. Encyclopedias, dictionaries, almanacs, and other sources of information are available on CD-ROMs. These computer discs are valuable resources for your research.

Measurement Systems

SI Measures (Metric)

Temperature
Ice melts at 0 degrees Celsius (°C)
Water freezes at 0°C
Water boils at 100°C

Length and Distance
1000 meters (m) = 1 kilometer (km)
100 centimeters (cm) = 1 m
10 millimeters (mm) = 1 cm

Force
1 newton (N) = 1 kilogram $\times$
   meter/second/second (kg-m/s^2)

Volume
1 cubic meter (m^3) = 1m $\times$ 1m $\times$ 1m
1 cubic centimeter (cm^3) =
   1 cm $\times$ 1 cm $\times$ 1 cm
1 liter (L) = 1000 milliliters (mL)
1 cm^3 = 1 mL

Area
1 square kilometer (km^2) =
   1 km $\times$ 1 km
1 hectare = 10 000 m^2

Mass
1000 grams (g) = 1 kilogram (kg)
1000 milligrams (mg) = 1 g

Rates (Metric and Customary)
kmh = kilometers per hour
m/s = meters per second
mph = miles per hour

Customary Measures

Volume of Fluids
8 fluid ounces (fl oz) = 1 cup (c)
2 c = 1 pint (pt)
2 pt = 1 quart (qt)
4 qt = 1 gallon (gal)

Temperature
Ice melts at 32 degrees
   Fahrenheit (°F)
Water freezes at 32°F
Water boils at 212°F

Length and Distance
12 inches (in) = 1 foot (ft)
3 ft = 1 yard (yd)
5,280 ft = 1 mile (mi)

Weight
16 ounces (oz) = 1 pound (lb)
2,000 pounds = 1 ton (T)

Health Handbook

Bicycle Safety

A Safe Bike

You probably know how to ride a bike, but do you know how to make your bike as safe as possible? A safe bike is the right size for you. When you sit on your bike with the pedal in the lowest position, you should be able to rest your heel on the pedal. Your body should be 2 inches (about 5 cm) above the support bar that goes from the handlebar stem to the seat support when you are standing astride your bike with both feet flat on the ground. After checking for the right size, check your bike for the safety equipment shown below. How safe is *your* bike?

headlight

horn

red rear reflector

white front reflector

clear reflector

pedal reflectors

clear reflector

Your Bike Helmet

About 400,000 children are involved in bike-related crashes every year. That's why it's important to *always* wear your bike helmet. Wear your helmet flat on your head. Be sure it is strapped snugly so that the helmet will stay in place if you fall. If you do fall and strike your helmet on the ground, replace it, even if it doesn't look damaged. The padding inside the helmet may be crushed, which reduces the ability of the helmet to protect your head in the event of another fall. Look for the features shown here when purchasing a helmet.

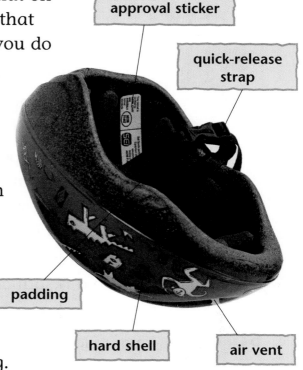

approval sticker

quick-release strap

padding

hard shell

air vent

Safety on the Road

Here are some tips for safe bicycle riding.

- Check your bike every time you ride it. Is it in safe working condition?

- Ride in single file in the same direction as traffic. Never weave in and out of parked cars.

- Before you enter a street, **STOP. Look** left, then right, then left again. **Listen** for any traffic. **Think** before you go.

- Walk your bike across an intersection. **Look** left, then right, then left again. Wait for traffic to pass.

- Obey all traffic signs and signals.

- Do not ride your bike at night without an adult. Be sure to wear light-colored clothing and use reflectors and front and rear lights for night riding.

Fire Safety

Fires cause more deaths than any other type of disaster. But a fire doesn't have to be deadly if you prepare your home and follow some basic safety rules.

- Install smoke detectors outside sleeping areas and on every other floor of your home. Test the detectors once a month and change the batteries twice a year.

- Keep a fire extinguisher on each floor of your home. Check them monthly to make sure they are properly charged.

- Make a fire escape plan. Ideally, there should be two routes out of each room. Sleeping areas are most important, as most fires happen at night. Plan to use stairs only, as elevators can be dangerous in a fire.

- Pick a place outside for everyone to meet. Choose one person to go to a neighbor's home to call 911 or the fire department.

- Practice crawling low to avoid smoke.

- If your clothes catch fire, follow the three steps shown here.

1. STOP

2. DROP

3. ROLL

Earthquake Safety

An earthquake is a strong shaking or sliding of the ground. The tips below can help you and your family stay safe in an earthquake.

Before an Earthquake	During an Earthquake	After an Earthquake
• Attach tall, heavy furniture, such as bookcases, to the wall. Store the heaviest items on the lowest shelves. • Check for fire risks. Bolt down gas appliances, and use flexible hosing and connections for both gas and water lines. • Strengthen and anchor overhead light fixtures to help keep them from falling.	• If you are outdoors, stay outdoors and move away from buildings and utility wires. • If you are indoors, take cover under a heavy desk or table, or in a doorway. Stay away from glass doors and windows and from heavy objects that might fall. • If you are in a car, drive to an open area away from buildings and overpasses.	• Keep watching for falling objects as aftershocks shake the area. • Check for hidden structural problems. • Check for broken gas, electric, and water lines. If you smell gas, shut off the gas main. Leave the area. Report the leak.

Storm Safety

- **In a Tornado** Take cover in a sheltered area away from doors and windows. An interior hallway or basement is best. Stay in the shelter until the danger has passed.

- **In a Hurricane** Prepare for high winds by securing objects outside or bringing them indoors. Cover windows and glass with plywood. Listen to weather bulletins for instructions. If asked to evacuate, proceed to emergency shelters.

- **In a Winter Storm or Blizzard** Stock up on food that does not have to be cooked. Dress in thin layers that help trap the body's heat. Pay special attention to the head and neck. If you are caught in a vehicle, turn on the dome light to make the vehicle visible to search crews.

First Aid

For Choking . . .

The tips on the next few pages can help you provide simple first aid to others and yourself. Always tell an adult about any injuries that occur.

If someone else is choking . . .

1. Recognize the Universal Choking Sign—grasping the throat with both hands. This sign means a person is choking and needs help.

2. Put your arms around his or her waist. Make a fist and put it above the person's navel. Grab your fist with your other hand.

3. Pull your hands toward yourself and give five quick, hard, upward thrusts on the choker's belly.

If you are choking when alone . . .

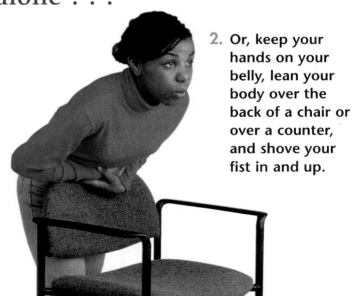

1. Make a fist and place it above your navel. Grab your fist with your other hand. Pull your hands up with a quick, hard thrust.

2. Or, keep your hands on your belly, lean your body over the back of a chair or over a counter, and shove your fist in and up.

For Bleeding . . .

If someone else is bleeding . . .

Wash your hands with soap, if possible.

Put on protective gloves, if available.

Wash small wounds with soap and water. Do *not* wash serious wounds.

Place a clean gauze pad or cloth over the wound. Press firmly for ten minutes. Don't lift the gauze during this time.

If you don't have gloves, have the injured person hold the cloth in place with his or her own hand.

If after ten minutes the bleeding has stopped, bandage the wound. If the bleeding has not stopped, continue pressing on the wound and get help.

If you are bleeding . . .

- Follow the steps shown above. You don't need gloves to touch your own blood.

- Be sure to tell an adult about your injury.

First Aid

For Nosebleeds . . .

- Sit down, and tilt your head forward. Pinch your nostrils together for at least ten minutes.
- You can also put an ice pack on the bridge of your nose.
- If your nose continues to bleed, get help from an adult.

For Burns . . .

Minor burns are called first degree burns and involve only the top layer of skin. The skin is red and dry and the burn is painful. More serious burns are called second or third degree burns. These burns involve the top and lower layers of skin. Second degree burns cause blisters, redness, swelling, and pain. Third degree burns are the most serious. The skin is gray or white and looks burned. All burns need immediate first aid.

Minor Burns

- Run cool water over the burn or soak it in cool water for at least five minutes.
- Cover the burn with a clean, dry bandage.
- Do *not* put lotion or ointment on the burn.

More Serious Burns

- Cover the burn with a cool, wet bandage or cloth. Do *not* break any blisters.
- Do *not* put lotion or ointment on the burn.
- Get help from an adult right away.

For Insect Bites and Stings . . .

- Always tell an adult about bites and stings.
- Scrape out the stinger with your fingernail.
- Wash the area with soap and water.
- Ice cubes will usually take away the pain from insect bites. A paste made from baking soda and water also helps.

▲ deer tick

- If the bite or sting is more serious and is on the arm or leg, keep the leg or arm dangling down. Apply a cold, wet cloth. Get help immediately!
- If you find a tick on your skin, remove it. Crush it between two rocks. Wash your hands right away.
- If a tick has already bitten you, do not pull it off. Cover it with oil and wait for it to let go, then remove it with tweezers. Wash the area and your hands.

For Skin Rashes from Plants . . .

Many poisonous plants have three leaves. Remember, "Leaves of three, let them be." If you touch a poisonous plant, wash the area. Put on clean clothes and throw the dirty ones in the washer. If a rash develops, follow these tips.

- Apply calamine lotion or a baking soda and water paste. Try not to scratch. Tell an adult.

▲ poison ivy

- If you get blisters, do *not* pop them. If they burst, keep the area clean and dry. Cover with a bandage.
- If your rash does not go away in two weeks or if the rash is on your face or in your eyes, see your doctor.

Being Safe at Home

When Home Alone

Everyone stays home alone sometimes. When you stay home alone, it's important to know how to take care of yourself. Here are some easy rules to follow that will help keep you safe when you are at home by yourself.

Do These Things

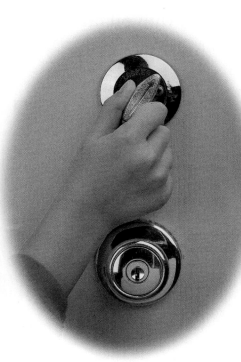

- Lock all the doors and windows. Be sure you know how to lock and unlock all the locks.

- If someone calls who is nasty or mean, hang up. Your parents may not want you to answer the phone at all.

- If you have an emergency, call 911 or 0 (zero) for the operator. Describe the problem, give your full name, address, and telephone number. Follow all instructions given to you.

  - If you see anyone hanging around outside, tell an adult or call the police.

  - If you see or smell smoke, go outside right away. If you live in an apartment, do not take the elevator. Go to a neighbor's home and call 911 or the fire department immediately.

- Entertain yourself. Time will pass more quickly if you are not bored. Try not to spend your time watching television. Instead, work on a hobby, read a book or magazine, do your homework, or clean your room. Before you know it, an adult will be home.

Do NOT Do These Things

- Do NOT use the stove, microwave, or oven unless an adult family member has given you permission, and you are sure about how to use these appliances.

- Do NOT open the door for anyone you don't know or for anyone who is not supposed to be in your home.

  - If someone rings the bell and asks to use the telephone, tell the person to go to a phone booth.

  - If someone tries to deliver a package, do NOT open the door. The delivery person will leave the package or come back later.

  - If someone is selling something, do NOT open the door. Just say, "We're not interested," and nothing more.

- Do NOT talk to strangers on the telephone. Do not tell anyone that you are home alone. If the call is for an adult family member, say that they can't come to the phone right now and take a message. Ask for the caller's name and phone number and deliver the message when an adult family member comes home.

- Do NOT have friends over unless you have gotten permission from your parents or other adult family members.

Being Physically Active

Planning Your Weekly Activities

Being active every day is important for your overall health. Physical activity helps you manage stress, maintain a healthful weight, and strengthen your body systems. The Activity Pyramid, like the Food Guide Pyramid, can help you choose a variety of activities in the right amounts to keep your body strong and healthy.

The Activity Pyramid

Sitting for more than thirty minutes at a time: Only Once in a While

Light Exercise: Two to Three Times a Week

Flexibility and Strength: Two to Three Times a Week

Twenty-plus minutes of continuous aerobic activity: Three to Five Times a Week

Stay active: Every Day

Guidelines for a Good Workout

There are three things you should do every time you are going to exercise—warm up, work out, and cool down.

Warm-Up   When you warm up, your heart rate, breathing rate, and body temperature increase and more blood flows to your muscles. As your body warms up, you can move more easily. People who warm up are less stiff after exercising, and are less likely to have exercise-related injuries. Your warm-up should include five minutes of stretching, and five minutes of low-level exercise.

Workout   The main part of your exercise routine should be an aerobic exercise that lasts 20 to 30 minutes. Aerobic exercises make your heart, lungs, and circulatory system stronger.

Some common aerobic exercises are shown on pages R26–R27. You may want to mix up the types of activities you do. This helps you work different muscles, and provides a better workout over time.

Cool-Down   When you finish your aerobic exercise, you need to give your body time to cool down. Start your cool-down with three to five minutes of low-level activity. End with stretching exercises to prevent soreness and stiffness.

Being Physically Active

Warm-Up and Cool-Down Stretches

Before you exercise, you should warm up your muscles. The warm-up exercises shown here should be held for at least fifteen to twenty seconds and repeated at least three times.

At the end of your workout, spend about two minutes repeating some of these stretches.

▶ **Hurdler's Stretch** HINT—Keep the toes of your extended leg pointed up.

▲ **Shoulder and Chest Stretch** HINT—Pulling your hands slowly toward the floor gives a better stretch. Keep your elbows straight, but not locked!

◀ **Sit-and-Reach Stretch** HINT—Remember to bend at the waist. Keep your eyes on your toes!

▲ **Upper Back and Shoulder Stretch**
HINT—Try to stretch your hand down
so that it rests flat against your back.

▼ **Thigh Stretch** HINT—
Keep both hands flat on
the ground. Lean as far
forward as you can.

▲ **Calf Stretch** HINT—Keep
both feet on the floor during
this stretch. Try changing the
distance between your feet.
Is the stretch better for you
when your legs are closer
together or farther apart?

Tips for Stretching

- Never bounce when stretching.
- Hold each stretch for fifteen to twenty seconds.
- Breathe normally. This helps your body get the oxygen it needs.
- Do NOT stretch until it hurts. Stretch only until you feel a slight pull.

Being Physically Active

Building a Strong Heart and Lungs

Aerobic activities cause deep breathing and a fast heart rate for at least twenty minutes. These activities help both your heart and your lungs. Because your heart is a muscle, it gets stronger with exercise. A strong heart doesn't have to work as hard to pump blood to the rest of your body. Exercise also allows your lungs to hold more air. With a strong heart and lungs, your cells get oxygen faster and your body works more efficiently.

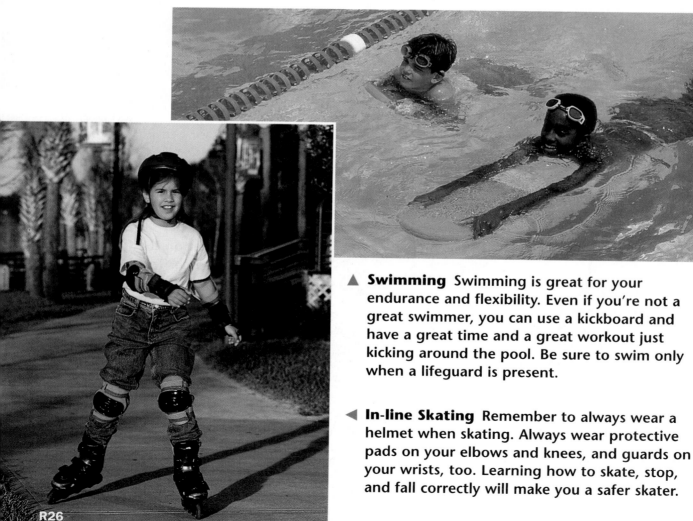

▲ **Swimming** Swimming is great for your endurance and flexibility. Even if you're not a great swimmer, you can use a kickboard and have a great time and a great workout just kicking around the pool. Be sure to swim only when a lifeguard is present.

◄ **In-line Skating** Remember to always wear a helmet when skating. Always wear protective pads on your elbows and knees, and guards on your wrists, too. Learning how to skate, stop, and fall correctly will make you a safer skater.

▼ Walking A fast-paced walk is a terrific way to build your endurance. The only equipment you need is supportive shoes. Walking with a friend can make this exercise a lot of fun.

▲ Jumping Rope Jumping rope is one of the best ways to increase your endurance. Remember to always jump on an even surface and always wear supportive shoes.

▼ Bicycling Bicycling provides good aerobic activity *and* a great way to see the outdoors. Be sure to learn and follow bicycle safety rules. And *always* remember to wear your helmet!

Good Nutrition

The Food Guide Pyramid

No one food or food group supplies everything your body needs for good health. That's why it's important to eat foods from all the food groups. The Food Guide Pyramid can help you choose healthful foods in the right amounts. By choosing more foods from the groups at the bottom of the pyramid and fewer foods from the group at the top, you will eat the foods that provide your body with energy to grow and develop.

Fats, oils, and sweets
Eat sparingly.

Meat, poultry, fish, dry beans, eggs, and nuts 2–3 servings

Milk, yogurt, and cheese
2–3 servings

Fruits
2–4 servings

Vegetables
3–5 servings

Breads, cereals, rice, and pasta 6–11 servings

Estimating Serving Sizes

Choosing a variety of foods is only half the story. You also need to choose the right amounts. The table below can help you estimate the number of servings you are eating of your favorite foods.

Food Group	Amount of Food in One Serving	Some Easy Ways to Estimate Serving Size
Bread, Cereal, Rice, Pasta Group	1 ounce ready-to-eat (dry) cereal	large handful of plain cereal or a small handful of cereal with raisins and nuts
	1 slice bread, $\frac{1}{2}$ bagel	
	$\frac{1}{2}$ cup cooked pasta, rice, or cereal	ice cream scoop
Vegetable Group	1 cup of raw, leafy vegetables	about the size of a fist
	$\frac{1}{2}$ cup other vegetables, cooked or raw, chopped	
	$\frac{3}{4}$ cup vegetable juice	
	$\frac{1}{2}$ cup tomato sauce	ice cream scoop
Fruit Group	medium apple, pear, or orange	a baseball
	$\frac{1}{2}$ large banana or one medium banana	
	$\frac{1}{2}$ cup chopped or cooked fruit	
	$\frac{3}{4}$ cup of fruit juice	
Milk, Yogurt, and Cheese Group	$1\frac{1}{2}$ ounces of natural cheese	two dominoes
	2 ounces of processed cheese	$1\frac{1}{2}$ slices of packaged cheese
	1 cup of milk or yogurt	
Meat, Poultry, Fish, Dry Beans, Eggs, and Nuts Group	3 ounces of lean meat, chicken, or fish	about the size of your palm
	2 tablespoons peanut butter	
	$\frac{1}{2}$ cup of cooked dry beans	
Fats, Oils, and Sweets Group	1 teaspoon of margarine or butter	about the size of the tip of your thumb

Preparing Foods Safely

Fight Bacteria

You probably already know to throw away food that smells bad or looks moldy. But food doesn't have to look or smell bad to make you ill. To keep your food safe and yourself from becoming ill, follow the steps outlined in the picture below. And remember—when in doubt, throw it out!

FIGHT BAC!

Keep Food Safe From Bacteria

CLEAN Wash hands and surfaces often.

SEPARATE Don't cross-contaminate.

CHILL Refrigerate promptly.

COOK Cook to proper temperatures.

TM

Food Safety Tips

Tips for Preparing Food

- Wash hands in warm, soapy water before preparing food. It's also a good idea to wash hands after preparing each dish.
- Defrost meat in the microwave or the refrigerator.
- Keep raw meat, poultry, fish, and their juices away from other food.
- Wash cutting boards, knives, and countertops immediately after cutting up meat, poultry, or fish. Never use the same cutting board for meats and vegetables without washing the board first.

Tips for Cooking Food

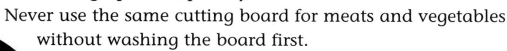

- Cook all food completely, especially meat. Complete cooking kills the bacteria that can make you ill.
- Red meats should be cooked to a temperature of 160°F. Poultry should be cooked to 180°F. When done, fish flakes easily with a fork.
- Never eat food that contains raw eggs or raw egg yolks, including cookie dough.

Tips for Cleaning Up the Kitchen

- Wash all dishes, utensils, and countertops with hot, soapy water. Use a soap that kills bacteria, if possible.
- Store leftovers in small containers that will cool quickly in the refrigerator. Don't leave leftovers on the counter to cool.

Sense Organs

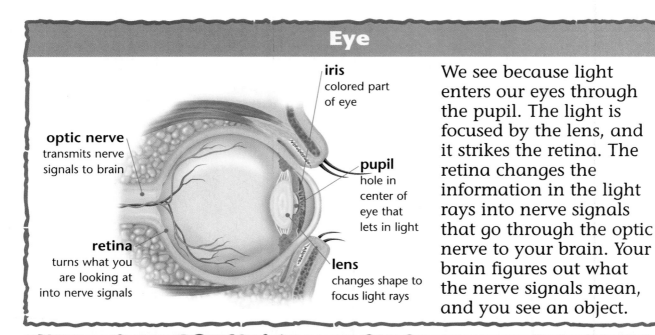

Eye

iris
colored part of eye

optic nerve
transmits nerve signals to brain

pupil
hole in center of eye that lets in light

retina
turns what you are looking at into nerve signals

lens
changes shape to focus light rays

We see because light enters our eyes through the pupil. The light is focused by the lens, and it strikes the retina. The retina changes the information in the light rays into nerve signals that go through the optic nerve to your brain. Your brain figures out what the nerve signals mean, and you see an object.

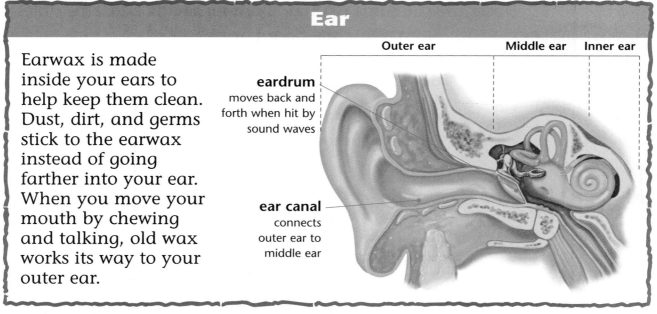

Ear

Earwax is made inside your ears to help keep them clean. Dust, dirt, and germs stick to the earwax instead of going farther into your ear. When you move your mouth by chewing and talking, old wax works its way to your outer ear.

Outer ear | Middle ear | Inner ear

eardrum
moves back and forth when hit by sound waves

ear canal
connects outer ear to middle ear

Caring for Your Eyes and Ears

- Have your eyesight (vision) checked every year.

- Wear safety glasses when participating in activities that can be dangerous to the eyes, such as sports and mowing grass.

- Wash in, around, and behind your outer ear. Do not try to clean your ear canal with cotton-tip sticks or other objects.

Nose

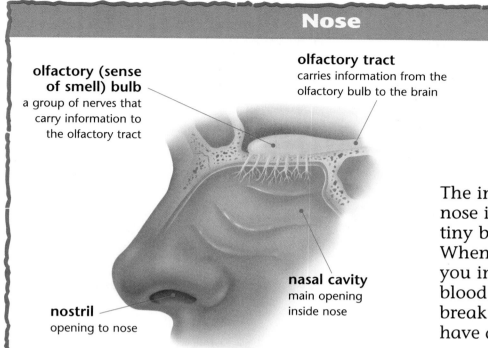

olfactory (sense of smell) bulb
a group of nerves that carry information to the olfactory tract

olfactory tract
carries information from the olfactory bulb to the brain

nostril
opening to nose

nasal cavity
main opening inside nose

The inside of your nose is lined with tiny blood vessels. When something hits you in the nose, these blood vessels can break and you can have a nosebleed.

Caring for Your Nose, Tongue, and Skin

- If you get a nosebleed, sit, lean forward slightly, and pinch just below the bridge of your nose for ten minutes. Breathe through your mouth.

- When you brush your teeth, brush your tongue too.

- Always wear sunscreen when you are in the sun.

Tongue

Germs live on your tongue and in other parts of your mouth. Germs can harm your teeth and give you bad breath.

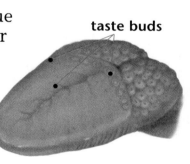

taste buds

Skin

protective outer layer

strong, springy middle layer

fatty lower layer

Your skin protects your insides from the outside world. It keeps fluids you need inside your body and fluids you don't need, such as swimming pool water, outside your body.

Skeletal System

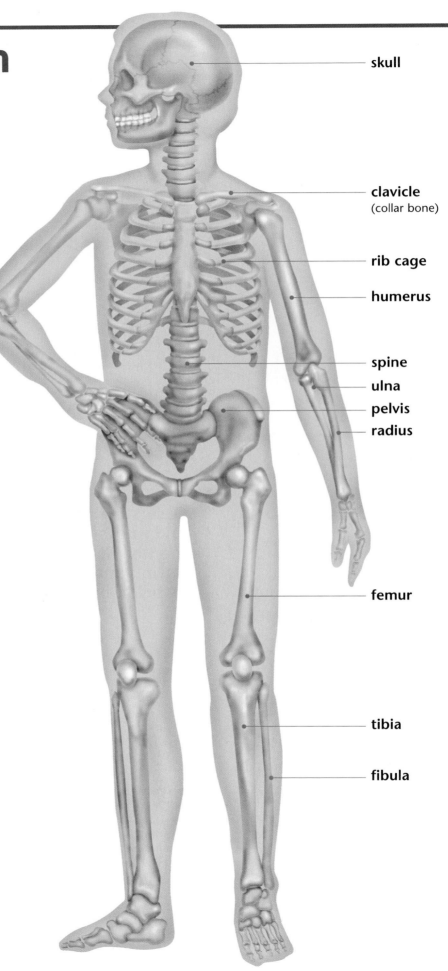

Each of your bones has a particular shape and size that allow it to do a certain job. You have bones that are tiny, long, wide, flat, and even curved. The job of some bones is to protect your body parts.

skull

clavicle
(collar bone)

rib cage

humerus

spine

ulna

pelvis

radius

femur

tibia

fibula

Bones that Protect

Rib Cage Your rib bones form a cage that protects your heart and lungs from all sides. Your ribs are springy. When something strikes you in the chest, your ribs push the object away instead of letting it hit your heart and lungs.

Your ribs are connected to your breastbone (sternum) by springy material called cartilage. The springy connection lets your ribs move up and down. This happens when your rib cage gets bigger and smaller as you breathe in and out.

cartilage

rib

sternum

Skull The bones in your head are called your skull. Some of the bones in your skull protect your brain. The bones in your face are part of your skull too.

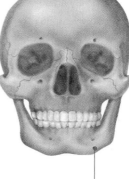

jaw

Caring for Your Skeletal System

- Calcium helps bones grow and makes them strong. Dairy products like milk, cheese, and yogurt contain calcium. Have 2–3 servings of dairy products every day.

- Exercise also makes your bones strong. When bones aren't used, they can become brittle and may break.

Activities

1. Look at the picture of the skeleton. Name a long bone. Name a short bone. Name a curved bone.

2. Put a tomato inside a wire cage. Gently throw a wad of paper at the cage. What happens? The cage protects the tomato in the same way your ribs protect your heart.

3. Measure around your rib cage with a string. How big is it when you breathe in? How big is it when you breathe out? Which measurement is greater?

Muscular System

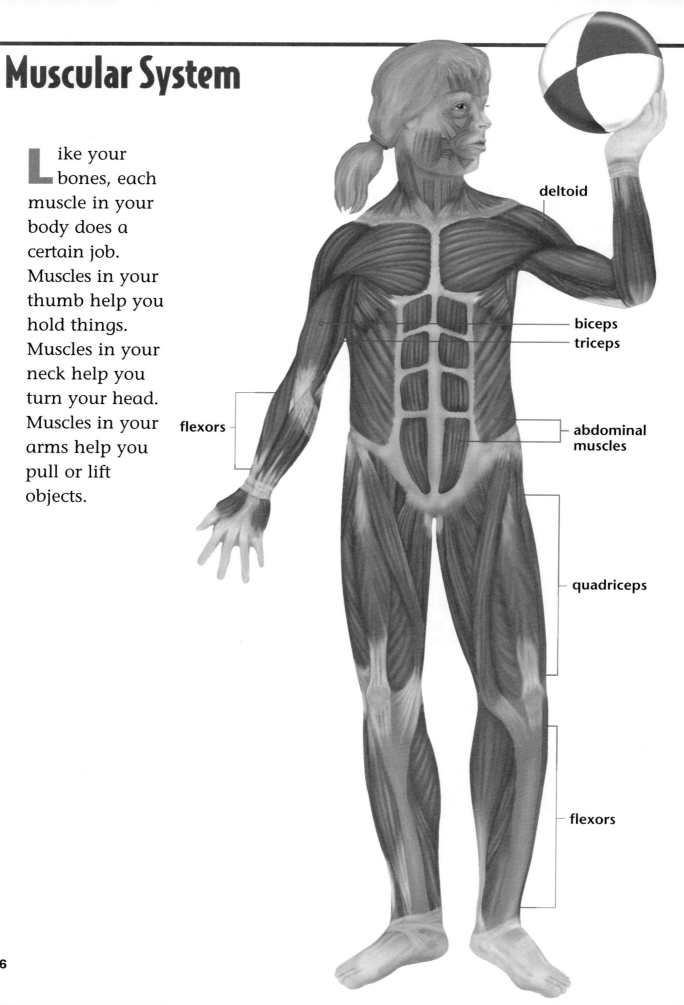

ike your bones, each muscle in your body does a certain job. Muscles in your thumb help you hold things. Muscles in your neck help you turn your head. Muscles in your arms help you pull or lift objects.

deltoid

biceps

triceps

flexors

abdominal muscles

quadriceps

flexors

How Muscles Move Your Body

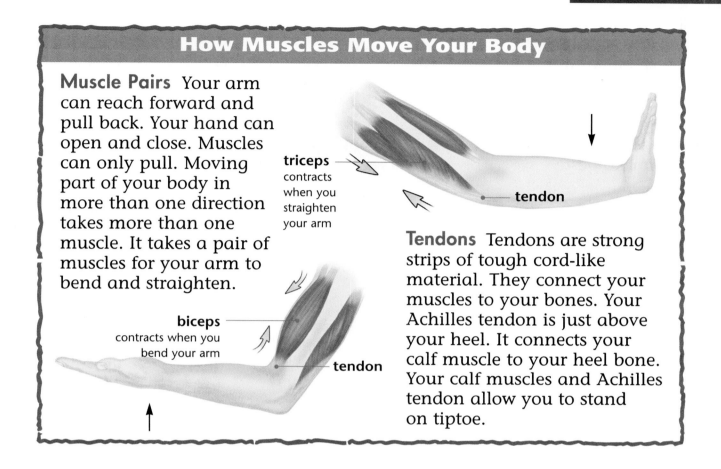

Muscle Pairs Your arm can reach forward and pull back. Your hand can open and close. Muscles can only pull. Moving part of your body in more than one direction takes more than one muscle. It takes a pair of muscles for your arm to bend and straighten.

triceps contracts when you straighten your arm

tendon

biceps contracts when you bend your arm

tendon

Tendons Tendons are strong strips of tough cord-like material. They connect your muscles to your bones. Your Achilles tendon is just above your heel. It connects your calf muscle to your heel bone. Your calf muscles and Achilles tendon allow you to stand on tiptoe.

Caring for Your Muscular System

- Exercise makes your muscles stronger.
- Stretching before you exercise makes muscles and tendons more flexible and less likely to get hurt.

Activities

1. Tie your shoe without using your thumb. What happens?

2. Pull up on a desk with one hand. With your other hand, feel which arm muscle is working. Now push on the desk. Which arm muscle is working?

3. Ask a friend to push down on your arms for one minute while you push up as hard as you can. When your friend lets go, what happens?

Digestive System

Food is broken down and pushed through your body by your digestive system. Your digestive system is a series of connected parts that starts with your mouth and ends with your large intestine.

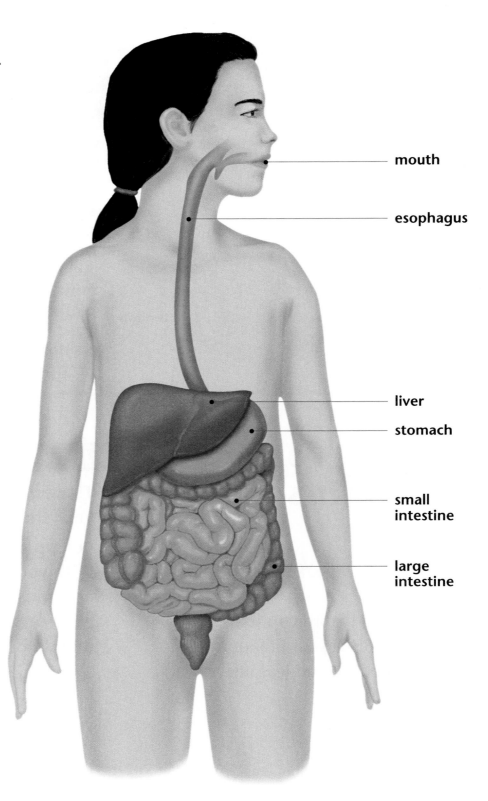

mouth

esophagus

liver

stomach

small intestine

large intestine

From Mouth to Stomach

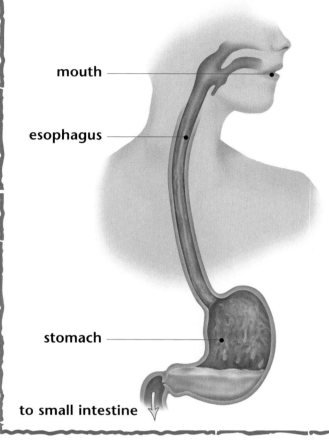

mouth

esophagus

stomach

to small intestine

Esophagus Your esophagus, or food tube, is a tube that connects your mouth to your stomach. After you swallow a bite of food, muscles in your esophagus push the food into your stomach.

Stomach Your stomach is filled with acid that helps dissolve food. The stomach walls are strong muscles that mix food with the acid. The stomach walls are protected from the acid by a thick layer of mucus. From your stomach, food moves to the small intestine and then to the large intestine.

Caring for Your Digestive System

- Chew everything you eat carefully. Well-chewed food is easier to digest.

- Do not overeat. Overeating can cause a stomachache.

Activities

1. Measure 25 feet (about 8 m) on the floor. This is how long your digestive system is.

2. Cut a narrow balloon so that it is open on both ends. Put a wad of paper in one end. Squeeze the outside of the balloon to push the paper through and out the other end. This is similar to how your esophagus pushes food to your stomach.

Circulatory System

Food and oxygen travel through your circulatory system to every cell in your body. Blood moves nutrients throughout your body, fights infection, and helps control your body temperature. Your blood is made up mostly of a watery liquid called plasma.

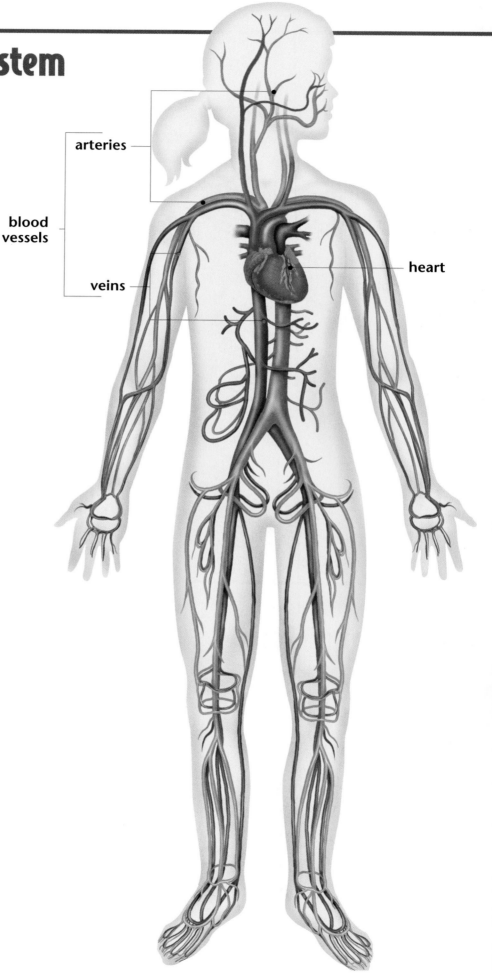

arteries

blood vessels

veins

heart

Blood Vessels

Arteries Arteries carry blood away from the heart. Blood in arteries is brighter red because it has come from the lungs and has lots of oxygen. Arteries bring oxygen and nutrients to all parts of the body.

Veins Veins carry blood to the heart. Veins have one-way valves that allow blood to move only toward the heart.

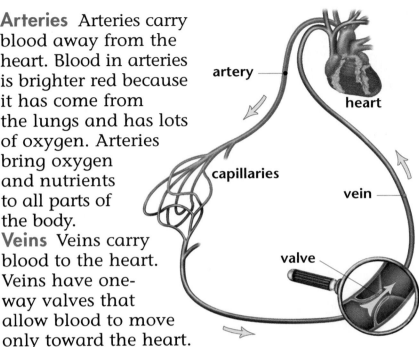

Capillaries Capillaries are very small pathways for blood. When blood flows through capillaries, it gives oxygen and nutrients to the cells in your body. Blood also picks up carbon dioxide and other waste.

Caring for Your Circulatory System

- Never touch another person's blood.

- Eat a healthy, balanced diet throughout your life to keep excess fat from blocking the blood flowing through your arteries.

- Get regular exercise to keep your heart strong.

Activities

1. Take the bottom out of a paper cup. Bend the top together like a clamshell. Hold the cup and drop a marble through from the bottom. Now try to drop one into the top. The clamshell-shaped cup is like the one-way valve in a vein.

2. Find the blue lines under the skin on your wrist. These are veins. Press gently and stroke along the lines toward your elbow. Now stroke toward your hand. What do you see?

Respiratory System

Your body uses its respiratory system to get oxygen from the air and get rid of excess carbon dioxide. Your respiratory system is made up of your nose and mouth, your trachea (windpipe), your two lungs, and your diaphragm—a dome-shaped muscle under your lungs.

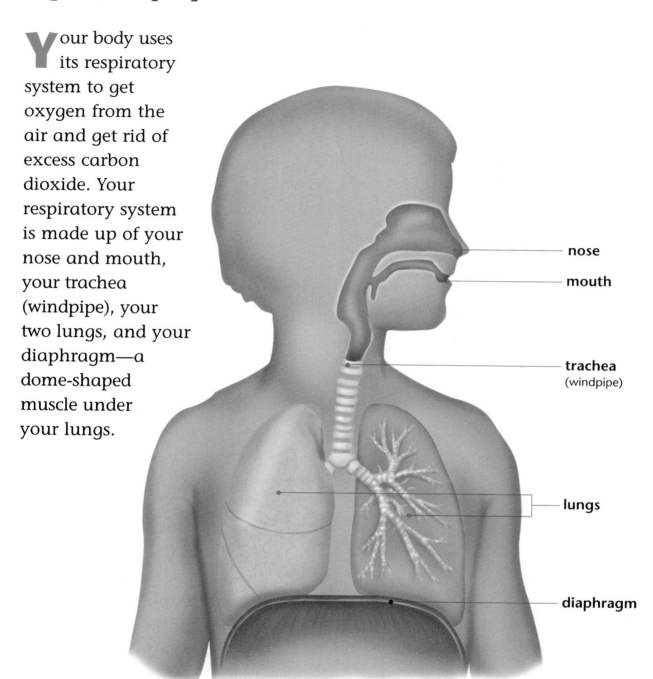

nose

mouth

trachea
(windpipe)

lungs

diaphragm

Breathing

When you inhale, or breathe in, air enters your mouth and nose and goes into your trachea. Your trachea connects your nose and mouth to your lungs. Your trachea divides into two smaller tubes that go to your lungs. Your lungs fill with air. When you exhale, or breathe out, your diaphragm pushes upward. Air is forced up your trachea and out your mouth and nose.

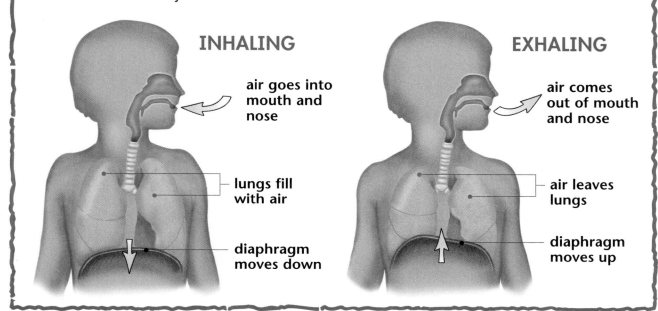

INHALING

air goes into mouth and nose

lungs fill with air

diaphragm moves down

EXHALING

air comes out of mouth and nose

air leaves lungs

diaphragm moves up

Caring for Your Respiratory System

- Exercise. When you exercise your body, you exercise your respiratory system too. Your muscles use more oxygen, so you breathe faster and deeper.

- Get enough sleep to help your resistance to colds.

Activities

1. Sit in a chair and count how many breaths you take in 30 seconds. Then exercise for two minutes. When you stop, count how many breaths you take in 30 seconds. Do you breathe more while sitting or after exercise?

2. Put your hand on your bellybutton and take a deep breath in and out. How does your hand move?

Nervous System

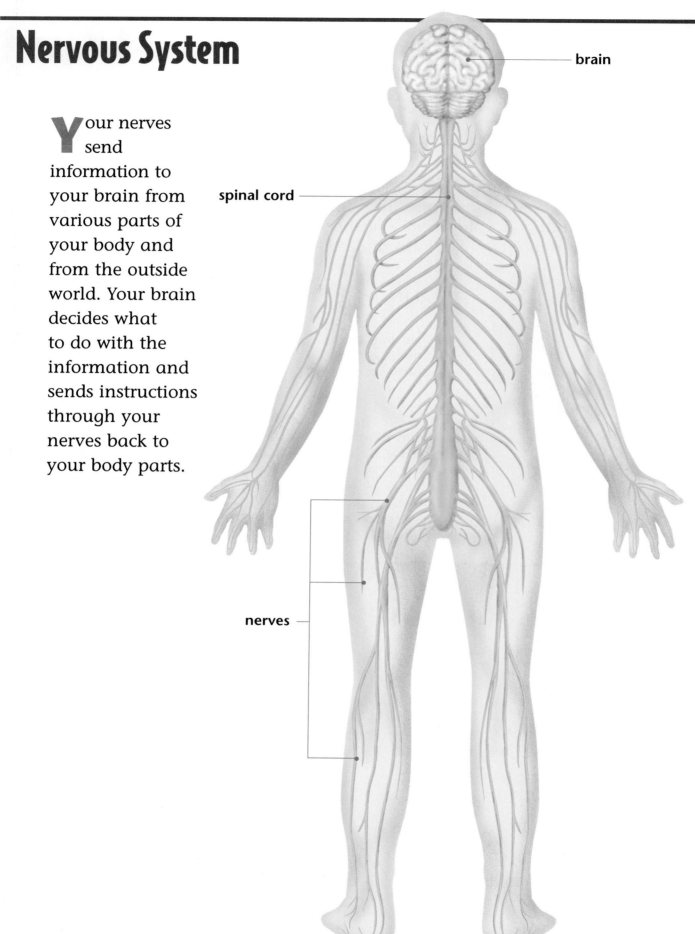

Your nerves send information to your brain from various parts of your body and from the outside world. Your brain decides what to do with the information and sends instructions through your nerves back to your body parts.

brain

spinal cord

nerves

Your Brain

Your brain is about two pounds of wrinkled, pinkish-gray material. It's protected by your skull and cushioned by a thin layer of liquid. The brain's main connection to the body is the spinal cord.

Different parts of the brain send signals to different parts of your body. For example, the part right behind your forehead tells your body how to move. The area near the base of your neck controls your breathing and heartbeat. If you are left-handed, the right half of your brain controls your handwriting.

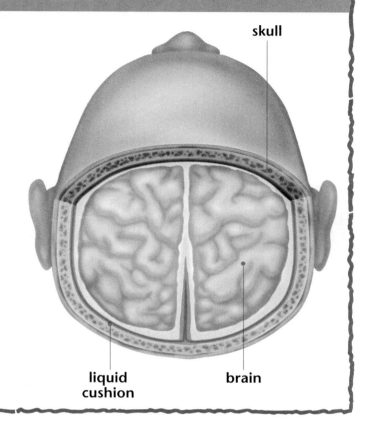

skull

liquid cushion

brain

Caring for Your Nervous System

• Many injuries to the brain are caused by car crashes. Wear your safety belt and sit in the backseat when you are in the car.

• Always wear a helmet when you ride your bike, skate, or use a skateboard.

Activities

1. Make a list of signals your nerves are sending to your brain right now. Also list instructions your brain is sending to your nerves.

2. Read a paragraph out of a book while the television is on. Do you know what the paragraph was about? Do you know what happened on television?

3. Write your name with your opposite hand ten times. Does your writing improve?

Glossary

This Glossary contains important science words and their definitions. Each word is respelled as it would be in a dictionary. When you see the ′ mark after a syllable, pronounce that syllable with more force than the other syllables. The page number at the end of the definition tells where to find the word in your book. The boldfaced letters in the examples in the Pronunciation Key that follows show how these letters are pronounced in the respellings after each glossary word.

PRONUNCIATION KEY

a	**a**dd, m**a**p	m	**m**ove, see**m**	u	**u**p, **d**one
ā	**a**ce, r**a**te	n	**n**ice, ti**n**	û(r)	**bur**n, t**er**m
â(r)	**c**are, **air**	ng	ri**ng**, so**ng**	yo͞o	**f**use, **few**
ä	p**a**lm, f**a**ther	o	**o**dd, h**o**t	v	**v**ain, e**v**e
b	**b**at, ru**b**	ō	**o**pen, s**o**	w	**w**in, a**w**ay
ch	**ch**eck, cat**ch**	ô	**or**der, j**aw**	y	**y**et, **y**earn
d	**d**og, ro**d**	oi	**oi**l, b**oy**	z	**z**est, mu**s**e
e	**e**nd, p**e**t	ou	p**ou**t, n**ow**	zh	vi**s**ion, plea**s**ure
ē	**e**qual, tr**ee**	o͝o	t**oo**k, f**u**ll	ə	the schwa, an
f	**f**it, hal**f**	o͞o	p**oo**l, f**oo**d		unstressed vowel
g	**g**o, lo**g**	p	**p**it, sto**p**		representing the
h	**h**ope, **h**ate	r	**r**un, poo**r**		sound spelled
i	**i**t, g**i**ve	s	**s**ee, pa**ss**		*a* in *above*
ī	**i**ce, wr**i**te	sh	**s**ure, ru**sh**		*e* in *sicken*
j	**j**oy, le**dg**e	t	**t**alk, si**t**		*i* in *possible*
k	**c**ool, ta**k**e	th	**th**in, bo**th**		*o* in *melon*
l	**l**ook, ru**l**e	t̶h̶	**th**is, ba**th**e		*u* in *circus*

Other symbols:
- • separates words into syllables
- ′ indicates heavier stress on a syllable
- ′ indicates light stress on a syllable

R46

absorption [ab·sôrp′shən] The stopping of light **(C106)**

amphibian [am·fib′ē·ən] An animal that begins life in the water and moves onto land as an adult **(A50)**

asteroid [as′tər·oid] A chunk of rock that orbits the sun **(B40)**

atom [at′əm] The basic building block of matter **(C16)**

axis [ak′sis] An imaginary line that goes through the North Pole and the South Pole of Earth **(B18)**

bird [bûrd] An animal that has feathers, two legs, and wings **(A45)**

chemical change [kem′i·kəl chānj′] A change that forms different kinds of matter **(C48)**

chlorophyll [klôr′ə·fil′] The substance that gives plants their green color; it helps a plant use energy from the sun to make food **(A20)**

circuit [sûr′kit] The path electricity follows from the battery, through the bulb, and back again **(C79)**

coastal forest [kōs′təl fôr′ist] A thick forest with tall trees that gets a lot of rain and does not get very warm or cold **(A89)**

comet [kom′it] A large ball of ice and dust that orbits the sun **(B40)**

community [kə•myoo′nə•tē] All the populations of organisms that live in an ecosystem **(A81)**

coniferous forest [ko•nif′ər•əs fôr′ist] A forest in which most of the trees are conifers (cone-bearing) and stay green all year **(A90)**

constellation [kon′stə•lā′shən] A group of stars that form a pattern **(B45)**

consumer [kən•soom′ər] A living thing that eats other living things as food **(E7)**

core [kôr] The center of the Earth **(E34)**

crust [krust] The solid outside layer of the Earth **(E34)**

deciduous forest [dē•sij′o͞o•əs fôr′ist] A forest in which most of the trees lose and regrow their leaves each year **(A87)**

decomposer [dē′kəm•pōz′ər] A living thing that breaks down dead organisms for food **(E8)**

desert [dez′ərt] An ecosystem where there is very little rain **(A94)**

ecosystem [ek′ō•sis′təm] The living and nonliving things in an environment **(A81)**

electricity [i•lek′tris′i•tē] A form of energy that people make by using other kinds of energy **(C63)**

endangered [en•dān′jərd] The term describing a species of organisms that are likely to become extinct **(A60)**

energy [en′ər•jē] The ability to cause change **(C62)**

energy pyramid [en′ər•jē pir′ə•mid] A diagram that shows that the amount of useable energy in an ecosystem is less for each higher animal in the food chain **(E14)**

environment [in•vī′rən•mənt] The things, both living and nonliving, that surround a living thing **(A80)**

evaporation [ē•vap′ə•rā′shən] The process by which a liquid changes into a gas **(C18)**

extinct [ik•stingkt′] When the last individual of a species dies and that organism is gone forever **(A60)**

fish [fish] An animal that lives its whole life in water and breathes with gills **(A52)**

food chain [fo͞od′ chān′] The path of food from one living thing to another **(E12)**

food web [fo͞od′ web′] A model that shows how food chains overlap **(E18)**

forest [fôr′ist] An area in which the main plants are trees **(A86)**

fossil [fos′əl] The evidence of an animal or plant that lived long ago **(A61, E46)**

fossil fuel [fos′əl fyo͞o′əl] A fuel formed from the remains of once-living organisms **(C64)**

fresh water [fresh′ wôt′ər] Water that has very little salt in it **(A100)**

gas [gas] A form of matter that does not have a definite shape or a definite volume **(C12)**

germinate [jûr′mə•nāt′] When a new plant breaks out of the seed **(A13)**

gills [gilz] A body part found in fish and young amphibians that takes in oxygen from the water **(A51)**

habitat [hab′ə•tat′] The place where a population lives in an ecosystem **(A81)**

heat [hēt] The movement of thermal energy from one place to another **(C80)**

igneous rock [ig′nē•əs rok′] A rock that was once melted rock but has cooled and hardened **(E38)**

inherit [in•her′it] To receive traits from parents **(A38)**

interact [in′tər•akt′] To affect one another or the environment to meet needs (said of plants and animals) **(E6)**

leaf [lēf] A plant part that grows out of the stem; it takes in the air and light that a plant needs **(A7)**

liquid [lik′wid] A form of matter that has volume that stays the same but which can change its shape **(C12)**

lunar eclipse [lōō′nər i•klips′] The hiding of the moon when it passes through the Earth's shadow **(B12)**

mammal [mam′əl] An animal that has fur or hair and is fed milk from its mother's body **(A42)**

mantle [man′təl] The middle layer of the Earth **(E34)**

mass [mas] The amount of matter in an object **(C24)**

matter [mat′ər] Anything that takes up space **(C6)**

melting [melt′ing] A process by which a solid becomes a liquid **(C18)**

metamorphic rock [met′ə•môr′fik rok′] A rock that has been changed by heat and pressure **(E38)**

mineral [min′ər•əl] An object that is solid, is formed in nature, and has never been alive **(E32)**

mixture [miks′chər] A substance that contains two or more different types of matter **(C43)**

molecule [mol′ə•kyōōl′] A grouping of two or more atoms **(C16)**

orbit [ôr′bit] The path an object takes as it moves around another object in space **(B34)**

phase [fāz] The shape the moon seems to have in the sky when observed from Earth **(B10)**

photosynthesis [fōt′ō•sin′thə•sis] The food-making process of plants **(A20)**

physical change [fiz′i•kəl chānj′] A change to matter in which no new kinds of matter are formed **(C42)**

physical property [fiz′i•kəl prop′ər•tē] Anything you can observe about an object by using your senses **(C6)**

planet [plan′it] A large body of rock or gas that orbits the sun **(A34)**

population [pop′yōō•lā′shən] A group of the same kind of living thing that all live in one place at the same time **(A81)**

predator [pred′ə•tər] An animal that hunts another animal for food **(E18)**

prey [prā] An animal that is hunted by a predator **(E18)**

prism [priz′əm] A solid, transparent object that bends light into its colors **(C110)**

producer [prə•dōōs′ər] A living thing that makes its own food **(E7)**

reflection [ri•flek′shən] The bouncing of light off an object **(C102)**

refraction [ri•frak′shən] The bending of light when it moves from one kind of matter to another **(C104)**

reptile [rep′til] A land animal that has dry skin covered by scales **(A55)**

revolution [rev′ə•lōō′shən] The movement of one object around another object **(B18)**

rock [rok] A solid made of minerals **(E34)**

rock cycle [rok′ sī′kəl] The process in which one type of rock changes into another type of rock **(E40)**

root [rōōt] The part of a plant that holds the plant in the ground and takes in water and minerals from the soil **(A7)**

rotation [rō•tā′shən] The spinning of an object on its axis **(B18)**

salt water [sôlt′ wôt′ər] Water that has a lot of salt in it **(A100)**

scales [skālz] The small, thin, flat plates that help protect the bodies of fish and reptiles **(A52)**

sedimentary rock [sed′ə•men′tər•ē rok′] A rock formed from material that has settled into layers and been squeezed until it hardens into rock **(E38)**

seed [sēd] The first stage in the growth of many plants **(A12)**

seedling [sēd′ling] A young plant **(A13)**

solar eclipse [sō′lər i•klips′] The hiding of the sun that occurs when the moon passes between the sun and Earth **(B14)**

solar system [sō′lər sis′təm] The sun and the objects that orbit around it **(B34)**

solid [sol′id] A form of matter that takes up a specific amount of space and has a definite shape **(C11)**

solution [sə•lōō′shən] A mixture in which the particles of two different kinds of matter mix together evenly **(C44)**

species [spē′shēz] The specific name used to identify an organism **(A60)**

star [stär] A hot ball of glowing gases, like our sun **(B44)**

stem [stem] A plant part that connects the roots with the leaves of a plant and supports the plant above ground; it carries water from the roots to other parts of the plant **(A7)**

telescope [tel′ə•skōp′] An instrument used to see faraway objects **(B48)**

thermal energy [thûr′məl en′ər•jē] The total energy of moving atoms in matter **(C80)**

threatened [thret′ənd] Describes an organism that is likely to become endangered or extinct **(A61)**

trait [trāt] A body feature that an animal inherits; it can also be some things that an animal does **(A38)**

tropical rain forest [trop′i•kəl rān′fôr′ist] A hot, wet forest where the trees grow very tall and their leaves stay green all year **(A88)**

vibrate [vi′brāt′] The quick back-and-forth movement of an object that produces sound **(C77)**

volume [vol′yo͞om] The amount of space that matter takes up **(C22)**

waste heat [wāst′ hēt′] The heat produced when a machine works to convert fuel energy into the energy of motion **(C88)**